People in Trouble

ALSO BY WILHELM REICH

The Cancer Biopathy
Character Analysis
Ether, God and Devil / Cosmic Superimposition
The Function of the Orgasm
The Invasion of Compulsory Sex-Morality
Listen, Little Man!
The Mass Psychology of Fascism
The Murder of Christ
Reich Speaks of Freud
Selected Writings
The Sexual Revolution
Early Writings; Volume One

Wilhelm Reich in Switzerland, 1927

WILHELM REICH

People in Trouble

VOLUME TWO OF

The Emotional Plague of Mankind

Translated by Philip Schmitz

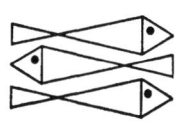

FARRAR, STRAUS AND GIROUX

NEW YORK

*Copyright © 1976 by Mary Boyd Higgins
as Trustee of the Wilhelm Reich Infant Trust Fund*
Menschen im Staat, Teil I *copyright © 1973 by
Mary Boyd Higgins as Trustee of the Wilhelm Reich Infant Trust Fund
Earlier translation published under the title*
People in Trouble (*The Emotional Plague of Mankind, Vol. II*),
*copyright 1953 by
the Orgone Institute Press, Inc.*

All rights reserved

Printed in the United States of America

First printing, 1976

*Published simultaneously in Canada
by McGraw-Hill Ryerson Ltd., Toronto*

Library of Congress Cataloging in Publication Data

Reich, Wilhelm, 1897–1957.
   People in trouble.

   Includes index.
   1. Reich, Wilhelm, 1897–1957. 2. Orgonomy. I. Title. [DNLM:
1. Politics. 2. Psychoanalytic interpretation. WM460 R347p]
RC339.52.R44A313   1976   615'.85   76–39776
          ISBN 0-374-51035-0 (pbk)

Love, work, and knowledge are the wellsprings of our life. They should also govern it.

WILHELM REICH

To the children of the future

Contents

The Silent Observer 3

Introduction 5

1. Wrong Directions 15
2. A Practical Course in Marxist Sociology 22
3. The Living Productive Power, "Work-Power," of Karl Marx 48
4. This Is Politics! 77
5. The Invasion of Compulsory Sex-Morality into Innately Free Primitive Society 118
6. Everyone Is "Enraptured" 135
7. Irrationalism in Politics and Society 158
8. The Psychoanalytic Congress in Lucerne, August 1934 224
9. Toward Biogenesis 254

Index 277

And so in the course of development all former reality becomes unreal, loses its necessity, its right to existence, its reasonableness. In place of the dying reality emerges a new, viable reality—peacefully, when the old is reasonable enough to die without struggle, violently, if it blocks the path of this necessity.

—Friedrich Engels, in *Ludwig Feuerbach* (1888)

People in Trouble

The Silent Observer

People in Trouble *is a translation of part of a German manuscript entitled* Menschen im Staat, *1937, to which other material, notes, and comments were added in 1944–45. Prior to its first publication in 1953, Reich, referring to himself as the Silent Observer, added further comments throughout the text. These comments, some signed "SO" and others unsigned, are enclosed in brackets or are preceded by the date "1952." The role of the Silent Observer is explained by Reich himself in this introductory note.* —Ed.

The Silent Observer (SO) in this autobiographical volume sees events in retrospect as of 1950–52—that is, while the oranur experiment was running its course. This experiment, which established unequivocally the existence of the primordial cosmic orgone energy in a practical and even socially penetrating manner, demolished every criticism, doubt, and distortion uttered by the enemies of orgonomy during the Norwegian campaign (1934–38) and by a few psychoanalytic slanderers (1934–47). The Silent Observer not only views these enemies objectively; he also includes the discoverer of orgone energy, Wilhelm Reich (WR), in his merciless criticism. The errors and stupid mistakes as well as the great strides and experiences from 1927 to 1937 constitute an important lesson for anyone who in the future may try to deal with human nature in a political rather than a scientific manner. Only the factual, not the political, way will finally come to grips with the sexual revolution of our times and master the emotional plague (EP).

The Silent Observer knows very well that the discovery of the primordial cosmic energy has rendered ineffective and outdated all petty political quibbling and all thinking in terms of class or of the unconscious. It is certain that in due time this discovery will provide useful new tools of thinking and acting for mankind in its struggle against the emotional plague, which undermines its most skillful and laborious endeavors. However, it seems tragically true that for many decades, perhaps centuries, to come, the politician and the mere ideologist will dominate the public scene and try to change human nature by way of ideas, programs, platforms, speeches, promises, illusions, maneuvers, and politicking of all kinds, without taking a single practical step to change conditions and to reestablish the natural laws of life.

This account of WR's experiences in the Socialist and psychoanalytic movements is being presented in an effort to help eliminate error and unnecessary blundering in the future. It is hoped that even the skillful, hidden slanderer, inside and outside the Communist Party, will feel enough respect for human suffering and searching to come out from his hiding place in the "bushes" and to desist from acts of abuse and misuse of candidness while this historical material is being exposed on the "meadow."

Introduction

This book comprises various writings from the period 1927–45.[1] It is not a compendium of sex-economic sociology; nor is it written in connection with a specific event. It illustrates the gradual maturing of insights over the course of nearly two decades, insights that finally fused into a composite view. Anyone who has worked in unexplored regions will realize that what is reflected in the final result is not a predetermined goal but rather the very path of the search itself.

The reader will ask why I emphasize this. The reason is simple: Natural-scientific thought bears witness to its own impartiality when it describes social events that occurred at various times and that reflect the paths both of error and of remedy. I did not write this book out of emotion or of preconceived theory. Nor did I write it as the result of an arbitrary thought process or because I envisioned a state of improved social organization. I gathered the insights summarized here just as a settler in an uninhabited wilderness must gather impressions and experiences if he wishes to survive.

Originally I was a clinician interested strictly in natural science and philosophy, not in sociology or even in politics. It was the spontaneous development of the science of orgonomy that led me, initially around 1919, into the area of individual and

[1] 1952: "1945" here refers to a plan only, conceived in 1945, to publish all historical material up to that year. Due to other commitments, only the period 1927 to 1939 was actually described extensively in a consistent manner. Other periods have been dealt with in separate papers.

social sex-economy. Sex-economy in turn was the precursor of the discovery of the orgone, i.e. cosmic life energy.

Looking backward from 1945, I must confess that my discovery of the orgone would not have occurred without the experiences described herein. It owes its very existence to the obstacles placed in its path by the irrational framework of human society and the character structure of the human animal in the twentieth century. Being compelled to recognize these obstacles as biopathic manifestations of life and not as coincidental strokes of fate, and being constrained to find means to overcome them, equipped me with the methods for orgone research. I suspected the existence of the orgone as little as did any psychoanalyst involved with drive psychology or any physicist or biologist involved with the earth's magnetism or cell division. As I have often stressed, what was remarkable was not the discovery of the orgone, but, rather, its *non-discovery* over a period of roughly 2,500 years, which was an achievement of repression. Two decades of clinical work with the human tendency to repress vital processes stimulated the quest for the cause of human irrationalism. Why, I asked, does man resist nothing so much as the realization of his own nature, his biological origin and constitution? I knew nothing of the biological degeneration of the human animal which has for thousands of years endangered his personal and social existence, chronically and in periodic catastrophes.

With this question, doubts arose in my mind as to the rationality of the human thought process, doubts that were never again to be quieted. As long as peace prevailed, my doubts received little nourishment. The neuroses Freud had learned to comprehend in a natural-scientific manner, although only psychologically, appeared to me and to everyone else as illnesses in otherwise healthy organisms. Had anyone proposed, prior to 1927, that so many human institutions had been essentially irrational, i.e. biopathic, for thousands of years, I would have been among the most vehement opponents. Meanwhile social developments throughout the world, emanating from Europe, have made a platitude of the fact that man and his society are mentally ill in the strictest psychiatric sense of the word. I was fortunate, or one might say unfortunate, in discovering this fact not in 1942, as did most people, but as early as 1927, when I began my research. The first encounter with human irrationality was an immense shock. I can't imagine how I bore it without going mad. Consider that when I underwent this experience I was comfortably adjusted to conventional modes of thinking. Unaware of what I was dealing with, I landed in the "meat grinder," a situation with which every sex-economist or vegetotherapist who has entered the field in the past ten years is well acquainted. It may be best described as follows: As if struck by a blow, one suddenly recognizes the scientific futility, the biological senselessness, and the social noxiousness of views and institutions which until that moment had seemed altogether natural and self-evident. It is a kind of eschatological experience so frequently encountered in a pathological form in schizophrenics. I might even voice the belief that the schizophrenic form of psychic illness is regularly accompanied by illuminating insight into the irrationalism of social and political mores, primarily in regard to the rearing of small children. What we term genuine "cultural progress" is nothing but the result of such insight. Pestalozzi, Rousseau, Voltaire, Nietzsche, and many others are its representatives. The difference between the experience of a schizophrenic and the insight of a strong creative mind lies in the fact that revolutionary insight develops, in practice, over long periods of time, often over centuries. Such rational insight floods the general perspective of the masses in social revolutions such as the American Revolution of 1776, the French in 1789, and the Russian in 1917. In time the "radical truths" become as self-evident as the irrational views and institutions were previously. Whether rational insight will lead to individual mental illness or to rational transformation of the social situation depends upon numerous factors. In the individual it involves above all the capacity for genital satisfaction and the rational organization of thought. On the broad scale of the masses, it depends upon the integration of natural-scientific knowledge with social necessity. However, it is a well-known fact that correct insight may arise prematurely in an individual, i.e. before social processes have achieved the same level of understanding.

The history of the natural sciences and of cultural development is full of examples to prove this contention.

The axis about which this book revolves is the impeding of the functions of simple and natural life processes by social irrationalism, which, once engendered by biopathic human animals, becomes biophysically anchored in the character of the masses and thus assumes social relevance. What is remarkable is that political irrationalism has been maintained instead of a rational organization of social life. [It is truly a devilish problem.] The biological energy expended irrationally in a lifetime of biopathic functioning would solve the towering mysteries of human existence if it were rationally channeled. No one active in biopsychiatry can deny this allegation. The dream of a better social existence remains a dream only because the thoughts and feelings of the human animal are blocked off from the simple and obvious. This fact became clear spontaneously in the course of events.

I myself participated in the social irrationalism in Central Europe for many years. Later I was a target of it in my capacity as a physician and research scientist. For years I was both a political man [i.e. a man vitally interested in social affairs] and a working man without ever realizing the incompatibility of work and politics. The politician in me perished but the working physician, research scientist, and sociologist not only endured but, so far, actually survived the social chaos. I had the opportunity to follow numerous political catastrophes at close range and experienced several of them personally: the collapse of the Austrian monarchy, the council dictatorship in Hungary and in Munich, the fall of Austrian social democracy and the Austrian Republic, the birth and fall of the German Republic. I experienced the Hungarian, Austrian, and German emigrations. Then followed in succession the fall of Czechoslovakia, Poland, Holland, Belgium, Denmark, Norway, and France. Personal and professional interests connected me with all of these countries. One fact stood out prominently in all this political ruination: once a politician crossed the borders of his own country, he became useless and unable to establish himself socially. If, on the other hand, a work-

Introduction 9

ing individual crossed the boundaries of his homeland, he was sooner or later able to establish himself financially and vocationally in another country insofar as he was not hindered by politicians. This one fact embodies an enormous truth. Politics is restricted inherently by national boundaries. *Work is essentially international and free from the constraint of any borders.* We shall be able to evaluate this fact in all its social implications only at the end of this book.

At present, there exist a number of groups in Europe and elsewhere which have based their new social orientation on my sociological writings from the period 1927–38. It is therefore imperative at this time to clarify my position: I still bear the entire responsibility for every natural-scientific, medical, or sociopedagogic claim made during that period, to the extent that corrections have not been made in later works or may be made in the future. The theoretical structure of sex-economy stands essentially unchanged, on firm ground; it has withstood the test of decisive social events. Since approximately 1934 orgone research has laid the experimental foundation for this structure, although it is by no means complete. Today, sex-economy is a recognized branch of natural-scientific research. However, none of the old political concepts found in my early sociological writings remain justified. They were discarded along with the organizations under whose influence they found their way into my writings. An extensive revision of the social concepts of my political psychology may be found in the preface to the third edition of *The Mass Psychology of Fascism.*[2]

The exclusion of the concept of political parties does not represent a regression to academic, socially disinterested natural science. Quite to the contrary, it is an immense step *forward*—leading away from the realm of political irrationalism into the rational thought system of natural work democracy. I do not and cannot know which of my old friends and colleagues have gone through this same process and which of them are still operating with outdated political concepts. Anyone who is acquainted

[2] Farrar, Straus and Giroux, 1970.

with my shorter essays on work democracy—for the most part published illegally between 1936 and 1940—will also be informed on the process of my own detachment from politics. Hence I would like to reject any attempts made to exploit my party commitments of more than fourteen years ago by calling them party politics. I would feel constrained to protest immediately and publicly if anyone ventured to exploit my name or my writings in support of socialistic, communistic, parliamentarian, or any other type of power politics. The danger of such exploitation is small, however; it could only be implemented through distortion of my findings. Experience shows that ordinary party politics and orgone biophysics react to each other like fire to water.

I am not and I have never been involved with power politics. I joined the Socialist and Communist cultural and medical organizations in 1927 in order to supplement, with mass psychology, the purely economistic view of society contained in Socialist theory. Technically, I was a Socialist and a Communist between 1927 and 1932. Factually, functionally, I have never been a Socialist or a Communist and I was never accepted as such by the party bureaucrats. I never believed in the ability of the Socialists and Communists really to solve human emotional problems. Accordingly, I never held any party position. I knew well their dry, economistic orientation and I wanted to help them since they played the role of "progressives" in Europe in the 1920's. I was never duped by politics, but I was slow in distinguishing "social" from "political" processes. I had a high regard for Karl Marx as a nineteenth-century thinker in economics. Today, I deem his theory far surpassed and outdated by the discovery of the cosmic life energy. Of Marx's teaching, I believe only the *living* character of human productivity will remain. This is an aspect of his work that is utterly neglected and was forgotten long ago in the Socialist and Communist movements, which fell victim to mechanistic economy and mystical mass psychology—a mistake one does not commit so consistently without forfeiting one's place in the book of history.

And finally, no trace of a distinction was made between a scientific view of society and the bestial, ignorant, despicable cruelties perpetrated upon working people by biopaths who knew how to attain power by way of intrigue. To confuse a Duncker or Kautsky or Engels with criminal murderers of the Moscow Modju type is the surest sign of a degenerate, scientifically incompetent, and confused mind. If anyone today claims to fight Communism he must prove that in addition to chopping off heads he knows what it is all about.

[1952: It is impossible to master functions of life if one does not live them fully. No miner can mine coal while avoiding coal mining. No engineer can build a bridge over a chasm without the actual risk of falling into it. No physician can cure an infectious disease without the risk of acquiring it himself. One who has never been married knows nothing about marriage, and no one who has never given birth to a child or at least assisted practically in the birth of an infant knows what it is like. This is the meaning of work democracy. When Malinowski decided to study ancient cultures, he went to the Trobriand Islands, where he lived with the people in their huts, sharing their lives and loves. In this way he discovered functionalism in ethnology. *To think functionally, you must live functionally.*

Similarly, when I decided to do work in preventive mental hygiene (today called "social psychiatry"), I had to—and I gladly, even enthusiastically did so—join the people at the very roots of society wherever and however they lived, loved, hated, suffered, and dreamed into an uncertain future. At that time in Europe, the so-called lower classes were organized under Socialist and Communist leadership. There were four to five million Communist and seven million Socialist voters in Germany alone, and those twelve million leftist votes were significant among Germany's approximately thirty million votes. One must have lived these facts to know what "leftists" are; one cannot possibly judge Europe from the American continent without having done so. It is also essential to know that in the late 1920's the orientation of the Communist Party in Austria and Germany was still predominantly democratic. It had not yet fallen prey to the red Fascists, as was the case in the 1930's.

This, then, was my field of work in social psychiatry, and my first steps soon met with the full evil force of the emotional plague of man. It was not long before I began to realize that *I was the first physician and psychiatrist to discover the emotional plague on the social scene and to find himself entangled in a deadly struggle with the worst epidemic disease which has ever ravaged mankind,* a struggle which continues to this day. This realization was a crucial prerequisite to mustering the skill and will to learn, which was indispensable if I was to survive.]

The concept of a natural work-democratic life process in society precludes political activity in the old sense. *We advocate factual processes, not ideologies.* The serious worker persists in his task under all circumstances and pleads its cause as valiantly as possible. This holds true for every vitally necessary work process. We inform the world how our work is organized. The participants in all other work processes are just as responsible as we for the outcome of this human society. We cannot dictate to the mining or food industries how they are to organize their specific tasks in a work-democratic fashion. Our task is to prevent cancer and other biopathies, and thus to foster the sex-economic principle in rearing small children and to administer the utilization of cosmic life (orgone) energy. We are doing pioneer work with our psychiatric and biophysical knowledge and uncovering the basic principles of the life process.

Numerous, age-old experiences tell us that at every decisive step toward social hygiene some powerful policy maker will obstruct our path. Here I must mention that through many years of patient effort, and supported by the practical success of our scientific endeavors, we have attempted to cooperate with responsible politicians of every stamp. We have, however, encountered only difficulty and have had to overcome the hazards and calumny for which they were regularly responsible. Every catastrophe which sex-economy was forced to overcome in its development was brought about by politicians: Communist and Socialist politicians, politicians in psychoanalytic and medical organizations, Christian government politicians, fascistic state politicians, dictatorial police politicians, and many others. The representatives of sex-economy have proven they are willing to cooperate. The politicians have proven they are enemies, not so much due to personal motives, but rather because of the fundamental motives of their existence. Hence the fault lies with them if representatives of sex-economy, political psychology, and orgone biophysics no longer take cognizance of them. Because we are working for the implementation of our social tasks we have no alternative but to automatically oppose politics of every sort.

Our social position is clearly and unmistakably set forth in this book, as in other writings. We want the world of party politics to be aware of this position so that no one may claim afterward that he "did not know." The experiences of these last terrible twelve years have taught us that politicians like to use the fruits of other people's honest work to solicit the vote. Once they have secured a sufficient number of votes and thus gained social leverage, they throw overboard the issue on which they rode to power, without principle or scruple. It is characteristic of them to dispose of the worker through calumny or the firing squad once they have appropriated the fruit of his labor. No lengthy consideration is necessary to see that a Lenin or an Engels could not have survived the Russia of 1930. An American Freud would have had equally poor chances of survival had an American Hitler risen to power on his ideas. Today these issues are banalities.

We do not know who the politicians of Europe, America, or Asia will be in 1960 or 1984. Our attitude has been determined by the political machinations which we experienced in the years between 1914 and 1944. It is in the nature of every brand of politics to jeopardize natural science when it puts the politicians' promises into practice. Those in power are not interested in eliminating the individual worker but rather in eliminating the ruling principle of work. They wish to exploit work, but they do not wish to grant it the right to control the direction of society.

These statements have no personal implications, as we do not know the politicians of future decades. However, I do not hesitate to warn against them: Overt enmity is preferable to treacherous friendship.

We are better armed against the irrational attacks of politicians today than we were years ago. Time is now also on our side rather than against us. Actually the attacks of the emotional plague on sex-economy usually boomeranged, but they still required a great deal of effort and money and repeatedly jeopardized our lives. Hence it is essential to continually expose the irrational nature of politics so that it is well defined and publicized should ever an individual suffering from the emotional plague again feel provoked by the presentation of facts. Of course, one cannot defend oneself against a shot in the back. But perhaps politicians will be content to refrain from murder if we assure them we do not intend to compete with them for power, and that we shall cede the field of demagoguery to them completely, limiting ourselves to our work with hapless human victims. Incidentally, assassinations would be of no avail; they would only create martyrs. The searching, the helping, the striving for truth and happiness would reappear a thousandfold. I hope I have made myself sufficiently clear.

1
Wrong Directions

Following the First World War (1918–27), there was no mention of a psychological interpretation of sociological processes. Social economists either were strictly oriented toward a Marxist economy or based their contentions, in the struggle against the Marxist value theory, on a type of economic psychologism as advanced, for example, by Max Weber or similar schools. In the nineteenth century Marx had traced the sociological and ideological processes of society to the development of economic-technical productive forces. His successors as well as his opponents, during and after his time, were correct in seeking the psychological factors underlying these forces. But the Freudian natural-scientific concept of depth psychology was, in essence, individualistically oriented. It had made little sociological headway and even that was in the wrong direction. (Cf. my sociological criticism of psychoanalytic attempts at sociology in *Der Einbruch der Sexualmoral,* 1932.[1]) Non-Freudian psychology dealt with surface manifestations and was merely a branch of philosophy or of the so-called ethical sciences. It could not yet be designated a natural science. It knew nothing of the unconscious instinctual life of the human organism and remained focused upon surface phenomena to the extent that it did not degenerate into ethics. Because of these historical developments the "psychological" schools of economics and sociology moved in wrong directions. They were unable to penetrate to the eco-

[1] *The Invasion of Compulsory Sex-Morality* (Farrar, Straus and Giroux, 1971).

nomic core of sociology or the biological [bioenergetic] core of human structure. Obviously, as a result, no trace could be found of a relationship between the biological sexual process and socioeconomic processes. Ethical conviction, a substitute for a natural-scientific explanation of the human striving for freedom, was also mentioned in Marxist circles; the gap in Marx's economic theory was already felt at the time but it could not be filled. Questions were raised about the role of man in the social process, his "essence" or "nature" [human character structure]. In this context we must mention the Belgian Socialist Hendrik de Man, who contrasted Marx's "materialistic socialism" with his own "ethical socialism." Thus the psychological gap in Marxist sociology was acutely felt but no one was able to name the missing factor in the comprehension of social processes. It was obvious to everyone that in addition to socioeconomic processes independent of man, there somehow also existed man's own decisive intervention through thoughts and feelings. Ethical views and demands intervened only where concrete knowledge about human nature was lacking. Strictly speaking, the concept of classes was sociological, not psychological, even though every "class" had its own interests, desires, needs, etc.

As became apparent later, the [biopsychological] gap in social science was, in fact, the absence of a well-founded, natural-scientific theory of sexuality. A sociology of sex could only gradually develop from such a theory. Not only was this insight intellectually distant, but if anyone had advanced the theory he would merely have encountered a gaping void. There were neither writings nor the experience that could have claimed to constitute a theory of sexuality exactly suited to fill the gap in understanding left open by Marx's social economy. There were indeed numerous thorough examinations of the "history of the family," but in these the family—which is merely the form in which human sexual life occurs—was erroneously assumed to be the basis of the biological sexual process per se. The question of "the family" is, in itself, full of irrational, emotional elements and leads back to ethics once again instead of to natural science. Thus neither the "problem of the family" nor the "question of procreation" (as "eugenics" or "population politics") was integrated into social economy. Today, after the experience of Fascism, we know that the age-old mystical and unscientific version of eugenics and population politics formed the basis for the development of the Hitlerian theories of *Lebensraum* and race. We now understand that Hitler's race theory developed precisely within the gap of sociology which could not be filled by purely economically oriented sociology. I attempted to substantiate this fact fully in my books *The Mass Psychology of Fascism* and *The Sexual Revolution*.[2] My interpretation of the gap is generally accepted today, to the extent that it is known: The issue was not the form of the family or the question of procreation but rather that which family and procreation had obscured from the very beginning, i.e. the biological pleasure function in the human animal and the social institutions in which this function has to take place.

However, during that time, around the First World War and for many years thereafter, the biosexual process was completely shrouded in darkness. Sexology, represented by great names such as Bloch, Forel, Ellis, Krafft-Ebing, Hirschfeld, and others, dealt with (and could only deal with) the biopathic sexuality of the time, that is to say, the perversions and procreation of the biologically degenerate human animal. Orgastic potency, the core of later sex-economic sociology, was discovered and described only between 1920 and 1927. I had as little to contribute to filling the biopsychological gap in sociology as anyone else. Only one thing became clear to me at the beginning of my studies of Marxist and non-Marxist sociology: the lack of concrete insight into human structure had been replaced and obscured in the conservative camp by ethical demands and in Marxist sociology by an "economistic," i.e. rigidly mechanistic, view of the societal process which, as I learned only much later, had already been vehemently opposed by Lenin during the time of preparation for the Russian Revolution. In economism, dead machines and technology are the only decisive factors. Man, as representative and

[2] Farrar, Straus and Giroux, 1974.

object of this mechanistic social process, drops out of the picture. This will be demonstrated later with concrete examples.

In short, *all endeavors to comprehend and reorganize society operated with no knowledge at all of the central biosexual problem of the human animal.* Fascist irrationalism has since forced the question of irrational human structure upon us. At the time, however, it lay entirely outside the domain of sociology. I became involved with these problems through a remarkable concatenation of my activities as a sexologist with important social events.

When I wrote my book *Die Funktion des Orgasmus*[3] between 1925 and 1927, I was already trying to utilize the question of genitality in a sociopolitical[4] way. This turned out badly. The entire chapter on "the social significance of genital strivings" was later deleted.[5] Under the influence of the psychoanalytic theory of culture, I had attempted to use unusable theories.

I also produced my "'Contributions to the Understanding of . . . ,'" harmless trifles which only through their accumulation become dangerous. They contained the usual mixture of half-truths and complete falsities. For example:

The war signified a collective lifting of repressions, particularly of cruel impulses, with the permission of an idealized father image, the Kaiser . . .

Thus I followed Freud's reflections on war and death: the war as an expression of the sadism of the masses! In 1805 it was a corporal and in 1933 again a corporal whom the multitudes made their "Kaiser." Today we know that it is not "the sadism of the masses," but the sadism of small groups to whom the masses, who have become biologically rigid, helpless, and authority-craving, fall prey.

---

[3] This work is not to be confused with Reich's later work published under the same title as Vol. I of *The Discovery of the Orgone*—Ed.

[4] 1952: The terms "social" and "political," which today I consider opposites, were still united in my thinking at that time.

[5] At the same time, it was enthusiastically published by Swedish Socialists.

Economic interests brought external limitations which were added to the individually conditioned [!] genital inhibitions. The proletariat is not burdened with such economic limitations of genitality [!], and since the pressure of cultural demands is also lower than in the property-owning classes, neuroses appear relatively less often. Genitality is freer, the worse the material conditions of life.

I was a naïve and harmless academician: There are "individually conditioned" genital inhibitions; the proletariat is unburdened by economic brakes on genitality; it has fewer cultural needs; the poorer the material conditions of life, the freer is genitality.

Neither Marxists nor Freudians criticized me. They were in agreement. Later, in their struggle against me, the Marxists attributed the "free sexuality of the proletariat" to poor living conditions. The psychoanalysts were satisfied because I did not remove the boundaries of morality between those human beings with and those without cultural needs. A leading Hungarian analyst once told me that the proletariat corresponded to the unconscious since it was without instinctual inhibitions, whereas the bourgeoisie corresponded to the ego and superego, for it had to keep the id in check. This statement was in complete accord with the psychoanalytic theory of culture which maintained that society was structured psychologically exactly like an individual. Everything was in proper order!

There were also obscure sentences having a core of truth falsely expressed:

Whoever has learned to know the inner readiness to accept and to increase economic necessity as a way out of inner conflicts, cannot believe in a thoroughgoing solution of social problems with the usual methods.

Neurosis was an "individual" psychic conflict. It had nothing to do with the social order, except for "a few hardships and injustices."

Freud's psychology began to penetrate Socialist circles through the influence of persons such as the Viennese counselor and pediatrician Dr. Karl Friedjung. He explained to the Social Democratic physicians in charge of public hygiene in Vienna that the child has a sexuality. The famous Freud had discovered this; it was a great finding. With this knowledge, one could further "sublimation of the instincts." The Social Democrats supported Freud. On his seventieth birthday, they made him a "citizen" (note: not an *honored* citizen) of the city of Vienna. Prior to Freud's discovery, one had not known where the devil, sexuality, had its dwelling place and therefore it could not be adequately fought. Now one knew and rejoiced that it could be fought better, more scientifically, and hence more successfully. Such slogans as "Sexual enlightenment on a scientific basis" and "Healthy sex education" appeared, representing the demand for instinctual sublimation and the scientific prevention of "living out." Psychoanalysts began to write books on sexual hygiene. They advocated the "education of the instincts," a term anyone could interpret as he pleased. Federn and Meng, both members of Socialist parties, wrote: "Under our social and economic living conditions, sexual abstinence may be necessary for valid general and personal reasons. *For the majority of human beings, abstinence is not injurious to health*" (*Das psychoanalytische Volksbuch*, 1927, p. 237). "*Accordingly, the utmost avoidance of outer stimuli* [!] *is necessary for the carrying out of true abstinence. . . . Sexual excitation can be decreased by cold baths and swimming. . . . Spontaneous erections which give rise to masturbation and cause sleeplessness stop if one holds one's breath as long as possible and repeats this several times . . .*" (*ibid.*, p. 240) (italics mine, WR). When in 1929 I wrote my critique of bourgeois sexual reform[6] I refrained from criticizing these ethical Socialists. I had no answer myself, and to criticize without being able to do better is easy. I still wrote in the name of psychoanalysis.

Why do "the world," "culture," and "society" not allow young men the natural satisfaction of genitality? Why are there such masses of psychically ill people? Why has Freud been so mercilessly opposed? Why do medical students hear nothing of

[6] *The Sexual Revolution*, Part I.

the overridingly important processes of sexuality? In analytic treatment, the social barrier against natural sexuality emerges clearly and distinctly. Where is the sense in this nonsense? I knew no answer and the literature on the subject offered only stereotyped information: Culture demands morality—chastity in girls, sexual asceticism until marriage, and abstinence during puberty. Otherwise there would be no systematic work and therefore chaos.

I began to study ethnology and sociology: Whence do sexual suppression and repression stem? What is their function?[7]

[7] Cf. my examination of this question in *The Sexual Revolution* and *The Invasion of Compulsory Sex-Morality.*

2

A Practical Course in Marxist Sociology
(Vienna, July 15 and 16, 1927)

I had just undertaken the first few steps to orient myself in the study of ethnological and sociological literature (Cunow, Mehring, Kautsky, Engels, etc.) when certain events caught me "theoretically unprepared" and taught me practical sociology.

Schattendorf, a small village in the Austrian province of Burgenland, had a two-thirds Social Democratic majority. On January 30, 1927, the Socialist Party called a meeting at 4 p.m. Even before the meeting began, monarchist-inclined individuals shot at the crowd without provocation from a tavern frequented by veterans. The skull of a war invalid, a former comrade in arms, was shattered. An eight-year-old child was shot, a six-year-old child critically injured, four members of the Schutzbund[1] received minor injuries. The snipers escaped unhindered.

Why did the threatened crowd not react in absolutely justifiable self-defense? How could the reactionary killers escape in a village composed of a two-thirds Socialist majority? The population turned the matter over to the courts in a disciplined manner. The next day several large plants shut down in protest. On February 1, 1927, the chairman of the Socialist Party of Austria and

[1] Protective guard. —*Trans.*

the Austrian labor union called for a fifteen-minute protest strike. This was unanimously carried out. No mass demonstrations were held in the streets although the Social Democratic opposition did have the means to demonstrate impressively against the murderous action of the Monarchists. "One did not wish to provoke the citizens and excite the workers." The end result was the fall of Social Democracy on February 14, 1934, brought about by the same monarchistic organization which in 1927 attempted to find out just how far it could go.

On February 3 a parliamentary interpellation took place in the National Assembly. The Social Democrats very politely asked the Christian Social, Hapsburg-minded government whether it was prepared:

1. "to vigorously prosecute those individuals responsible for the killings in Schattendorf";

2. to dissolve the local veterans' organizations in the province of Burgenland.

The debate ended without a decision. The trial—I believe it was held on July 14, 1927, in Krems—ended in the acquittal of the killers, apparently by monarchist-inclined reactionary judges.

At 10 a.m. on July 15, 1927, a physician came to my office to keep his usual appointment for analysis. He told me that a strike of the Vienna Workers' Union had broken out. Several people had already been killed; the police were being armed; and the workers had already occupied the inner city area. At this I discontinued the session and walked down to the Schottenring, which was close to my home. The police headquarters were located on one of the streets I passed on my way. A number of policemen were standing there; they were being handed rifles from a truck. On the Schottenring long lines of workers marched in the direction of the University. They were dressed in work clothes and walked in groups, some of them keeping in step, but they were unarmed. I noticed especially the composure in their faces and the serious determination of their bearing. They were not singing or shouting. They walked in silence. From the University, the columns of the Schutzbund marched in the opposite direction toward the Danube embankment. Bystanders asked where they were going. The answer was: "To quarters." No one understood. Here a clash was brewing between heavily armed police and factory workers, and the troops of the Workers' Union, which had been organized for years for just such an occasion, were going back to their quarters. A week later, the general consensus was that the Social Democratic Schutzbund could have prevented the bloodshed that subsequently occurred by putting up barriers before the police. During the term of office of the Social Democratic City Council, Vienna had at its disposal a fifty-thousand-member Schutzbund with military training. If the encounter was to have been avoided the workers would have needed protection from the police. No one knew what went on within the Executive Committee of the Social Democratic Party. The first summary of events by the Socialist Party of Austria came out twenty-four hours later, on July 16.

I am reporting here from the standpoint of a mere onlooker. I was among those tens of thousands present at the time who were both onlookers and targets of the police. The reality of such days and hours during the "war of the classes" differs from the description in official reports on civil and class struggles. In these reports the conflicts, according to theory, are fought out between "capitalists" and "workers." In the streets, however, people actually run, scream, shoot, and die! I saw no capitalists on the street, only thousands and thousands of workers in and out of uniform, women, children, physicians, and spectators. The indelible impression remained that *people were warring here with their own kind.* The police who shot a hundred people in those two days were Social Democrats. The workers were Social Democrats. The Schutzbund was Social Democratic. The crowd was predominantly Social Democratic. Was this class conflict? Within the same class? In a city administered by Socialists? Here for the first time those misgivings arose concerning the irrationalism of politics in general which found their answer twelve years later in the formulation of natural work democracy. It was a practical example of the biopsychological gap in Marxism!

I continued with the crowd to the Schottentor. An armed police contingent was marching to the Palace of Justice, which was ablaze. The troops, for the most part Social Democrats, were looking toward the ground; the police officers walked with a constrained gait as if they had something to hide. Groups of people of every age and vocation were everywhere; not just the youth, but older women and office workers—in short, people one would see in the downtown area of any city on a normal day. Many called out to the police: "Don't shoot! Don't be fools! Whom do you want to shoot down?" A group at the Vienna Bank Association screamed furiously: "Worker killers!" and "You are workers yourselves!" The police hung their heads even lower. Their faces betrayed even more confusion. The first casualties had already occurred. The excitement was tremendous. But thousands upon thousands of people were still merely nonparticipating onlookers.

I walked on to the Rathaus Park. Suddenly shots rang out nearby. The crowd dispersed in the direction of the Ring and hid in the side streets. Several minutes later they slowly emerged again, like curious children whose fear had been overcome by defiance and boldness. When a crowd runs, one feels an irresistible urge to run with it. Several people screamed: "Stop! If you run away the police will shoot even more." Shooting continued in the park. Mounted police rode into the crowds. Ambulances with red flags arrived and drove off bearing the dead and wounded. It was not a riot per se, with two antagonistic factions, but simply tens of thousands of people, and groups of policemen shooting into the defenseless crowd. Only at the Palace of Justice was there a regular battle. Soon we saw flames mounting. Rumor had it that several police stations had been stormed. Four policemen had been killed at the Palace of Justice, compared to a hundred casualties among the crowd. The mob was so dense there was no access to the building, not even for the police.

Several policemen were stripped of their uniforms and forced to crawl away in shame in their underwear. The uniforms were symbolically hanging from flagpoles. I marveled at the crowd's clemency. There were enough people to tear the policemen to shreds and still they were peaceable and complaisant. The police passed unmolested among them even though people in the immediate vicinity were being shot down like rabbits. I could not understand this. How could the crowd look on and do nothing, absolutely nothing at all, to prevent the bloodshed? "Sadism of the masses"? The news that the Palace of Justice was afire was enthusiastically cheered by all. "That shack had it coming." Justice existed only for princes and the rich anyway. There was grumbling, to be sure, and mourning for the dead; but there were no actions that could have been termed *resolute*.

The Palace of Justice was occupied by young workers. They had driven the police out and now, in righteous fury, were throwing the records out of the windows into the street below, where they were set aflame. The Schutzbund was nowhere to be seen. The Social Democratic mayor of Vienna, Karl Seitz, drove a fire truck through the crowds toward the Palace of Justice but was unable to get through. The crowd would not move aside and simply allowed the building to burn down. Here and there killing was taking place automatically. Whenever a policeman or group of policemen felt the urge to do so, they shot blindly into the masses. For hours people continued to be shot down. I ran home to tell my wife, who could not believe it and felt it was all utterly impossible, as did, I am sure, hundreds of thousands of others in Vienna on that day. I asked her to come and witness it with her own eyes, and I walked to the University with her. We stood between the University building and the Arcaden Café with a crowd of three or four hundred watching the fire. Everyone felt that the blaze was a just response to the acquittal of the two Heimwehr[2] Fascists who had shot a worker and a youth *for no reason* and had just been permitted to go free. This was not objective justice but simply a "pact with murder." Approximately two hundred meters from the Town Hall there stood a phalanx of policemen with rifles lowered. We saw them gradually begin to move. They approached slowly, very slowly! When they were only about fifty paces from the unsuspecting onlookers, the officer in charge stepped aside and gave the order to fire. I saw several policemen raise their gun barrels and shoot over the

---

[2] A political organization; literally, Home Guard. —*Trans.*

people's heads. Many, however, fired straight into the crowd, which scattered. Dozens of people lay on the ground. It was hard to tell whether they were dead, wounded, or merely trying to protect themselves. I jumped behind a tree and pulled my wife after me. The police phalanx was now positioned parallel to the Schottenring. They no longer used their rifles but just stood there, two hundred meters away as before. Again I had the feeling of watching "a senseless machine," nothing more. A stupid, idiotic automaton lacking reason and judgment, which sometimes goes into action and sometimes does not. And this was what governed us and was termed "civil order." It ruled and prescribed whom I was allowed or not allowed to love, and when. *Machine men!* This thought was clear and irrefutable. Since then it has never left me; it became the nucleus for all my later investigations of man as a political being. I had been part of just such a machine during the war and had fired just as blindly on command, without thinking. "Lackeys of the bourgeoisie"? "Paid executioners"? Wrong! Merely machines!

Some of these machine men had enough life left in them at least to be ashamed. They averted their eyes or shot over the heads of the crowd. A living being does not fire blindly without knowing at what he is shooting and for what reason. Life had to have died within those who did so. This was not changed by the fact that the machines moved spontaneously, mechanically. If these mechanical men did not exist there would be no war. But how did they work? What controlled their actions? Who created them and why? How could living beings degenerate thus? This problem was not to be solved by attributing it to "corruption" or the "bourgeoisie." That was obvious. Being uniformed was also not the cause, although undoubtedly "organization" had something to do with the mechanization of humans. The psychologist Le Bon had studied mass mechanisms of this kind, and Freud based his *Group Psychology and Ego Analysis* on Le Bon's claims. Using the hierarchic organization of the army, the Church, and political groups as examples, he attempted to prove that under regimentation man divests himself of his individuality and identifies with the leader or the idea. He ceases to be himself and reaches back to infantile phases to implement identification. Moreover, the "primal horde" situation comes into play again: The sons submit to the all-powerful father and because of their guilt feelings identify with him "for culture and civilization." I quietly added: "and for peace and quiet." [SO: Witness the "quiet and order" in the middle of the twentieth century brought about by such culture and civilization!]

Freud's claims were correct. Servile identification with the leader could be directly observed, as could the loss of the individual ego and the effect of an abstract idea as well. But still . . . I was not satisfied. These explanations eternalized the facts and anchored them in biological lawfulness. The family was, after all, a biological institution and thus everything the family constellation engendered was biological as well! Therefore, there can be no possibility of change. Therefore, policemen for all eternity will, in this irresponsible fashion, shoot at people observing a fire. Therefore, these people will—for all eternity—set palaces of justice on fire and allow themselves to be shot down like rabbits and react complaisantly. And this is supposed to be progress in the development of culture! Is this culture? It is said that culture demands "renunciation of the instincts." Therefore, this crowd, despite its numerical advantage, renounced lynching those few policemen for reasons of "instinct renunciation," in order to qualify as civilized, in order not to act out the destructive death instinct, in order to sublimate their drives, in order to secure civilization. Yes . . . but . . . the police, the "representatives of civilization," fired indiscriminately at harmless masses of people. Where was the sublimation of *their* drives? And the "objective" judges had unhesitatingly acquitted outright murderers! Was *that* securing culture? Impossible! Somewhere an enormous deception lay hidden. Freud was hypocritical in this. But Freud was an honest, upright man! Why would he be hypocritical? Did he know? Certainly not. But then, why his firm, confident claims regarding cultural morality and the necessity for repression of the instincts? I felt an honest and very real urge to attack the police and simply to strike out blindly in every direction just as they had fired blindly into the crowd. Only the thought that I would stand alone restrained me. I had the strange feeling that my action would seem ridiculous, even to the individuals who had been shot at so recently. My strongest reaction was: The mistreated masses themselves would not understand! Otherwise they themselves would have reacted spontaneously! They did not need me to set them an example. I thought perhaps cowardice was influencing me and that a real Communist would certainly have jumped at the throats of the police under such conditions. However, the Communists and the Social Democratic leaders were nowhere to be seen. The latter had tried in vain to persuade the crowd at the Palace of Justice to allow the fire to be put out. I felt that the masses were unquestionably in the right and not their leaders. The judges who were meant to uphold and practice justice had pronounced murderers innocent.

In Alser Street, in front of the University clinic, I encountered a working woman who had just visited her son in the hospital. She cried out in despair: "Where are the Communists? They should beat those policemen to a pulp! They have shot my son!" But there were no Communists around. One or another may have been present as individuals, but not as "leaders of the proletariat." Only on the following day did the Communists distribute leaflets. [SO: The "Communist" already appears here as one who rectifies injustice by mere proclamation. In doing so, he hooks on to the yearning for justice in people, who then become gullible stooges of the red Fascists.]

In numerous illegal meetings I had learned that at such times the party had to "consolidate, direct the struggle as a leader, and ensure the best possible outcome." In isolated sessions behind locked doors, the Communists dreamed of mass revolts that would lead to the triumph of the revolution. Now the revolt against social offenses had erupted spontaneously. The leaflet came one day too late. Similarly, when the German bank crash occurred in July 1931 and everyone was waiting for the Communists, their poster arrived in Berlin eight days later when the "mood" had already passed. In the same way Russia came to Spain's aid several months too late, with "We did not know how to mobilize the masses," "We were still too weak," etc., etc. But when one is "still too weak," or does not yet "know how to mobilize the masses," it is a crime to call oneself the "only leader of the proletariat," to stand by helplessly in such catastrophes, undertaking nothing for the protection of the masses, and afterward to continue to agitate to revolt with full force, depending upon the occasion—for or against a strike, for or against bourgeois democracy, for or against a pact with Hitler or a war with Germany, for or against birth control, for the abolition of market economy, and for the oil trade with Italy in the Abyssinian war— in short, to be without forethought or conviction.

All this was unknown to me at the time. I, too, was waiting for the Communists. Hadn't they accomplished the Russian Revolution? They would take care of everything. They were no doubt still deliberating. On the same day, I had a Communist doctor register me in the medical group of the Arbeiterhilfe, one of the affiliates of the Austrian Communist Party.

[1952: The Arbeiterhilfe (Workers' Help) consisted mainly of people who were not party members but sympathized openly with the Russian Revolution. It and the Rote Hilfe (Red Help) were organizations similar to the Red Cross. In the early 1930's, however, there were many instances in which they were used for political purposes without the consent or even the knowledge of their membership, which was nonpolitical. My later conflict with the German Communist Party leadership over the Sexpol organization I had built up was characterized basically by the same pattern. I always maintained that the mental hygiene clinics had to be socially oriented but suprapolitical. However, the Communist Party leadership, in the service of Moscow, was already deeply entangled in power politics and intent on misusing the original purposes for which these organizations had been founded. It is the same today—everywhere. In this conflict which started around 1930, I strenuously opposed the Communist politicians who had obviously begun to develop and to organize all the trends which a few years later (1934–35) led them into fullfledged Fascism.

Awareness of the sharp contradiction between the factual (social) and the power-political approach to human problems

A Practical Course in Marxist Sociology 31

was never again absent from my sociological work. The factual approach maintains that social organizations, including economic ones, should be determined by the needs of the population. This was the way I had interpreted the Marxist economic theory. However, it became clear in our first clashes that the party ideologists had an entirely different interpretation of Marxist economics. To them all action and thought had to be oriented to "productive power," that is, to nothing more than machines. It is obvious that the industrial-mechanistic point of view and my functional one could never agree, since they led to opposite, mutually exclusive directions of social development. Today, these two views characterize two inimical camps. In 1927 I had very little knowledge of all this. I was soon to learn the hard way to distinguish sharply between a society determined by the needs of the people and one based on power machines. The poverty in Russia and the marked tendency toward poverty in Socialist England are clear expressions of complete disregard for human needs as the basis of social structure.

If we add to the economistic interpretation of Marxism the confusion of state with society and a misinterpretation of the relationship between individual and society (which meant the state), we can begin to comprehend the agony into which people slid unwittingly and unwillingly. We can also appraise the importance of clear thinking and the correct handling of scientific ideas for the benefit of the human community. I would suggest to the reader that he view all events as they roll by us on the following pages from the standpoint of this sharp contradiction in approach to human existence.]

I did not wish to censure or criticize but merely to help as best I could. When I heard from members of the Schutzbund that Otto Bauer[3] had told representatives of the gas and electric workers to "do what you like" and had then abruptly walked away, I felt acutely the enormity of the situation. However, I did not leave the Socialist Party of Austria. I decided to work socially as a physician wherever I could. Let me emphasize this: I was

[3] Leader of the Austrian Socialist Party. —*Trans.*

apolitical, a scientific worker, a physician with a highly successful private practice and wealthy American pupils. I was a member of the bourgeoisie.

The Palace of Justice burned to the ground. Every thoughtful person understood the motive for the fire. [SO: It was a true mass emotion, a genuine reaching out for justice. Twenty years later, traitors and well-hidden spies, misusing such emotions in order to kill justice everywhere, would enable red Fascists to march in. But why?]

The inner city was gradually cleared. Approximately a thousand critically wounded persons were lying in the overflowing hospitals. The conflict had claimed more than a hundred casualties because the Schutzbund had turned their backs. No one could have envisioned the reverse, namely, that in 1934 the Schutzbund would bleed to death and that the masses, their trust betrayed in 1927, would stay away.

In the suburbs, especially Ottakring and Hernals, there was more fighting on July 15. In the evening of that day, my wife and I walked through the desolate streets. The fighting had subsided. We encountered many agitated people, women in tears, and men who desperately asked what could be done to prevent further bloodshed. There was still no sign of the "only leader of the proletariat." We decided to visit a friend who lived in the vicinity; her father was in a Social Democratic organization and one of her brothers was even a Social Democratic functionary. We arrived and were amazed to find the dining-room table set and decorated with flowers; they were expecting guests. I was without a jacket and tie. The gory events appeared not to have penetrated this room. In my agitated state of mind I suddenly felt out of place and ludicrous in this cool, reserved atmosphere. I wanted to leave but was asked to stay. Then the guests arrived. A very intelligent conversation about the events of the day began in truly cultured Viennese fashion. It was obvious that no one knew what had really happened. They spoke of the bloodshed as they might ordinarily have spoken of Goethe. We said goodbye and took our leave. We had both remained polite. I would have liked, at the very least, to have overthrown their table, but I was sufficiently well-bred to discipline myself. I was a leading assistant in the Polyclinic Hospital and the superior of these Social Democratic colleagues.

July 16 passed with fighting in the northern suburb of Ottakring, but only isolated groups were involved and the crowds stayed away. Several people were killed and a number wounded. The police either patrolled the streets with special commando trucks loaded with carbines pointed upward, or rode self-confidently and brutishly through the side streets. It was horrible. Early in the morning of the third day the streetcars began to run again and the newspapers resumed publication. The everyday appearance of a large city was restored as if nothing had happened. However, a great deal occurred from that time onward. On July 15, Austrian Social Democracy had enkindled the forces of its own downfall in 1934. No one was aware of this; people simply debated and argued about the tactics and strategy of the "proletarian class struggle." Although it was not true, the Social Democrats accused the Communists of inciting people to set the fire that Seitz had tried to extinguish. This argument did not end until their common downfall in 1933 and 1934. The ruling party, led by the Catholic priest Ignaz Seipel, and various representatives of the wealthy bourgeoisie condemned the "revolt." No one spoke or wrote a word of explanation or pacification to the effect that such conflicts should be prevented for all time. The political parties, whether Christian Socialist, Liberal, or Communist, accused each other, threatened, negotiated, and maneuvered politically, but no one could be found to get at the root of the matter. Getting at the root of the matter would have required discovering and declaring that politics in itself is entirely irrational and a social disease. This would have necessitated dissolving all political parties. It would have been senseless to complain or to appeal to the conscience of the politicians. Their attitudes are a part of their social misfunction. One can either recognize them or stop them from functioning, but complaining serves no purpose.

The Social Democrats disclaimed all responsibility for the revolt although their organization had participated in the massacre. As one looks back on their organizational and, in part, their personal liquidation by the royalists in February 1934, several problems raised by the July revolt become quite clear. At the time, I knew of no one who could have discerned or grasped these problems. It is much easier to recognize them today after history has taught its cruel lessons. Hindsight is easy. One alters history only when one recognizes in time the processes and problems that are obscured from the general public. Social catastrophes result from the very obscurity and insurmountability of that which one would like to prevent. To this day, the energies of world reformers usually exhaust themselves in the observation that what has happened *had* to happen. But, to supplement a phrase by Marx, it is important not only to interpret the world, but to *change* it as well! Our politicians have remained interpreters and recorders, or else highway robbers. Changing the world radically requires honesty, courage, a scientific approach, and foresight, character traits no politician possesses.

The actual problems of the July revolt were:

Why were the masses of mistreated people so helpless?[4]

Why did the "reactionary" sons of workers and farmers shoot down workers and farmers?

Was it really a question of workers rioting against capitalists in the streets? Or was it the oppressed against the oppressed?

Did the middle class really only vacillate between the two other classes? Why did it not, in view of its own miserable economic situation, spontaneously and naturally take sides with the industrial workers?

It was impossible to pose such questions at the time. This would have required the complete exposure of political irrationalism as it occurred in the subsequent fifteen years. In contrast, the workers' movement had only the following facts:

Austrian Social Democracy was numerically strong. After gaining 3 mandates in the election of April 24, 1927, it comprised 71 seats as opposed to the 85 of the Christian Socialist Party bloc. Let us note that these 85 Christian Socialists and German Na-

---

[4] SO: Why, in forty years of social misery, did not a single sound, deep-reaching thought come from among the millions of workers? Why no action, no step toward peaceful living?

tionalists had not been elected by capitalists but by many hundreds of thousands of working people. In Parliament as well, it was not a matter of capitalists versus the working class, but of representatives of socialist-inclined working people versus those of Christian, monarchist, and German nationalist inclination. I am aware that this is an example of the clarity of hindsight.

The number of Social Democrat votes had increased, but power and courage had declined. In 1926, when the national population was 6 million, the Socialist Party of Austria received over 1,535,000 votes, against 1,312,000 votes in 1923. And in Vienna, with a population of 1.8 million, it received 694,000 votes in 1926, against 571,000 in 1923. When the party convention in Linz declared that nothing could prevent a power take-over once an outright majority was reached, there were numerous party members who felt that the day the 51 percent point was reached would be a day of dire catastrophe because then they would be compelled to assume power. But what to do with their power?

[There was *no bridge whatsoever* between what the Socialists promised (peace, brotherhood, "bread and freedom," a Socialist government, etc., etc.) and the true, deeply rooted character structure of the people which reproduced daily its own miseries of which they knew nothing and did not want to hear anything.]

It is my contention—contrary to that of many politicians— that it was not personal timidity or malice which prompted Otto Bauer's dangerously irresolute politics. I feel it was his complete insecurity as to what to do with the masses after a take-over, which repeatedly made him indecisive. Their helplessness was more frightening than their servility. Yet neither the helplessness nor the servility of the human masses was recognized or acknowledged. I do not know whether Otto Bauer ever even considered them. To do so would have been "heresy" against Socialist views, until the triumphant advance of Fascism made answers to these questions absolutely necessary. The numerous lofty political arguments for and against democracy obscured the central issue, namely, whether the working masses are capable of building a free society. They are certainly able to destroy the old authoritarian social institutions, as was demonstrated by the Russian Revolution.[5] The very successful propaganda of the reactionary organizations was based on the objection that one may not destroy the old unless one is able to replace it with the new. There was no answer to this, nor was there relevant historical experience—not even in Soviet Russia.

In general, there was fear of a breakthrough of mass rule. Very few people admitted this openly; many covered it with political slogans. No one was acquainted with the abysmal depths of the problem of human character structure. We were infinitely far from theoretical and practical organizational measures for solving this problem. The readiness of the masses for freedom was considered self-evident. No one could doubt this without being called a reactionary. (As was demonstrated later, there existed a definite fear of the basically conservative nature of the masses, which no one dared to confront.)[6] To do so would have undermined the entire basis of the political propaganda which, in accordance with the Coué method, employed fantasies of an ideal future society and illusions of human freedom. I lived through this phase, as did many others. One was socialistic by inclination but rejected, especially in vital areas, the foundation of a free development. It would have appeared insane to speak of the incapacity of the masses for freedom and their fear of freedom as was done later in 1935.

In 1927 there was no basis upon which a factual evaluation of the conservative attitude of the democratic leaders and the masses in every walk of life could have been made. This became possible only after the collapse of the Austrian and German democratic movements had conspicuously raised the question of the masses' capacity for freedom. It is easier initially for reactionary politicians to deal with the masses because they do not try to solve basic social problems. Their actions are determined by nationalistic sentiments and their success is based on complete disregard for and negation of the working masses' vital needs.

[5] SO: To date, the Socialists and Communists have failed to prove that they can build a new, free society. They have even failed to state this dry fact as a first step toward improvement.

[6] SO: This is largely so to this day, 1952.

A Practical Course in Marxist Sociology

The movements for freedom on the other hand, whether Socialism, Communism, Liberalism, or other, have an immensely difficult task; the number of questions and problems to be solved is limitless. The Socialists and Communists certainly knew the laws of capitalist economy and the outlines of a "socialistic society" as conceived by Socialist pioneers. Democrats of other persuasions believed in the possibility of peaceful and gradual reforms without taking into consideration the activity of the political reactionaries. Every gap in the Socialists' body of knowledge constituted an advantage for the reactionaries. The hesitant, halfhearted liberalism of the democratic-bourgeois faction in regard to strivings for freedom, and their frequently less hesitant liberalism toward the reactionaries, paved the way for the impending catastrophe.[7] For all of the democratic organizations, recognition of human anxiety and incapacity with respect to freedom would have been second in importance only to the mastering of daily tasks and the control of international social processes. For seven years (1927-34) I struggled within the workers' movement and in liberal organizations to evaluate the role of the people in the social process and to determine how to handle their subjective views and actions correctly. It was a matter of clarifying the role which biopsychic phenomena play in the development of society and of comprehending fundamental life processes above and beyond their economic basis. There was no information available which would have been of practical use. Hence everyone felt a gap which no one was able to fill. All factions raised arguments in opposition to freedom tendencies, and each was correct in some respect: the conservatives in demanding concrete plans for reconstruction and in fearing social chaos; the Social Democrats in their belief that the social revolution demanded by the Communists was an impossibility; the Communists in claiming that Social Democratic politics were a "betrayal" of the cause of freedom, that they constituted a strengthening of the reactionary political position and would finally lead to ruin. On the other hand, the Christian Socialists could not keep a single campaign

[7] The same phenomenon emerged in the Second World War, 1939-44, in the attitude of the English and American democracies.

promise, the Social Democrats were leading the masses to destruction, and the Communists were correct in theory (which is very easy) but not in practice. In 1927, they acted as a kind of admonishing conscience. Ten years later in Spain and France, they adopted the same practices they had accused the Social Democrats of using in 1927 in Germany and Austria. And between 1936 and 1942, they slipped into the pact with Hitler and further into complete confusion and the betrayal of their views. They carried on the war against Hitler in Russia as an authoritarian, dictatorial nation, not as possessors of a solution to the contradictions that were causing world chaos.

The basis of all mistakes made by all parties and of all the catastrophes they caused—no matter how well-meaning or honest they may have been—was the ideological confusion of the working population, its exclusion from practical control of the work process, and its incapacity for freedom, which was unrecognized at the time owing to the parties' fear of the masses. Their point of departure was not the life and suffering of the masses but an "ideology practiced in the interest of the masses" and used to brainwash them. The bizarre and even ludicrous debates in Parliament following the July revolt in 1927 may be grasped and evaluated only from this perspective. I shall cite but a few examples. A systematic chronicle of these events is not intended here.

The tactics of the bourgeois democratic governments were the same everywhere; they were unyielding and relentlessly opposed to the Socialist parties. They took ample advantage of the serious gaps in the Socialist world-view which revealed the Socialists' political weakness and lack of principle, as well as the guilt feelings of their leaders. They let no opportunity pass to increase the Socialists' insecurity or to appeal to their bourgeois political conscience. The Catholic prelate and Christian Socialist Federal Chancellor, Ignaz Seipel, a man clever, hard, and knowledgeable about psychology, recognized the weakness of the Socialists immediately. He supported the acquittal of the murderers in the Schattendorf trial. He said the jurors had had no other alternative, after the press campaign by the Socialists. They had to view the killing as "a political affair" and not a private act. This attitude was shrewd; the Social Democrats had portrayed the shooting as an individual act of murderers and had appealed to the conscience of the government. However, this government did not consider questions of conscience but rather the economic interests of big industry, of property owners, and of the Church, and this they did not deny. The Social Democrats were embarrassed that the rioters had correctly recognized the political character of the matter. Hence their first action was to draw a sharp line between themselves and the revolt. In his rebuttal speech before the National Assembly on July 26, 1927, Otto Bauer said that, in regard to the casualties, it was everyone's moral duty first of all to examine his own conscience. "Hence I wish to utter no word of accusation before openly confessing any fault on our part which may be revealed by an examination of our consciences." He then continued, naïvely exposing the Social Democrats' fear of their own mass support, and said the party itself might have held a demonstration "with all possible security so that order would not be disturbed." This would have given the demonstration "a political sting" and justified it. Bauer deplored the conduct of the Christian Socialists. "Shooting is popular nowadays, and shooting at citizens seems to awaken feelings of gratitude."

Bauer tried to stir the members of the ruling party emotionally. He said he understood when guards shot in self-defense, but that most of the casualties had been caused by an inhumane method of clearing the streets. Why did Bauer, a powerful man, with thousands backing him, not have the streets closed off immediately? The army and police force were still predominantly Social Democratic. They would not have opened fire had not the brother organization, the Schutzbund, been withdrawn. Bauer had not been confronted with the question of seizing power but only with the task of achieving the realistic goal of preventing the massacre, supported by his own authentic power. He would not have had to go begging in Parliament had he rationally used his power in Vienna to keep the peace. Because of his insecurity with the masses and the Christian Socialist government, he attempted to avoid civil war at any cost. Civil war had resulted nevertheless, and Bauer was unable to prevent it in 1927 or in 1934; he had merely lost it.

The masses go where they see strength, courage, and determination. There they feel secure. Every clear, decisive action increases the confidence of the masses and the strength and courage of their organization. It is better to lead a civil war *with* the masses than to have the police lead it against them. [Consider Lincoln's decisions in the American Civil War.]

Bauer demanded a statement by the government in favor of the arrested Socialists and sacrificed a general strike for it. However, "the government gave no explanation, *we* made the sacrifice. I will stand by what I did; I advised my friends to strike and I am proud of that. The beginning of this movement was something which must necessarily have aroused the reservations of every individual with a conscience, but its conclusion was a triumph of organization and of discipline." But only until 1934! Bauer appealed to the reason of the Christian Socialist government and to its statesmanlike insight. "Hold me back or else I shall have to shoot against my will!" This was the way Bauer functioned. Finally, in 1934, he did have "to shoot" after the battle had long been lost. But Bauer could not have acted otherwise. He really did not know what to do. [SO: Appeasement is always the expression of a lack of knowledge as to how to act.] He would certainly have carried through courageously to the end had he seen the issue in its entirety. He later proved that he was personally not a coward.

He made the right demands but they could not always be fulfilled. In 1927 there was no one competent to say how Otto Bauer should have handled the situation. Most people knew or sensed that his actions were wrong; some people even thought he was laying the groundwork for a catastrophe. But would these critics have done a better job in his place? I say no! No one had the ability. There are phases in the social development of a movement which correspond to the demands of urgent life-forces. Then there are phases which only partially correspond to these demands and in which one can already perceive mistakes without being able to avoid them. One can explain which mistakes lead to negative results but cannot yet say how the developmental process could be turned in a positive direction. In such phases, a responsible leader [It is said that a thousand heads are better than one; unfortunately, they often see and know much less than one alone] should be able to: (1) see that mistakes are being made, (2) look for the possible negative consequences, (3) make the movement aware of both, and (4) mobilize all forces in the movement which are capable of working together to reverse the trend.

These are only the indispensable prerequisites for avoiding an impending catastrophe. They do not in themselves avoid it but merely prepare the ground for further possibilities. When the actual events lead to success or cause defeat, insight and comprehension are sharpened. Only in the course of the battle for the new are its most important weapons forged. At the beginning, only a yearning for freedom (in itself powerless) and a theory about the goal (also powerless per se) are operative. They do not gain power over people and hence over reality until they are in harmony with historical development and only insofar as they solve the real problems of human existence, step by step, and constantly correct themselves in relation to reality.

No individual or movement can anticipate, control, or successfully master all the questions the future will raise. Moreover, the spirit of opposition is also actively plotting and its cunning increases in direct proportion to the number of those yearning for freedom. Sometimes the movement is struck by a catastrophe. This happened to the Russian Socialists in 1905 when their revolt was crushed. However, a defeat of this nature, tragic as it may be, still lies on the path toward success, to the extent that no glaring errors were made beforehand. The inability to grasp and to solve everything immediately cannot be counted as a mistake. But it is an unpardonable mistake not to be aware of this and to hinder, and even take punitive action against, the initiative to fill in these gaps. In the long run no movement can escape the consequences of this inferior manner of operating. If one is prepared for the consequences of incomplete knowledge, in other words the possible success of the opponent, then a setback does not necessarily mean complete failure. The German and Austrian workers' movement brought about its own downfall by refusing to recognize the gaps in its body of knowledge, by being arrogant about the success it achieved, by leaving the pioneers of the movement out in the cold, by underestimating the opposition, and by physically and spiritually undermining the masses who supported it. However, even these errors and self-destructive actions were not an expression of malice or cowardice but were very deeply rooted. The gap that had to be filled required knowledge and action contrary to the entire structure of Socialism as it existed until 1934 and to the whole ideology as it was maintained organizationally up to that point. The whole concept of Socialism, to the extent that it concerned the transformation of man, was incorrect, often basically false, and very frequently anti-socialistic. To explain and prove this, even in the briefest terms, would fill a hundred pages. There is far too much to be clarified.

When a movement with a certain goal, a circumscribed ideology, contradicts essentially itself, it will be crushed by its opponent. It crushes itself, so to speak, because it rejects its own goal, which is then taken up by other social forces. When the aims of a movement are broad but lack clarity while the collective will toward a common goal is indomitable, then the entire society is threatened with ruin. This situation materialized with the victory of German Fascism in 1933. Although thirty-five million Germans wanted Socialism in that year, Hitler was victorious, as grotesque as it may sound, with his reactionary and limited but courageous and shrewd tactics. The socialistic will of a population of seventy million people lived under the specter of barbarism, shabby tricks, and war as the center of their lives. No one was able to comprehend this, to grasp it in time, and to prevent it. The workers' movement collapsed because it did not understand the thousand-year-old problem which the Fascist movement had brought to light. It was a basic problem of human society, and in this—but only in this—was German Fascism progressive. I am convinced that the question it raised will be solved not by Fascism but rather by the aggressive advance of science. It was the

A Practical Course in Marxist Sociology

question of the role of human beings in the technical developmental process of society, a misunderstood and even abused issue. The life work of numerous secular geniuses, the sacrifice of millions of people, and all the suffering of a thousand years of human history were needed to formulate it, to grasp it, and to attain the first childlike beginnings of a solution.

To introduce the exposition of this problem I must return to Otto Bauer and the maltreatment he received from his opponents in 1927.

Bauer had cleared his conscience before the opposition. He then appealed to reason, to the government's "judgment." It had to try, he said, "to quiet the agitated masses with a gesture indicating that this may not continue and that the government does not wish you to abandon yourselves further to blind hate." What fear of mass indignation! Certainly Bauer sensed the complexity of human structure. He simply did not know that this structure had been created by the oppressors. He believed in its biological, i.e. unchangeable, nature since even Freud, the greatest psychologist of the century, had proven scientifically that biologically immutable destructive drives exist in man. To unleash these drives would unquestionably lead to chaos. Bauer's Christian Socialist opponents, however, were not theorizing about destructive drives, introverted or extroverted. They were not even considering burdening themselves with the problem of how "to make evil people good." Their maxim was: Beasts should be under lock and key; make short work of them; put them in chains. Hitler was the end product of this attitude. [SO: The Socialists and Communists have no answer either and nothing to offer here except, again, brutal force against the people, as used in red Fascist Russia.]

After Bauer, Kunschak, the leader of the Christian Socialist government party, spoke. He rejected an investigation. He was not interested in whether any police agents had overstepped their authority, but solely in who was responsible for the tragedy. "The Christian Socialists will convey their gratitude to the Chancellor."

The Christian Socialist Vice-Chancellor, Hartleb, declared that he assumed all responsibility for the police intervention.

Gürtler of the Christian Socialists answered Bauer: "We would gladly have granted you this moral success (the pacification and distraction of the masses), but we cannot simply overlook the fact that you were no longer in a position to achieve it. . . . *A revolution is as much a calamity for you as for us.*" [How true!] And Otto Bauer, the initiator of the revolutionary program in Linz, had to listen to this without being able to give an answer. Gürtler was right. A mass revolution would have been a disaster for Bauer and his party, who would not have known how to handle it. Would the masses have known? Or the Communists? Let us wait for an answer.

The Christian Socialist Aigner recognized Bauer's deep emotions as "honest and heartfelt." "However," he said, "during his speech I had the impression that here stands the responsible man of that party which for years has led these unfortunate victims before the guns of the executive power of the state through unrestrained agitation in the press and the spoken word." And Grailer remarked, "In the future when you raise your arm to strike, you may expect the heavy blow to fall upon *yourself.*"

How gruesomely correct these reactionaries were in the final analysis! How could they be so confirmed in their opinion when they had absolutely nothing to offer the human masses, either their supporters or their opponents?

What did the Communist Party of Austria, which because of its convictions considered itself the real "leader of the workers," have to say about all this? [SO: What would any of the "freedom" politicians have had to offer? WR, at that time, was deeply involved in these problems, but he was far from knowing that no politician had anything whatsoever to offer, and that the events of 1927 were only a small link in the chain of mass murders which occurred in the following decades.]

The masses of manual laborers belonged to non-Communist, Christian Socialist, and Social Democratic worker organizations. On every possible occasion the Communists demanded the arming of the workers, the dissolution of antagonistic organizations, a general strike, etc., etc. When the workers were involved in actual fighting, the Communists came too late (Spain, July 1936)

A Practical Course in Marxist Sociology

or had no contact with the mass movement and no leadership (Austria, February 1934) or curbed the mass movement (Germany, October 1933). However, they always laid claim to leadership because of their "convictions."

This brings us to the question of why, assuming its program is valid, the Communist movement has no contact with the mass movement? The answer to this is not to be found in any of the polemic writings but in the evidence that, after 1918, the masses had a different concept of Socialism than the Communists, that their desires were full of contradictions, and finally that although the Communists knew, theoretically, the principles of socialist economy [which they later abandoned] they never had the slightest idea of the real life of the masses.

For years the Communists had encouraged what finally took place spontaneously on July 15. On the evening of July 14 they called a meeting of their plant representatives, about eighty people, "who said they were making an attempt to lead the workers out of their shops, but were not convinced their efforts would be successful. If successful in prevailing upon the workers to walk out, a quiet demonstration was to take place." ("Vienna is red—with the blood of the workers." —letter to Inprekkorr,[8] July 19, 1927.)

They "analyzed" the causes of the spontaneous movement with all the latest subtleties of their "Marxist-Leninist" method, the only one suited for leadership. In an anonymous pamphlet put out by the Association of International Publishing Houses, Berlin, 1929, they arrived at certain conclusions. The causes of the July revolt were attributable to:

1. The Social Democratic tactics of evasion and persuasion toward the bourgeoisie. (This would mean that the Social Democratic workers rose up on July 15, 1927, because they were infuriated at their hesitant leaders, whom they subsequently followed completely for another full seven years until 1934.)

2. The Austro-Marxist habit of "accompanying all compromise with radical speeches and gestures . . ." Please note care-

---

[8] International Press Correspondence. —*Trans.*

fully: The workers took to the streets because of the radical language used by the Social Democrats. The individuals in the Christian Social government made the same claim.

3. The "poor economic situation of the workers." In Austria the economy was booming in 1927—and two casualties had mobilized the workers. In 1932, there was dire need and crisis; there were continuous killings everywhere—and not one single worker took to the streets. The matter is more complicated than the "only leaders of the proletariat" had indicated in their premise.

4. "The main reason for this sudden outbreak is the lack of a revolutionary people's party with revolutionary leadership recognized by the masses." Please read this sentence carefully several times: The main reason for "the revolt" was the lack of a revolutionary people's party. If, however, such a party had existed, no revolution would have taken place. Between 1930 and 1933, as Hitler rose to power, there was a revolutionary people's party. At that time no sudden revolt occurred. The statement thus seems correct but is nothing but confusing nonsense, an expression of the complete factual and theoretical loss of direction on the part of Lenin's successors. Where were the units the Soviet Russians had trained in the "strategy and tactics of class struggle"? And why were the masses who desired the revolution not willing to recognize this leadership either now or then? [SO: Why did the red Fascists have to steal and murder their way into power even after the Second World War?] Why, then, all the demands for a general strike and the proclamations of the plant representatives such as those at the "Heimwehr" demonstration in Pottendorf? Why, then, the Coué-type proclamations and agitation for a general strike? It is not my intention here to recapitulate the story of the Communist movement. I have merely attempted to indicate the level on which politics was operating and the ideology into which the struggle for recognition of mass psychology was placed.

At the end of July 1927, I had a discussion with Freud on the Semmering. It seemed to me that he lacked all understanding of the revolt and viewed it as a catastrophe similar to a tidal wave. I would like to emphasize that, other than the spontaneous

A Practical Course in Marxist Sociology

angry eruption of the masses over the unjust verdict in Schattendorf, there was no response, in either intellectual or political circles, which shed any light on the events. Neither before nor after July 15 had the working population shown any inclination to place the revolt in an intelligible social context. Their reaction to the Schattendorf verdict was the burning of the Palace of Justice in Vienna, for which they paid with thousands of dead and wounded. They did not respond at all to the far more serious and dangerous abuse of their civil rights by reactionary political forces in the following years until the downfall of their organization in February 1934. [This is a good historical example of mass-psychological irrationalism.]

I would have given my thoughts free rein if I had known the answers to the many questions which rushed one after another through my mind. To be sure, everyone was talking about everything in a hit-or-miss way. As I listened to this talk, the feeling of the senselessness of politics must have taken possession of me for the first time. Never had I seen any relationship of politics to the actual life of human beings, but clinical work had convinced me that one must have experienced a thing completely in order to judge it correctly. Thus I began practical political-sociological work.

3

The Living Productive Power, "Work-Power," of Karl Marx

A brief comment to avoid any possible misunderstanding. I have portrayed the figures of capitalists and property owners in anything but glowing colors. In this context, however, such individuals have been referred to only insofar as they personify economic categories or champion certain class conditions and interests. I view the development of an economically based form of society as a natural historical process, and my theory holds the individual less responsible for prevailing conditions than does any other. Man remains the product of his social environment regardless of how far he may rise above it in a subjective sense.

—Karl Marx, *Capital*, preface to the first edition (1867).

FOREWORD

This article was written in 1936 as the sociological illusions in the Soviet Union assumed the character of constitutional statutes ("Introduction of Soviet Democracy"). The article was not published at the time. There is a twofold reason for its publication now.

1. Scientific, i.e. truthful, thinking is more necessary in this miserable human society than ever before. Armed conflict will not change the misery one iota. Although German Fascism has been defeated by military power, the fascistic human structure continues to thrive in Germany, Russia, America, everywhere. It will metastasize underground, seeking new forms of political organization, and without fail will lead to a new catastrophe

The Living Productive Power, "Work-Power," of Karl Marx

unless responsible groups throughout the world decide quickly and energetically to protect and advance the truth. Only political lies are protected and advanced today. This can be predicted with certainty.

From the scientific standpoint, which is the only possible perspective, the following explanation is altogether permissible: Karl Marx discovered vital facts having far-reaching social consequences, but the realization of these consequences is impossible because knowledge and techniques are not yet adequate to produce a sufficiently rapid change in human emotional structure. There can be no objection to this viewpoint, which contains hope for the future. One may hail Marx or condemn him. That is a matter of choice. But one may not under any circumstances, if one lays claim to common decency, refer to Marx and then distort his scientific findings for the purpose of political maneuvering. We may not distort an established truth without sooner or later making ourselves accomplices of Fascism, that past master of deceit. Even if changing the human situation to correspond with true scientific claims is impossible, the misery of daily life must under no circumstances tempt us also to crush humanity's only hope, the truth.

[The emotional plague affected Marx's theory of value in the following way: In their attempt to arouse the emotions of the masses and to win them over, the party politicians forgot about the unemotional explanation of the value of work-power. They attached to the factual concept of "surplus value" feelings of resentment, hatred, envy, and the urge to pocket surplus value oneself. Thus the fruitful and promising findings of Marx got lost in a heap of irrational emotions which not only led to no practical achievement but brought ruin to the whole workers' movement.

True, the emotional plague is able to win masses, conquer nations, destroy populations, but it is unable to provide even one constructive measure for the improvement of economic misery. True, the emotional plague can shoot to pieces, burn, or otherwise destroy millions of trees. But there can be no dictatorship over the growth of trees; one cannot prescribe to a tree how fast and how much it should grow. On the other hand, scientific research into the laws of tree growth can provide the means of preventing damage to trees, of improving the conditions under which trees grow faster and better. Scientific fact finding corresponds to the mastery of obstacles in the way of unfolding life.

This example shows clearly the biological function of natural science as contrasted with the destructive function of every manifestation of emotional plague. What political groups in Europe and America fight as "Marxism" has nothing to do with Marx's economic teachings. Similarly, the various "Marxist" parties of today have nothing in common with Marx's science.]

Ten or more years ago one was severely reprimanded if one tried to alter a single line of Karl Marx's writings and one would have been ostracized for declaring scientifically that Marxist economy badly needed to be supplemented by a scientific mass psychology. Yet, recently Marxism was "revised" in the Soviet Union. Official state economists "discovered" that Marx was incorrect in claiming that, in Socialism, no surplus value would be produced and accumulated, that this was a specialty of capitalism.

Here lies the distortion: Nowhere in Marx's economic theory is there any mention that, in Socialism, the production of surplus value would cease to exist. This "revision" is meaningless; actually it is nonsense because what has been corrected was never proposed.

The basic problem of Karl Marx was not whether surplus value is or is not produced in Socialism. The problem involved the nature and origin of surplus value and the question of who manipulates it. Surplus value is produced because of the particular character of living productive power. The fundamental difference between living and dead productive power forms the core of Marx's economic theory.

A determination of the nature of living productive power, and through this of the origin of surplus value, then leads to the sociological question of who acquires the surplus value. It is always appropriated by the owners of the social means of production: in private capitalism, by the individual capitalist; in state capitalism, by the state; and in free work democracies,[1] by the society of workers (as seen historically in primitive societies and envisioned by Karl Marx in the genuinely democratic society of the future).

One may form one's own opinion of this statement, accept it enthusiastically or detest and reject it, but one may not distort it. Shifting the problem of surplus value production from its nature, origin, and appropriation to the question of "whether it exists" is an illegitimate distortion of scientific findings. The following corrections have nothing at all to do with political sentiments but only with a vital interest in protecting the body of scientific knowledge. In our day, it is not superfluous to emphasize that scientific questions such as these are not to be disposed of by means of the firing squad, that most modern instrument for settling human arguments.

2. The second reason for the publication of this article at present is the consonance of Marx's analysis of living productive power in surplus value with the orgone-physical investigation of biological activity in the human animal. Since approximately 1928, sex-economy has been aware of the fact that Karl Marx's living productive power is identical with what orgone biophysics refers to as the "work function of biological energy." I would like here and now to express my deep human and scientific satisfaction that a thinker and researcher of the stature of Karl Marx elevated a specific life function to the very core of his "dry" economic theories. Working humanity owes him gratitude, for he was the first to achieve this. Allowing him to practically starve, continually defiling his name, falsely ascribing claims to him which he never made, and appropriating his practical scientific achievements without credit to him—all add to humanity's al-

---

[1] Work democracy is based essentially on two facts:

a. A worker is anyone who does socially necessary work, i.e. not only the manual worker.

b. Social responsibility rests with the society of the workers and not with private individuals or individual state functionaries.

ready heavy indebtedness to Marx. It is not Marx who is at fault. It was my duty as a scientist to make clear what an unthinkable social mentality is attempting to blur.

Wilhelm Reich
Orgonon, July 1944

In the summer of 1927, while living with my family in the town of Lans near Innsbruck, I studied *Capital* by Karl Marx. After carefully working through the first hundred pages of argumentation regarding surplus value, I realized that Marx signified for economics what Freud had meant for psychiatry. His basic views were simple, self-evident, and contradicted all the traditional concepts. Pre-Marxist and non-Marxist economists, on the other hand, attempted to deduce profits from the "natural value" of inanimate material, and from currently available and invested capital, etc. Before Marx, the economists had claimed that the value of commodities was determined by the ratio of supply and demand. Marx proved that this causes only slight price fluctuation and that the value of commodities is determined by the human "work-power" expended upon them. Marx said that a tree, in itself, is of no "value" as long as human effort is not "added" to it. Only when the tree has been felled, sawn into pieces, processed into boards or poles, does it gain "value" for mankind. This holds true of everything which has "value." Air has no "value"; it is free because it may be consumed without additional human effort. The hide of an ox also has no value until human hands process it into shoes.

Marx differentiates between constant and variable capital. Constant capital is composed of inanimate raw material and inanimate machines. They yield no profit of themselves until human work, i.e. variable capital, transforms them into commodities, into use value. Since money can be lent for interest, the value of capital lies in its yielding money over again, whether through investments in business (industrial capital) or through loans (bank capital). Money, according to Marx, is only paper, issued to facilitate transactions based on a social convention. It has no value of itself, aside from the effort expended to produce the bank notes and coins. It receives its actual value only through what it represents, what it can be exchanged for, such as a commodity. However, not only inanimate but also living commodities are bought. The entrepreneur pays the worker for the use of the commodity "work-power." Work-power can be bought and sold exactly like any other product. If I am a shoemaker and sell a pair of shoes which I made, they no longer belong to me. Similarly the labor which a machinist sells to an owner of capital no longer belongs to him. Just as the buyer of the shoes may use the intrinsic value of the shoes as he pleases, the entrepreneur may do as he pleases with the work-power he has bought, and may exploit it however he pleases. This is not "wrong" but entirely legal according to the laws of market economy.

Marx defined the concept "capitalist" scientifically. It is not, as is commonly assumed, an individual who possesses a lot of money, but a person who is able to buy and make use of the work-power of others on the basis of the laws of market economy. If, as a doctor, I am proficient in my field, cure numerous patients, and discover good methods of healing, then many sick people will come to me. They pay for my time and, along with this, for the value of my work-power. In order to do my work I must repeatedly renew my work-power, that is, I must eat, house myself, buy clothes, etc. This constitutes one part of the value of my work-power. But with this alone I could not carry on my specific work. I need, additionally, certain training which requires work and money, continuous expenditure of effort for further development, instruments, etc., upon which others have exerted their work-power. I pay for all this with portions of my work-power. Hence the patient must pay not only for my work-power but for all the work-power expended upon him through my work. This is done through the conventional value substitute "money," by means of which I, in turn, may purchase the results

The Living Productive Power, "Work-Power," of Karl Marx

of other people's effort, such as shelter, food, clothing, etc., i.e. use values. As long as I myself work, I am not a capitalist no matter how much money I earn. However, if I were to employ, let us say, four doctors, pay them a fixed salary of two hundred kronen a month, and use their eight-hour work-power to treat patients for me, *then* I would be a capitalist. Then I would be "exploiting" the work-power of others and appropriating the value of their work-power in the form of money. In eight hours, I myself could treat eight patients and earn eight hundred kronen in twenty-five working days. Four doctors, however, could earn four times as much, namely thirty-two hundred kronen. While I would have to pay the four doctors a total of eight hundred kronen, I could keep what was left of the thirty-two hundred kronen they had earned, thus acquiring twenty-four hundred kronen through the exploitation of other people's work-power *without having worked for it myself*. According to the laws of market economy, I would not be considered a swindler but would be acting entirely within the law. No one could prosecute me or accuse me of wrongdoing.

Karl Marx's great accomplishment lies in having disclosed the secret of the living commodity, work-power, its dichotomous character, and the difference between exchange value and use value. If a person has produced a pair of shoes which he does not plan to use for himself, the shoes have no use value but rather exchange value. He can exchange them for peas, meat, or money. As a value replacement, he receives approximately the value of the work-power necessary to produce them. The work-power, as has been stated, is measured in work-hours, the average number of work-hours expended. The purchaser, however, does not buy the shoes for their exchange value but for their use value. He must have them to satisfy a need, in this case to protect the soles of his feet while walking. He is entitled to have the *complete* exchange value of the shoes, which he paid for in the form of money or meat, returned to him in the form of serviceability of the shoes. *The exchange value and the use value of a dead commodity in which human work-power is objectified are identical.* On the other hand, the only living commodity, work-power, functions differently precisely because it is a *living* power. In it the exchange value and the use value are not identical. The use value is far greater than the exchange value.

Every type of worker, i.e. the person who creates use value, sells his commodity, work-power, to the entrepreneur just as the shoemaker sells a pair of shoes, and according to exactly the same laws of market economy. But the worker must reproduce his commodity himself by eating, buying clothing, and finding shelter. For this he must work, let us say, three hours a day if we again measure the value of food, shelter, and clothing in terms of average labor necessary for the reproduction of work-power. These three hours constitute, according to the laws of market economy, the exchange value of his work-power. The capitalist, therefore, does not cheat the worker in paying him for the exchange value of his commodity, work-power, the value of three hours of work a day. At least he does not cheat him according to the laws of market economy in which human work-power is negotiable like any other commodity. But the buyer of this commodity, e.g. the owner of a factory, uses the laborer's work-power, not for three hours a day (in keeping with its reproductive value as measured in work-hours), but rather for eight or even ten hours. This means that the use value of the labor expended by the worker (eight hours of work) is greater by far than the exchange value for which he is paid (three hours of work). The profits of market economy arise from the difference between the lower exchange value and the far greater use value of work-power. If a wealthy purchaser of this commodity buys the work-power of a thousand or ten thousand workers as use value, he utilizes the latter at a corresponding multiple of its exchange value. This is because a thousand or ten thousand workers now transform inanimate material, dead capital, into commodities by adding their work-power a thousand or ten thousand times. Their labor is collective, but the appropriation of the value of the commodity is individual ("capitalistic"). If a shoemaker produces two pairs of shoes a day in his shoeshop, he receives the exchange value of two pairs of shoes. If, with improved machinery, he produces ten pairs of shoes a day instead

The Living Productive Power, "Work-Power," of Karl Marx

of two, he can collect the exchange value of ten pairs of shoes. If, however, he is a worker in a shoe factory which continually improves its machinery, he nevertheless receives no pay increase as exchange value for his labor despite the increased production of use value. The utilization of his work-power by the capitalist has remained approximately the same although the "exploitation" has risen because the exchange (=use) values he now produces have greatly increased. But the product is not at his disposal. He simply continues to sell his commodity, work-power, in compliance with the laws of market economy, at the market price for three hours of work. Anyone who supports himself by selling his work-power is a worker. Anyone who purchases the exchange value of this commodity and exploits its use value is—due to the difference between exchange and use values of living work-power—a capitalist in the Marxist sense of the word.

According to strict Marxist scientific principles, it is a mistake to hold the capitalist responsible for exploiting the individuals who produce these values. Contrary to the views of narrow-minded Socialists, neither the individual capitalist nor the capitalist class is "at fault." The essence of the exploitation lies in the nature of economically structured class society based on market economy. This is what makes it possible for an individual—by whatever means—to acquire sufficient capital to enable him to purchase other people's work-power and make use of the difference between the exchange value and the use value of work-power. The economic swindling of the worker is based on the conditions of capitalistic production and not on human intent.

Comprehension of the following paradox in the reasoning and propaganda of the Marxist parties is indispensable for an understanding of natural work democracy. On the one hand, they were strictly economistically oriented; the character structure of human beings as they are in reality was completely excluded from their thinking. As became apparent later, any consideration of human character structure in the struggle for genuine democracy was sharply opposed. On the other hand, Marxist propaganda did not operate with the "material" facts of human biological and social existence, but essentially with secondary, neurotic drives such as hate, jealousy, power mania, etc. I am aware that the followers of Marx will take my statements as a grave insult. It is not my intention, however, to insult anyone but merely to reveal the facts which helped to bring on the catastrophe. Using a simple example from my medical practice, I would like to illustrate the difference in attitude between Marxist party politicians and those making work-democratic efforts toward freedom. When one is confronted with a neurotic child suffering from insomnia and learning disturbances, even a superficial conversation will reveal the child's neurosis as the result of faulty upbringing by a neurotic mother. At this point it would serve no purpose whatsoever to condemn the neurotic mother or to provoke the child's hate against her. Establishing the harmful influence of the mother in rearing her child serves only *one* purpose, namely to cure the child's neurosis. Realization of this fact enables me to intervene and be of assistance. Without knowledge of this fact, revolutionary moral indignation or the kindling of hate in the child could help neither child nor mother. The ill mother who caused her child to become neurotic is not "bad" or "evil"; she has not "oppressed" the child or "exploited the child's helplessness." She is the tool and, together with her child, the victim of an unfortunate sexual-social situation.

Exactly the same holds true for the "exploiting capitalist" and the "exploited worker." The kindling of hatred within the worker against the capitalist, the arousal of jealousy, the use of defamation, the instigation to murder, etc., will not change the commodity laws of societies based on private economy or state capitalism. The laws say: "I, the possessor of capital, will pay you, laborer, farmer, technician, scientist, etc., thirty or fifty dollars a week so that you can provide food, shelter, and clothing for yourself and your family, in other words reproduce the exchange value of your commodity, work-power. You will sell me your work-power for eight hours a day regardless of how large the exchange value (use value) of the product which you produce in these eight hours is, even if this exchange value is three or five times as great as the value you must produce and use in one day to provide for yourself and your family." The owner of capital and the worker do not enter into a relationship with each other as human beings, a relationship determined by free will which they can change whenever they please. They are both the objects of a certain social relationship which functions on the basis of historical development and dominates them both, independently of their will.

The reader's understanding of the development of sex-economic sociology and mass psychology which led to the discovery of natural work democracy in 1939 depends completely upon his viewing the Marxist analysis of the laws of market economy in a factual, natural-scientific manner, without rage or love, without ethical or moral judgment. Our first concerns must be *facts* and *functional laws,* not ideals and aspirations. Real aspirations can only be based on real statements of fact.

One of the main causes for the chaotic misery into which human society repeatedly falls is the fact that politicians usually base their idealizations and endeavors—whether well intended or not—on irrational, emotional value judgments, rather than on facts. Anyone who is acquainted with my writings knows that I have always been aware of the importance of emotions, but only those emotions and aims that are based firmly in reality. I have always opposed unfounded, illusory, or irrational ideals and aims.

The discovery of the above-described law of market economy and the paradox peculiar to the living commodity, work-power (*exchange value less than use value, as opposed to dead commodities whose exchange value equals the use value*), is a scientific finding, neither good nor bad, but simply *true*. It has nothing to do with ethics or morals. The capitalist who pays for the exchange value of the worker's commodity, work-power, and then utilizes its far greater use value is not motivated by an evil intent. Personally he may be either a scoundrel or a well-intentioned man. Usually he is not even aware of the mechanism to which he owes his wealth. He is entangled in the process and subjected to all the consequences of the laws of market economy, such as competition with other firms and plants, the usual economic crises, etc.

In stating this, I neither attack nor defend the capitalist. I do not wish to obscure the fact that I personally do not care for the character of the typical capitalist who devotes all his thoughts, actions, and emotions exclusively to the earning of money, who substitutes the power of money for natural love and is an artist in taking but an amateur in giving, with no understanding of the joy it can bring. This, however, must not be allowed to prevent my distinguishing between the human traits of a certain capitalist and the laws of market economy whose agent he has become through inheritance or enormous effort.

I also do not wish to conceal the fact that I consider the discovery of this economic law by Karl Marx one of the greatest accomplishments ever achieved by human thought. Although market law was discovered by Marx to have existed during the last three hundred years of capitalistic machine civilization, it extends far beyond this period into the ancient history of human society to a point in the obscure past when society gradually ceased to produce use values and shifted more and more to the production of exchange values, i.e. commodities. This process ran parallel to the development from a natural economy to a monetary economy. Parallel to this, in turn, ran the reversal from sex-affirmation, which guaranteed the natural self-regulation of sexual energy, to sex-negation and the emotional plague.[2] Karl Marx's discovery has changed the entire countenance of society on this planet. In thousands of economists and sociologists, it has awakened a sense of that which we see before us today as modern social economy. There are countless economists and sociologists who have never read Marx, or have even rejected him, but who nevertheless show the influence and bear the mark of his economic and social theory in their practical work. It was not Ricardo and Smith but rather Karl Marx who brought the laws governing modern technical development to the level of general human consciousness. The numerous liberal and Socialist organizations would never have kept step with this development had they not been, either consciously or unconsciously, under the

[2] Cf. *The Sexual Revolution* and *The Invasion of Compulsory Sex-Morality*.

spell of Marxist sociology. I know from experience that there are many responsible capitalists who regard Marx highly and understand him better than do many socialistic party politicians.

These positive qualities of Marx's achievement do not change the fact that his sociology, understandably, contains serious omissions, above all a lack of comprehension of man's biological roots and the fact that he is governed by his instincts. Party politicians replaced these factors with unscientific ethics, unfounded slogans of freedom, and formal, bureaucratic "freedom organizations." One cannot replace scientific insight with slogans, ideologies, illusions, and theses without losing one's way and forfeiting one's goals. I do not know how many economists in the Soviet Union are consciously aware that, according to the strict criteria of Marx's value theory, a market economy still exists there with all its peculiarities, including the paradox of exchange and use value of work-power, and with it the exploitation of human labor. It is irrelevant whether the "state" or the "individual capitalist" does the exploiting. The essential issue is whether society is determined by the individuals who create surplus value arising from the difference between use and exchange values or by those who merely use surplus value, be it state or individual capitalist.[3] Over the course of twenty years I have not heard one Soviet social economist mention this fact. According to Marxist principles, Socialism, i.e. the abolition of market economy, does not prevail in the Soviet Union—but, rather, capitalism, to be more precise, state capitalism without individual capitalists.

The functioning of market economy is responsible for capitalism and not the individual capitalist or the state. Only when this perspective has been clearly and unmistakably grasped can one evaluate the social effects of market economy on human life and proceed to the question of whether and how a thousand-year-old market economy could be abolished and replaced by an

[3] SO: "State" and "society" represent two basically different social facts. There is a state which is above or against society, as best exemplified in the Fascist totalitarian state. There is a society without a state as in the primitive democratic societies. There are state organizations which work essentially for social interests, and there are others which do not. What has to be remembered is that "state" does not mean "society."

economy based on use values. Planned economy, into which economy everywhere increasingly develops, automatically expedites the transition from market economy to an economy of use. Commodities are produced to satisfy needs, not merely to be sold for a profit. To the extent that the Soviet Union had a planned economy, it developed into an economy of use, but wherever it engaged in foreign trade it necessarily adhered to market economy. These facts are neither good nor bad but actual processes. Therefore it is not party politics but Marxist socio-scientific work which will reestablish sociology and economy and enable them to move in a forward direction.

I must emphasize once again that the basic element of Marx's discovery of the value theory and, along with that, of the essence of human work in general, is biological or biosocial in nature. This central fact evaded party politicians. Living work-power alone (variable capital) creates values, and not inanimate (constant) capital!

The reader will inquire why I admit to being such a strong advocate of the Marxist value theory. It is not out of political sentiment or the recognition of social misery, but simply because I know of no sociology other than Marx's which corresponds more closely or is more relevant to my own discovery of the laws of biological energy. Both the natural organization of work as a biological fact (and not as a moral or political postulate) and the findings of orgone biophysics require recognition of the actuality and distinctiveness of the living commodity "work-power." Facts such as these have a singularly weighty and decisive influence when supported scientifically from two independent perspectives, regardless of whether they represent the views of a mystic, a capitalist, or an unscientific Socialist who sees himself as a liberator.

To recapitulate: The production of goods for society is collective; their appropriation in capitalism is individual, not social. The producer of goods, the working man, does not have the product of his work at his disposal. He is a salaried worker, that is, he receives the exchange value of his commodity, work-power, paid in accordance with the law. Capital as a social force is

The Living Productive Power, "Work-Power," of Karl Marx 63

symbolized by the private or state ownership of the means of production, of land and buildings, and stands in contrast to salaried labor. These two, the owners of capital and the salaried workers, represent the two economic classes. Their interests are antithetical. It lies in the nature of capital to want to realize a profit. It can be profitable only if it yields interest, and this in turn is possible only if it acquires "surplus value" from the difference between the exchange value and the use value of workpower. The worker, on the one hand, naturally wishes to increase his wages; the capitalist has the equally natural wish to keep them low or even reduce them. Hence two classes confront each other hostilely. The socioeconomic laws of market economy are the cause of this situation which is then maintained by specific institutions.

Marxist economy unquestionably has the same significance for economics as the Freudian theory of unconscious psychic life has for psychology. Both presuppose a certain factually based view of the laws which govern contemporary human life. The functional theory of life cannot be grasped if one is not acquainted with these preconditions.

Marx's theory manifests all the indications of an unabashed boundlessness, as does all great human thought. The fact that this boundlessness yielded to political narrow-mindedness when Marx himself could no longer assert his fiery temperament is in itself a problem of Marxist sociology. Even before then, he had kept a certain distance from his pupils, saying, "I am not a Marxist!"

I am not a Marxist either, but I do believe that I understand Marx's vast greatness and minute shortcomings. Let us return to his great ideas and findings. He was very consistent and had to pay for this with voluntary exile, dire poverty, and persecution.

It was formerly believed that man, the leader, the genius, "makes history"; Marx thoroughly extinguished the spark of this illusion. Of course man makes history, who else? Certainly not machines! However, man can make his own history only under certain circumstances which control him. Human will and the striving to achieve goals are dependent upon the level which society has reached and on the current state of technological mastery over nature. Daedalus and Icarus had wished to fly, but could not. They simply lacked the knowledge and technology to produce gasoline and construct motors capable of carrying a certain weight through the air. True, human imagination and activity are the sources of every social impulse, but they themselves are determined and limited by their times. Copernicus and Galileo were not able to take from man his feeling that the earth is preeminent and unique. They were severely punished because their era did not know what to do with their discoveries. There were no astronomers and stratosphere pilots who needed the knowledge of the earth's revolving around the sun. *Anyone who values his life had better not be too far ahead of his own time.* We shall see that only through Marx himself are we able to grasp the reasons for his inability to achieve success during his lifetime and for the crushing defeat of his movement, because of complete irrationality, fifty years after his death. Without Marx we can comprehend neither Marx nor Marxism and, consequently, the extreme reaction of metaphysics, Fascism.

All vital, effective human beings are interested in improving life. If, then, the repeated claims of metaphysicians are correct that man makes history "of his own free will," we should have been living in a paradise for a long time. The fact that we are far from paradise and, on the contrary, are suffocating in the opposite realm, verifies the correctness of scientific sociology. Humans have created among themselves "unconscious" relationships and conditions which now control them. They built machines to produce greater quantities more easily. Now they are being decimated, driven to starvation, and ravaged by the same machines. Man discovered the technology of the motion picture and scores of actors lost their jobs. Silent films yielded to sound films and thousands of cinema musicians became unemployed. The faster and easier it becomes to build houses, the closer people have to crowd together in their apartments. The more wheat or coffee that is harvested, the faster it is dumped into the ocean and the less millions of people have to eat. This is an absurdity which certainly demands most intensive scientific scrutiny. Capitalist

The Living Productive Power, "Work-Power," of Karl Marx 65

economy is a profit economy. It produces commodities but not primarily necessary commodities. The economy does not serve the satisfaction of needs; rather, the needs are created, suppressed, or shifted in keeping with the laws of profit economy. World economy does not ask how many Chinese or Africans are going barefoot, but it does hold yearly conferences to effect slight changes in gentlemen's and ladies' footwear and then advertises "new shoe fashions" as indispensable, vital necessities. The film industry does not consider which educational, medical, or technological problems of humanity might be presented in order to "raise cultural standards." Instead it provokes perverse, sadistic feelings within people to make its product more salable. There is not one film which has really solved a human problem. Very few even touch upon vital issues and most simply provoke pathological desires. Films do not serve man but the purpose of profit making.

Profit economy thrives on overpowering its competition. Competition, so-called free private enterprise, destroys small ventures and consolidates the larger ones into concerns or trusts which continually increase in strength. In this way "capital becomes concentrated in the hands of the few" and the impoverishment of the masses progresses. Shoe factories have ruined the shoemaker, as have agricultural machines the farmer with his plow. The more powerful capitalist destroys the smaller capitalist who has already crushed the artisan. The erstwhile class of free tradesmen is transformed into a host of technologically specialized employees and predominantly untrained manual laborers.

Rationalization of the economy then produces unemployment instead of a reduction of work-hours. If business is good and the demands high, more and more is produced, without limit. Every capitalist in the world functions in this way in order to earn more money, to keep in step and not be left behind. When demand is exhausted, the trend begins to slacken and the capitalists are left with their stockpiles, which become increasingly difficult to dispose of. This, in turn, produces an economic recession and the whole process moves in a vicious circle. The entrepreneurs lay off workers, causing the buying power of the population to drop. Banks fail because commerce in money and goods breaks down. This destroys small capital and reduces buying power once again. The already lowered buying power of the populace increases the stagnation of distribution, which necessitates further layoffs, and so forth. Wages are cut, work-hours may even be increased without monetary compensation, or decreased with commensurate salary reduction, and neither labor nor industry really understands the process. That was the status of the economic situation in 1930.

Society is not merely an aggregate of individuals living and working side by side. Life in society is determined by the resultant activity of all forces within and among men, and mutual interdependency is the decisive factor. The "well-ordered, legal state" is not a reality but a dream, an illusion exactly like the "harmony of the consummate personality" in antiquated ethical psychology. Since man is aware of only a minute fraction of his own interrelationships, he is unable to govern or change them. Thus interpersonal relationships assume the character of inescapable destiny. The average person views his social position as such. Those who see through this network of social dependencies and the exploitation mechanisms become "class-conscious," the bourgeois with his capital and the laborer with his work-power alike. The former can exploit better and more cunningly, whereas the latter is better able to resist exploitation successfully. Thus ran the theory of the Marxist parties. This contradiction cannot be resolved within the capitalist system. Either producers control the means of production, or the owners of capital do. Simultaneous control is unthinkable. The desire to exploit other people's work-power is under no circumstances reconcilable with the desire not to submit to exploitation. Any attempt to unite these concepts would result in awareness of the exploitation process. Capital and labor can coexist "peacefully" only when exploitation is concealed from the awareness of the exploited party. Anyone who does not admit this but struggles against it is labeled a "Communist agitator." Marx was the greatest Communist agitator to date because no one demonstrated as clearly as he the

The Living Productive Power, "Work-Power," of Karl Marx 67

manner in which the value of the commodity work-power was created.

But Marx did not pose the question of how those who were exploited and suppressed would react to the exposure of their own condition. The Marxists never doubted that the suppressed individuals would welcome the awareness and the message of liberation; and this mode of thought was rational and entirely correct. Unfortunately, however, man's thoughts and actions are not always rationally determined. Irrational, impracticable, and distorted thinking and acting also come into play. Freud had already proved this, but at the time no one could foresee that the workers' movement would ever be confronted by this question as a pressing, cardinal issue. Two antagonistic camps formed around Marx and Freud and competed with each other for recognition of their interpretations of life in society. My attempt to combine those theories—which later, of course, was frustrated —began at this point.

Marxist sociology pointed out the economic processes which determine interpersonal, i.e. social, relationships. Freudian psychology, in contrast, demonstrated that the unconscious forces which control human thought and action are, in the final analysis, instinctual biological forces. The result was the coexistence or, more correctly, the confrontation of natural-scientific sociological and natural-scientific psychological interpretations of human existence.

Karl Marx claimed: "Objective socioeconomic conditions and processes, independent of conscious human will, determine your thoughts and existence."

Sigmund Freud claimed: "Psychic instinctual forces, which in the final analysis originate in as yet unknown biological sources of energy and are independent of conscious human will, determine your thoughts and existence."

The socioeconomic conditions, namely the Marxist productive forces, are active outside man's biopsychic apparatus in such things as technological development, work conditions, family conditions, ideologies, organizations. Freud's psychic instinctual forces, on the other hand, are active within the depths of the biopsychic apparatus and are removed from the sphere of conscious human volition, as are Marx's socioeconomic productive forces.

The two scientific interpretations of human existence appear to contradict and mutually exclude each other. Consequently the sociological and psychoanalytic schools of thought were in sharp conflict. Marxist social economists who had exerted a profound influence on public life in Germany and Austria viewed psychoanalysis, and psychoanalysts viewed Marxism, as undesirable and "dangerous" competition in the interpretation of social and individual existence.

Both schools, however, had in common their search for and description of an objective process, unknown to man, which was active behind the surface phenomena of ideology, value judgments, ethics, social demands, etc. In this, both employed a genuine natural-scientific method, similar to physics, which seeks behind the phenomenon of motion the laws of motion, or behind the spark of a battery the functional laws of invisible electrical energy. Both removed the psychologisms and ethicisms which cling merely to the surface phenomena in psychology as well as in economics.

It was an enormous achievement of the human intellect to progress from empty, factually unfounded although well-intended, demands and moral judgments to the essence of actual processes. From such facts alone, not from empty demands, was it possible for a reality-adjusted, non-utopian, practical experiment in the improvement of individual and social existence to develop.

The economists, philosophers, and psychologists of Marx's time held to the metaphysical theory that man determined his destiny through his "free will." They were unable to free themselves because this view offers illusory comfort within the chaos of natural events. As we know, illusions have always attracted human sensibilities more than tangible reality has. The illusion of determination by man's own free will or by the supernatural, namely fate and providence, serves two irrational purposes: first, these illusions place man above his helplessness in relation to nature (including his own drives), and second, they veil his feelings of impotence and his anxiety by making him feel Godlike. This last illusion found its highest expression in the Hitlerian outbreak of the emotional plague. As we know today, but did not know in 1928, this was the achievement of irrationalism in the masses and not that of an individual who had failed utterly in every attempt to function rationally.

The second function of the free-will theory has a rational core, although it is ultimately deceiving. This is the function of imbuing man, when he feels helpless, small, and impotent, with enough courage to continue his existence even when knowledge of processes and procedures is lacking. Man must exist, with or without knowledge; for this he requires the emotional strength of illusion. Illusions are not merely irrational impressions but also strength-giving attitudes. The proverbial faith that can move mountains originates here. The success of Hitlerian mysticism demonstrated clearly that mysticism, which has its basis in human emotions, is capable of producing greater social effect than scientific knowledge.

Hence we recognize the illusion as justified and necessary but only where man has not progressed to real knowledge. If we absolutely and automatically condemn illusion as such, we can easily slip into an intolerant and unproductive attitude toward achievement based on illusion. The accomplishments in the Soviet Union, for example, in regard to economic reconstruction and removal of the crassest social injustices, resulted from the illusion of "building Socialism." The illusion of mechanistic natural science in its struggle against the efforts of religion and mysticism to discover the "essence of the soul," led to great achievements in the fields of physiology and colloid chemistry.

But the danger and harmfulness of illusion are far greater than the real gains it yields. Achievement stemming from illusion never equals practical achievement generated by real knowledge of processes and procedures. From the beginning of time, illusionary world-views have appeared repeatedly in opposition to man's rational striving to limit the realm of the unknown and expand the field of knowledge. Illusions lead, with inevitable regularity, to reactionary and regressive social institutions. This has been demonstrated by developments in the Soviet Union as well as by the inhibiting influence exerted by mechanistic natural science upon efforts to understand living functions. Hence, if I have demonstrated here a rational function of illusion, it does not imply that the arduous struggle for scientific expansion of the sphere of human power need not be ceaselessly carried forward. If I cannot walk on a leg, I will use a crutch if necessary in order to move about. But by the same token I will certainly discard the crutch as soon as I have regained the natural use of my leg.

Now, the metaphysicians and mystics of all sorts, owing to the emotional gratification of their self-esteem gained through illusions, vehemently opposed Marxism and Freudianism. The cries of *"I am so very free, superior, so God-like, master of myself and nature"* did not alter in the slightest their dependency upon psychic irrationalism on the one hand and socioeconomic processes on the other. This tragic dependency found expression clearly and unmistakably in the world catastrophe of the last decade. Marx and Freud were indispensable forerunners of serious progress in mastering these two types of human dependency. They also parallel each other inasmuch as both erected their scientific edifices upon yet undiscovered biological or biosocial principles.

Marx's entire concept of socioeconomics was based on the living nature of human work-power as a basic biological activity peculiar even to primitive living organisms. Man does not differ in his work function from other animals by the fact that he works; all living creatures do this or they could not exist. He differs from other animals in his attempt to improve his work function by inventing tools. We already know, through Karl Marx, that man's misfortune lay in this social differentiation from other animals, that he became a slave of the tools he himself invented. Most Marxists, to judge by their publications, have overlooked the fact that it is *living* work-power which, through the difference between its use and exchange values, has determined the social mechanisms of patriarchal civilization. In his philosophical writings, Marx stressed repeatedly that man with

The Living Productive Power, "Work-Power," of Karl Marx 71

his *biological organization* is the final "precondition of all history." Marx, of course, knew nothing of the concrete nature of this "biological organization," nor could he have known, inasmuch as the science of biology itself was not aware of it and the specific biological energy, the cosmic orgone, was only discovered between 1936 and 1939.

The two objective, basic, biological functions of living matter, "work" and "sexuality," or the "pleasure process," were each treated at the beginning of the twentieth century in separate scientific systems, i.e. in Marxist sociology and in Freudian psychology. The sexual process led a pitiful existence in the Marxist system under the misleading heading of "family development." The work process, in turn, was relegated to an equally pitiful position in Freudian psychology, likewise under misleading headings of "sublimation" and "hunger drives" or "ego instincts." Far from contradicting each other in principle, the two scientific systems actually met (completely unbeknown to their founders) in the *biological basis of all living matter, the biological energy of all living beings,* whose activity splits, in accordance with our energetic-functional method of thought, into work on the one hand and sexuality on the other.

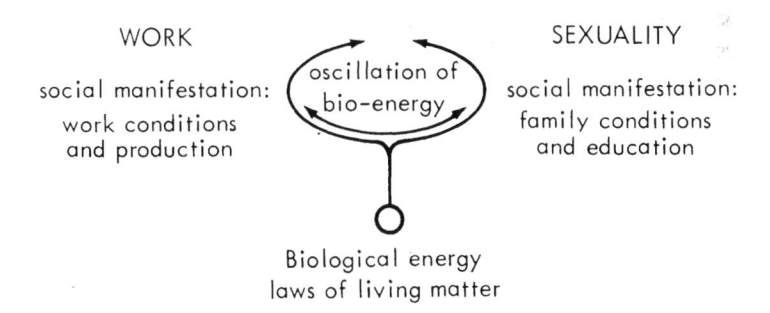

WORK — oscillation of bio-energy — SEXUALITY

social manifestation: work conditions and production

social manifestation: family conditions and education

Biological energy laws of living matter

Elaborating on this functional, simultaneously identical and antithetical character of biological energy was reserved for sex-economic research. Of course, I had no idea of this at the time. My attempts between 1928 and 1930 to reconcile two scientific systems led me, by means of the logic of factual research, to the method which finally triumphed in the discovery of the orgone, the specific biophysical energy, in 1939. I doubt that I would ever have succeeded in discovering the orgone had I not applied sociological criticism to Freud's psychology in hard, everyday practical work over a period of years, and if I had not discovered the gap in Marxist socio-economy and filled it with the concept of "character structure."

The laws of biological energy, of the orgone, encompass the basic mechanisms of both work and sexuality, and thus the emotional forces within, without, and between human beings. These laws underlie rational as well as irrational endeavor, the urge to do scientific research on the unexplained as well as the mystical belief in the existence of an unknown all-powerful being.

The basic biological mechanisms of life are not simply a mechanical sum of sexual and work functions. They constitute, rather, a third factor simultaneously identical and antithetical as well as more fundamental. Sex-economy and orgone biophysics are therefore not the sum of Marxist and Freudian concepts but new disciplines based on sociological and depth-psychological insights, which led, from the incompatibility of these concepts, to the discovery of a third concept common to both.

Although this is clear today, it was far from clear in 1928. But let us return to the experiences which constituted the milestones in the course of this development.

Following that July 15 which so tragically demonstrated the basic mechanisms of class society, I began to study Engels in addition to Marx. It was only natural that a psychoanalyst should find his book *The Origin of the Family* extremely interesting. The contradiction between Marxist and Freudian explanations of the family was painfully obvious. Although they appeared to be correct on decisive issues, both could not be simultaneously valid. Engels led me to Bachofen and Morgan; I pored over *Das Mutterrecht* and *Urgesellschaft*. Since these works were in sharp contradiction to Freud's views, I felt constrained to delve into the most important ethnological writings. For four years I found myself in a chaos. Then light was shed upon one of the central enigmas of primitive human history. This I described in the context of another book, *Der Einbruch der Sexualmoral* (1st ed. 1932, 2nd ed. 1936).[4]

The actual secrets of the social function of sexual suppression were revealed in the practical experiences afforded me by my sexological work among Viennese adolescents. The years between 1927 and 1930, when I moved to Berlin, were years of great doubt. During this period I gathered material for *Der Einbruch der Sexualmoral*. In 1929 the short work *Sexualerregung und Sexualbefriedigung* was published and in 1930 *Geschlechtsreife, Enthaltsamkeit, Ehemoral*.[5] Also during these three years I formulated the sociological critique of psychoanalysis. A Russian version of my paper "Dialektischer Materialismus und Psychoanalyse" was published in 1929 in the *Journal of the Academy of Sciences* in Moscow. It appeared in German in the periodical *Unter dem Banner des Marxismus*, and subsequently in the Austrian edition of the periodical *Imago*, 1930.

In 1928, I founded the Socialist Society for Sex-Counseling and Sex-Research with several Viennese physicians. Based on sex-economic principles, it established the first sex-counseling centers for workers and business employees in Vienna. Over the course of these years I became acquainted with the inner functioning of the revolutionary movement of that time. ["Revolutionary" is not to be considered identical with "communistic."] Not a single line of what I wrote later is conceivable without this experience. The basis for my parting with Freud was also laid during this period in connection with the formulation of the most important sex-economic insights, including "character analysis" (in the form of various clinical articles), and the clarification of the question of masochism, with which I was able to refute his death-instinct theory. Until that time I had opposed it without a counter-theory. Several decisive social experiences also occurred in these years which later formed the basis for my book *The Mass Psychology of Fascism*. Since they exerted a most profound

---

[4] *The Invasion of Compulsory Sex-Morality.*
[5] Part I of *The Sexual Revolution.*

influence on my socio-psychological work, I shall begin by describing them.

I made the decision to commence sociological work following a conversation with Freud. I explained my plans and asked him for his opinion. Sex-counseling centers were to be opened and psychoanalytic insight applied on a mass scale in the form of social sex-economy. In this way it was designed to serve the general public. Freud agreed wholeheartedly. He knew as little as I where this would lead. When I explained the necessity of treating the family problem rigorously, he replied: "You'll be poking into a hornet's nest." ("*Hier greifen Sie in ein Wespennest.*") His attitude toward the "Russian experiment" was critical but sympathetic. Correct sociological views had already begun to call into question the psychoanalytic interpretation of primitive history. While the psychoanalytic ethnologist Roheim was uncritically and unscrupulously interpreting this and that, Malinowski's warnings were heard in London. In 1926 Malinowski's paper on the Oedipus complex in matriarchal societies appeared. He and Jones were engaged in a dispute over the question whether the family was a biological or a socio-historical institution. Jones contended that the biological Oedipus complex was the "*fons et origo*," the source and origin of everything—society, law, rights, culture, etc. Malinowski claimed that the Oedipus complex took on a different form in matriarchal societies due to variations in the social structure. Freud remained neutral in this. Everyone sensed that these questions were not merely an academic pastime. They touched upon the great Russian revolution in a very definite, but as yet not very tangible, form. Freud mentioned in conversation that it was conceivable that the "light would come from the East." Quite a statement from an academic professor! Freud asked me whether I would be able to handle the extensive work in the technical seminar, at the Polyclinic, in private practice, and in the sex-counseling centers, all at the same time. We agreed that one could only wait and see whether it was possible. He thwarted an attempt made by leading functionaries of the psychoanalytic association [in particular, Paul Federn] to use this opportunity to oust me from my position as leader of the

The Living Productive Power, "Work-Power," of Karl Marx

seminar. It was not to be taken out of my hands if I desired to continue leading it (letter dated November 22, 1928). For a long time I did not see through this concern for my excessive work load. The conflict within psychoanalysis in regard to its social function was immense long before anyone involved noticed it.

Seen in today's light, the fall of the Austrian Social Democratic Party did not signify just the fall of one political party; its decline was rather the symptom of a social process which was drastically revealed in the rise of Hitler's National Socialist Party and over the course of the next ten years produced the extraordinary insight that politics is altogether unfounded, unscientific, irrational, and an expression of biopathic human structure and thought. In essence, politics is organized gratification of the party followers' biopathic emotions, formulated into a political platform. There is no such thing as good politics in one place and bad in another. In essence, politics always proves that certain social situations, owing to a lack of concrete knowledge, cannot be mastered scientifically. With attention fixed upon the differentiation between good and bad politics, one is unable to approach the matter of politics itself and of what is concealed from our sight. Three decades (1914–45) of bloodshed were needed to discover the quiet, rational work process and natural work democracy behind the tumult and turbulence of politics.

From 1927 to 1934 I myself was in the midst of this turbulence. Since the sciences were not socially oriented and social chaos nevertheless seeped into the smallest crevices of daily life, all hope was placed in "good politics" and not in natural science. The following accounts serve to prove that I—along with millions of others—put my hopes in political activities instead of anchoring them to my work on human beings.

It is incorrect to accuse the Austrian Social Democrats of pursuing "bad politics." They were trapped in the irrationalism of politics just as were the English Conservatives under Chamberlain who signed a pact with the German Fascists to "save the peace." Political reactionaries always openly acknowledged the general nature of politics, realistically and unequivocally—the lying, fraudulence, irrationalism, and naked violence. The practice of conceding or appeasing is, in the strictest sense, neither "bad" nor "good" politics but an admission of factual insecurity in the face of strong political reaction for which the irrational character structure of the masses serves as firm support.

Truth cannot prevail through politics. Politics and truth contradict each other. If the advocates of truth attempt to compete with politics, they are unquestionably condemned to perish. This was the fate of the Austrian Social Democrats between 1927 and 1934 and also of the English under Chamberlain. Genuine democratic politics are and can basically never be anything but radical, merciless exposure and abandonment of every kind of politics.

Here we encounter enormous difficulties. Day-to-day human existence demands a myriad of practical solutions. It is the essence of natural science that it can make only slow progress in furnishing practical answers to questions of existence. Mysticism and politics fill the gaping fissures with illusions and promises of satisfaction. This means that natural-scientific regulation of social life cannot dispose of political, illusional mass leadership overnight. Personally I have no solution for the dilemma between realistic and illusional leadership. But it is my responsibility to expose such difficulties and not to conceal them. This at first arouses the erroneous belief that one can quickly fill the gaps in understanding. However, I do believe that it is possible to replace politics with a different form of mass leadership. The road which led to these decisive conclusions was tortuous and full of pitfalls.

4

This Is Politics!

After the crushing moral defeat on July 15, the mighty Austrian Social Democracy slowly but surely lost ground. The former Social Democratic Foreign Minister, Renner, uttered prophetic words: "The Austrian working class is so strong that it cannot be conquered; it can only fall through its own mistakes." The mayor of Vienna, Seitz, said in his concluding speech at the party convention following July 15, "We are so convinced that democratic developments will lead to our goals that we do not need to assist them with violence." I shall chronicle the subsequent events briefly.

On November 1, 1927, the Social Democratic party convention unanimously accepted a "resolution." Political reactionaries had armed Fascist groups but the Socialist Party had saved Austria from civil war. From 1923 onward, it had emphasized that it was "ready at any time for serious negotiations on disarmament." They said the Linz Program had recognized class cooperation in the form of a coalition government, but a coalition would not be possible as long as the Catholic and nationalist bourgeoisie wished to dissolve the Socialist Party. The Social Democrats, however, wanted to prevent a civil war and were ready to cooperate with anyone willing to help. They said they would employ force in one case only—namely, if the political reactionaries attempted to overthrow the democratic republic or usurp the rights of the working class which the republic had guaranteed. Stricter discipline was necessary: "No demonstrations without the concurrence of all concerned. No strikes in vital industries without consent of the entire labor union association!" The republic was to be transformed into a "true republic of working individuals in town and country."

And this is what happened in the process of appeasement:

In August 1927, the Christian Socialist-controlled National Assembly passed a number of reactionary school laws *without prior debate*.

In the same month, the leader of the Social Democratic Schutzbund and the workers' athletic clubs canceled their August 7 meeting in Graz, which had been in preparation for months.

At the beginning of August, Seitz ordered the dissolution of the Social Democratic Gemeindeschutzwache,[1] organized after the massacre of July 15.

At the end of August, the election of staff representatives of the Vienna police force resulted in five Christian Socialists and one Independent Trade Unionist as opposed to five Independent Trade Unionists and one Christian Socialist prior to this.

In September 1927, the National Assembly resolved to reduce the unemployment benefits of older workers. A proposal of amnesty for the accused of July 15 was defeated by the Christian Socialist government.

In October 1927, Otto Bauer publicly confirmed a weakening of Social Democracy before a convention of the metalworkers' union. He suggested "peaceful democratic development." The union leader, Domes, advocated technological rationalization. Pitzl, the representative of the International Association of Trade Unions, was excluded.

In the same month, Dr. Renner demanded a coalition government with the Christian Socialists, who rejected this, however, through Dr. Schmitz.

On October 16, 1927, the election of soldiers' spokesmen resulted in 9,000 Socialist votes yielding 118 mandates and 6,000 Christian and German Nationalist votes yielding 220 (!) mandates. The Socialist Party lost 2,000 votes and the conservatives

---

[1] Municipal guard. —*Trans.*

This Is Politics! 79

gained 3,000 through internal gerrymandering. The army staff commission was now composed of two Socialist Party representatives instead of nine, and seven conservatives instead of none.

On November 21, 1927, the Styrian assembly nullified the immunity of assemblyman Wallisch, a courageous, honest, forthright man. He was executed in 1934 by the Christian Socialist Dollfuss government.

On December 11, the Social Democrats were severely defeated in the federal police elections.

On January 18, 1928, in the official elections of the Tyrolean legislative assembly, the Social Democrats were excluded.

On February 20, the landlords scored a parliamentary victory in presenting a bill to reduce rent control, which was greatly favored by the populace. Later, they succeeded in having it passed and the Social Democrats proclaimed it a "victory for the Socialist Party"—a victory inasmuch as the outcome was not worse!

On March 3, the Social Democrats were completely defeated in an election of police staff representatives.

On March 16, the election of plant representatives in the Donawitz steel mills resulted in a gain of Socialist votes from 1,991 to 2,404, a loss of Communist votes from 706 to 227, and a gain in government votes from 131 to 951! Donawitz later became a bastion of the semi-fascistic Heimwehr organization.

On March 18, representatives of the labor boards, together with representatives of the chambers of commerce and agriculture, founded an "Economy Commission" to accomplish a mutual rationalization of industrial leadership. One year later this rationalization aggravated the economic crisis which had such horrible effects in Austria.

Between April 5 and 10, there were mass layoffs in the mines owned by the Alpine Montangesellschaft[2] in Seegraben, which were designed to purge the company of Socialists. Although the employees demanded a strike, the council of employee representatives rejected their demands as a result of pressure from

---

[2] An Austrian mining corporation. —*Trans.*

party officials. (On February 14, 1934, not one major industrial firm struck, while the Social Democratic Schutzbund bled to death.)

On May 11, the Christian Minister of the Armed Forces, Vougoin, announced that any soldier who had participated in May Day celebrations would be discharged.

On May 12, there was a spontaneous protest strike in the Hüttenberg mines against political terror in the operations of the Alpine Montangesellschaft. The union leaders were against the strike.

Between May 16 and 22, numerous partial strikes occurred in the Styrian and Carinthian mining and steel industries. The movement was so powerful that the union directors felt constrained to "spearhead it." [Red Fascist talk.] There were mild threats, negotiations several days later, and the strike was called off, but the workers struck again.

On June 3, a strike began among female jute workers in a large factory near Vienna. They worked ten hours a day for the miserable wage of sixty schillings a month. Their traveling time to and from work was three hours a day. Children were actually dying of hunger. Together with several friends of mine, I took some of the children in. The strike ran aground because there was neither strength nor courage behind it.

The founder of the Heimwehr, Steidle, announced that the first large Heimwehr demonstration would take place on October 7 in Wiener-Neustadt, a town with a population composed strictly of industrial workers, having a Social Democratic majority. Following the events of July 15, 1927, he had very quietly, and under the protection of the Christian Socialist administration, begun to organize his Heimwehr in the Tyrol. In those days, had a member of the Heimwehr ventured into a working-class district in Vienna he would have been soundly beaten. The Socialist Party said that one should not bother them, that they were not dangerous but merely exhibitionists, and that the best way to prevent their gaining power was to ignore them. (On February 14, 1934, in the same working-class districts, the Heimwehr demolished the workers' homes with cannons.)

A year of defeats had so embittered the members of the Social Democratic Party that its leaders could no longer afford to simply tolerate the extreme provocation of the political reactionaries. That would have sealed their fate within their own ranks. Therefore they called for a demonstration to counter Steidle's, on the same day and in the same town, Wiener-Neustadt. They had striven to avoid a confrontation but had continually weakened their own position only to be forced to proceed, devitalized, against the entire platform—until February 14, 1934, when they were defeated.

The Christian Socialist government was so sure of a victory and yet so fearful of Heimwehr competition that as a security measure it ordered the army, the local police, and federal police to Wiener-Neustadt for that same date.

The Communists also did not want to tolerate the situation. (On December 21, 1927, the Communists had organized their Rotfrontkämpferbund,[3] fashioned after the German model. Thälmann, later head of the German Communist Party, had come to Austria for the occasion.[4]) They "mobilized" their Arbeiterwehr for October 7 with the express objective of disturbing the demonstrations of all three antagonistic groups in Wiener-Neustadt. Thus an organization of approximately 250 unarmed men set out, with all the earnestness of revolutionary courage (I say this without sarcasm), to "disturb" organized troops numbering approximately 40,000, or, more accurately, to prevent their demonstration; and this with utter seriousness, deep conviction, and absolute determination to win. I can testify to this because I was one of those 250 people. On that day I became aware of the power of ideology independent of its economic basis and learned to evaluate it correctly. On that day I first began to understand the misuse of that power: how the psychologically inept and therefore futile mass labor movement misused the workers' right-

[3] Red Veterans' League. —*Trans.*
[4] This group was subsequently outlawed on April 27, 1928, but actually remained in existence under the title of Arbeiterwehr. It comprised a total of 250 members, about 150 of whom lived in Vienna. In the entire country the Communist Party had approximately 3,000 members, most of whom were unemployed.

eous earnestness and desire for freedom. On that day I saw clearly that the socially suppressed individual is entirely different psychologically from the way the rigid sociology of class antagonism describes him or would like him to be. I saw that the socioeconomic structure of a given society in no way coincides with the mass-psychological structure of its various social strata; that people in the same socioeconomic situation stand in opposite camps, grouped together by irrational ideologies bearing no relation whatsoever to the practical aspects of their lives. The decisive issues of life which meld these antagonistic camps of socioeconomic equals into one large community are not even expressed in politics, let alone treated justly. I saw, in short, that the real life of the working masses is lived on a completely different level from that on which the tumult of politicians and party politics rages. The present position of political psychology was born on those days: Down with *all* politics! Let's get to the practical demands of life! Nevertheless, ten years passed before this position matured consciously into the concept of work democracy.

Excitement over the demonstrations of armed organizations in Wiener-Neustadt was limited to political circles which constituted only a minute fraction of the entire working population. The Communist Party of Austria issued an "order" that the Arbeiterwehr was to proceed to Wiener-Neustadt in small groups without "attracting attention." The three physicians in the Arbeiterwehr were to join the Kampftruppe[5] with rucksacks full of first-aid supplies. I packed my rucksack, said goodbye to my wife and children (it was questionable whether I would ever return), and left to join a very courageous woman doctor with whom I was acquainted.

It was Saturday and I was convinced that rucksack and tourist attire would not attract attention. Everything was to be highly "illegal." We were so brimming with rage over the "fascistic provocation" and the "impending betrayal by the Social Democratic Schutzbund leaders" that we had no difficulty in stifling the question of what we were actually going to *do*. All we

[5] Combat troop. —*Trans.*

This Is Politics! 83

knew was that "it is a Communist's duty to set a good example in the class struggle" and "rise to lead the proletariat in case of civil war." And indeed there were in Wiener-Neustadt, on that Sunday, approximately 15,000 armed members of the Schutzbund, the champions of labor. We devoted no thought to how we should actually manage to "spearhead" them. There had to be a way, if we only showed enough courage. I must emphasize that we were no fools but respected physicians with lucrative practices and numerous influential connections; we were skilled workers. A doctor I was treating at the time was to "conquer" Wiener-Neustadt with a different troop.

I met my female colleague in the hall of South Station. We both looked very "innocuous" and our rucksacks "attracted no attention." The vast hall resembled an army camp. Hundreds of Schutzbund members stood about waiting to be searched for weapons by the police. Numerous plainclothesmen, called "bulls" for their typical facial expressions, mingled in the crowd "inconspicuously," eyeing the "elements threatening national security." We recognized them immediately and they recognized us. We were all so inconspicuous we could not possibly overlook each other. Approximately fifty equally inconspicuous members of the Arbeiterwehr were standing around too, but we studiously avoided looking at one another. Therefore every detective knew we belonged together. The police and gendarmerie were being loaded into trains by the hundreds. They left first, followed by the Schutzbund. We, the revolutionary leaders of the proletariat, ordained to sway the enthusiasm of 15,000 Schutzbunders the very next day, inconspicuously bought third-class tickets for the local train to Pottendorf, a small village near Wiener-Neustadt. From there we hoped to approach Wiener-Neustadt without attracting any attention. We were even clever enough not to ride directly into the city after hearing that civilians would not be allowed through. We felt reassured while sitting in the railroad car with several dozen comrades. We spoke in banalities; no one mentioned a suspicious topic. Secret police were among us and we recognized them. Several were stared at so long that they finally left on the pretense of reporting something to the gendarmerie. Friends told us that someone very inconspicuous would be waiting for us in Pottendorf and when we arrived, there was actually someone waiting on the platform, a worker, recognizable a mile away as a functionary. Needless to say, there was instant recognition. He whispered quietly that we should follow him to a certain inn. The Social Democratic mayor of the town was as incensed as the Communists and had offered his inn as quarters for the night. When we got there, hundreds of Schutzbund members were sitting around. We drank some beer and then the innkeeper led us to a large dance hall, where we were to spend the night. As time passed, small groups of Arbeiterwehr members arrived from all directions. Some had not been able to afford the train fare and had left Vienna the day before to walk the forty kilometers to Pottendorf. We ate lightly and anticipated the next day's events. What would the outcome be? None of us knew what was supposed to happen, but we had learned that in times of civil war every Communist advances to be a leader of thousands; the results would tell the story. We lay on the floor, using our rucksacks as pillows. Sleep was impossible.

During the night a small group arrived from Vienna. One of them, a young unemployed worker, lay down beside me and we immediately struck up a conversation. He lived with his old mother and wanted to fight *for her sake*. The situation, he said, could not go on this way; that mob had to be beaten to a pulp; together with the Schutzbund we could do it; the day of reckoning had finally come. He had been unemployed for two years and was barely subsisting with his mother on unemployment benefits. Only infrequently could he find odd jobs and if he were caught his benefits would be cut off. And now they were even beginning to reduce the benefits. In a short time they would stop it altogether, and that would mean hunger and breadlines. Even his shoes were worn through at the soles after the long hike, but this didn't bother him. Tomorrow would straighten things out. We became good friends and shared bread and bacon. Several hours passed. Approximately a hundred people were sleeping or talking quietly in the hall. All were waiting for the big day. It dawned.

Around 7 a.m. someone looked out the window. The building was surrounded by gendarmerie with fixed bayonets. Confusion broke out. What now? Someone shouted, "Let's beat them up!" Others said, "Let's wait and see what's going on." Then a gendarme with two men entered the room and said in a genial Viennese dialect, "Children, pack your belongings, the train to Vienna is waiting for you." Cries of protest were heard: "We'll go wherever we want to," and the like. The officer said he knew only that orders were orders and he had been assigned to transport the entire group in these quarters to the railroad station. I was delegated to negotiate. I told the officer that we first wished to discuss the matter among ourselves. He left and we held a short conference. Some were in favor of yielding; others shouted that it would be cowardly to submit to arrest so easily. If that were the case, it would be better to fight. Someone called out, "With what?" We decided that each position should be "upheld" by one speaker and then a vote taken. And so it went. The "reasonable" speaker said it was senseless to attempt anything under these conditions. We had fallen into a trap—period. He said we had to feign going home and then try to force our way back. The other speaker answered that revolutionaries simply didn't do things that way. It was a disgrace to the revolutionary spirit. What would people say? They would just laugh. And he wasn't far from wrong. No one knew how the vote would turn out. I thought with horror of the impending bloodshed. The memory of July 15 was still fresh, and we were unarmed. Were we to defend ourselves bare-handed, surrounded by heavily armed gendarmes? At the same time, I felt rage welling up within me over the disgrace being inflicted upon us. I didn't vote. The situation was hopeless; the majority voted for surrender. It was really degrading.

Later, we discovered that the Social Democratic innkeeper had discussed the matter with the gendarmes the night before. He had lured us into a trap.

Someone went out and informed them. We packed our rucksacks and walked out into the courtyard. We were arranged in rows of four flanked on either side by gendarmes and marched off. The cry went up, "We should at least sing." We sang the "Internationale" loudly. Sleepy, *indifferent* faces could be seen in the windows of this working-class suburb. We could almost hear them saying, "They're just leading some Communists off." The Communists were not in good standing with the majority of workers. They only disturbed the deep-seated, peaceful development of Socialism.

At the railroad station we entered the row of empty cars awaiting us. Two expressionless gendarmes were posted on every platform with fixed bayonets on their loaded rifles. The train began to move. In a few minutes it came to an abrupt stop; someone had pulled the emergency brake. It was released and we were on our way. Again the train stopped and then finally started up. Everyone was in a miserable frame of mind. One man suggested that we beat up the few gendarmes on the platforms, but most were opposed to this. Suddenly it occurred to us that the police would be expecting us in Vienna. To be put on their "list" meant the loss of a job for many. This *must* not be allowed to happen. But how to prevent it? Someone had a marvelous idea: Just outside Vienna we would simply get off when the train stopped. Would the gendarmes shoot? That was uncertain! When the train stopped at the appointed station, the word was passed along, "Everybody out." We took our rucksacks and got off. The gendarmes were dumbfounded. "Where do you think you're going?" they asked. "To Vienna," we all called out. We walked off and they watched us leave, astounded. They didn't know what to do. The engineer also watched us. One worker made a kind of speech and said we had been "illegally" arrested, that we had wanted to go to Wiener-Neustadt, that this was the rule of the bourgeoisie. And that it was! Nevertheless, the Social Democratic engineer only gave us a blank stare. The railroad workers, who had been the most revolutionary group of Austrian workers in 1918, were not interested in lending support. We walked the rest of the way. The third physician, with his troop, was actually met by the police when his train arrived in Vienna, but we passed the police like a group of harmless tourists, which we actually were.

Only very few members of the Arbeiterwehr reached Wiener-Neustadt. When they tried to pass out pamphlets among the Social Democratic Schutzbund, they received a terrible thrashing. In Wiener-Neustadt absolutely nothing happened. With field artillery and machine guns, 15,000 sons of farmers and workers in state uniform kept an equal number of farmers' and workers' sons in green uniform apart from the same number of farmers' and workers' sons in gray uniform. All this ran under the heading of high politics and class warfare, defense of country, and defense of the working class. No one saw it in that perspective at the time, but everyone must have sensed in some way how ridiculous it all was; otherwise, millions of German-speaking workers could not possibly have become the victims of Hitlerian *Volksgemeinschaft*[6] fantasies several years later. How many victims were needed merely to demonstrate that in reality the "war of the classes" is not fought between capitalists and workers but among the oppressed themselves? Removal of the mental inhibition which keeps this insanity from being recognized immediately would be in itself a tenfold reward for the struggle against it! From that time onward, my understanding of this insanity remained one of the most substantial factors in my striving to find the meaning of "freedom."

Other lessons were learned as well which took many years to mature.

Two hundred unarmed, genuinely revolutionary individuals set out to storm 40,000 armed and uniformed non-revolutionary individuals of the same society. That is absurdity raised to the twentieth power. How was it possible nevertheless? I have already mentioned that we were no fools. We fancied we knew more than the masses, and we did know much more, but not nearly all the indispensable facts necessary to gain a victory for human freedom instead of simply making ourselves ridiculous.

---

[6] National community. —*Trans.*

These 200 souls (myself included) honestly believed that if they were subjectively for freedom and thought logically, the others would also "soon have to see the light." Furthermore, according to "party" theory "the others" had already seen the light. It was only force that prevented them from turning their knowledge into action. These 200 Communists were convinced that if the economy broke down objectively, if wages were reduced objectively, and the most basic strivings for freedom objectively suppressed, the population would naturally and automatically be roused to indignation. This line of thinking was the basis of all revolutionary politics in Germany and Austria until 1933. But the conclusions were wrong and caused the workers' movement to collapse, wherever it did not flee back into the establishment it had previously attacked. Every possible compromise was made and every correct principle of the socialistic movement sacrificed, every single one. And all for this one reason: the complete inability, amid the confusion of daily tasks, to keep one's head clear for correct insight into living reality. This reality, this life in its infinite variations, which was yearning for freedom, lay in the gutter and was trodden under foot until it decomposed. The representatives of the concepts of freedom were themselves not free; the social suppression they were struggling against existed in themselves. They were afraid to think, afraid to confront life's realities. I have the right to speak as I do. I was one of the few who, year after year, in complete devotion to the cause of human freedom, pointed out the practical realities. But we also were not free, although we wrote about it, formulated it, and tried to make those responsible comprehend. We too were bound by antiquated concepts and were unable to understand much of what we felt. With feelings alone, however, indispensable as they may be in a struggle, one cannot transform a world of rigidified custom. Life seems to have great difficulty in becoming aware of itself. Awareness means reflecting on one's own origin, structure, and desolation. The human will, which undertook to order life according to rational laws, was itself a conglomerate of irrational feelings. The psychoanalytic movement, with hundreds of specialists all over the world, rejected the thesis that psychic health is possible only if love is fulfilled. Marxism rejected the fact that the psychic function constitutes the actual dynamic force of history even if preconditioned by the historical and economic framework. Both theories were reflections about life, for the purpose of bettering our mastery of life's requirements. But they occurred simultaneously and were bound to their time. The times were against life. This world existed only by devastating life. But no one yet knew what life was.

The complete triumph of organized political irrationalism, the collapse of economistic rationalism, and the threat to the national existence of vast human masses by the emotional plague, were further catastrophes necessary before the intellect could apply itself to the freedom problem. Until 1934 it was suffocated in formal, bureaucratic, mechanical "freedom devices." [SO: Those forms of "liberation" would never attain true liberty. Twenty years later an imperialist Russia, led by a son of the working class, would threaten to conquer the world under the guise of liberation. In place of government by the toiling men and women in all professions, a minority of political crooks and spies and armed gangsters would destroy even the last possibility of freedom—the freedom to talk about freedom.]

Part of the human animal's tragic fate is that it does not learn to think logically in peaceful times and that it must be provoked and threatened with extinction before it realizes its dangerous errors in thought and action and stops suffocating rational, vital thinking in itself. The triumph of scientific thought lies in the fact that it always remains correct over a long period of time despite its lack of social power and influence amid the tumult and confusion of everyday politics. It is a genuine guideline and the only perspective which guarantees social progress practically.

I can formulate my own experiences as follows: During the confusing years between 1927 and 1937, my writings on social psychology and mental hygiene were a mixture of natural-scientific fact finding and political notions I had borrowed from the organizations in which I worked professionally. Had I not blended the natural-scientific facts which I discovered with ideological party catchwords I could not have presented them in any of the political organizations. Nevertheless, real facts and processes inevitably come to light sooner or later.

1. Blending natural-scientific facts with political phraseology was to no avail. When the hard facts began to effect social changes the party politicians intervened sharply.

2. Today, not one political catchword is still valid. They were lost forever amid the social chaos.

3. My natural-scientific findings of 1928 are still correct; more, they have achieved great significance. On the other hand, all party-related expressions in my writings at that time have proven false and useless and have had to be struck from my works on mass psychology. All this occurred not by my own or someone else's choice but exclusively as a result of the permanence of natural science and the transience of political slogans.

Unfortunately, natural-scientific thought, either in physical or social areas, has not managed to provide an international organization capable of sparing the helpless, naïve working masses the bloodshed of trial and error in the day-to-day tumult of politics—an organization capable not only of recognizing irrational action in time but also of eliminating it. One of the greatest mysteries of man's irrational structure is why vital functioning, including rational thinking, is so feared.

MASS PSYCHOLOGY AS SEEN FROM "BELOW"

In reading newspaper reports of parliamentary committees, or government reports on social conditions, one often has the feeling that the social existence of the human animal takes place and is exclusively regulated in diplomatic meetings, federal budget conferences, parliamentary election speeches, and the drafting of bills. When social catastrophes occur periodically, the ensuing social chaos brings concrete problems of life to the surface. One is then astonished to see that there was no mention of these social processes in the newspapers, debates, conferences, and resolutions. "National politics" and "social existence" suddenly appear to stem from two different worlds which have absolutely no connection with one another.

I would like to contrast the Austrian parliamentary debates held after July 15, which were described earlier, with a segment of social reality as I experienced it from "below."[7]

One of the basic tenets of social sex-economy is that the chaos of human society results from irrational psychic mechanisms which arise out of the biopathic structure of the human animal. Had I not participated naïvely in these social irrationalisms, I would have remained imprisoned in economic sociologisms or academic interpretations of the "social unconscious." The economic process is the basis, but not the vital content, of social existence; furthermore, society has neither an unconscious nor a death instinct nor a superego. Here is an example of reality:

The Communist Party in Vienna organized demonstrations of the unemployed on certain occasions. With untiring effort party officials announced the demonstrations in the newspaper *Rote Fahne* and organized them as well as possible through the distribution of leaflets in unemployment offices and in the working-class sections of the city. Since I was a well-known physician in Vienna, my collaboration in the form of moral support was heavily relied upon, and justifiably so. I was known to the various unemployment committees, spoke on problems of hygiene at meetings, and participated in almost every demonstration although I never had a specific political function. I was offered a chair on the Executive Committee and was nominated for the post of national assemblyman, but I declined as I had neither the time nor the inclination. The demonstrations, however, impressed

[7] In 1943, when I read Wendell Willkie's book *One World*, an American best seller, the contradiction became clear once again. Unquestionably, Wendell Willkie is one of the most honest, democracy-minded exponents of human liberty and we can only agree with his views and intentions. However, the weakness of his book lies in its portrayal of the problems of democracy "from above," from conversations with statesmen and military leaders, from conferences and social actions *above* the level of the people. Wendell Willkie did not stress the *unofficial*, the *private*, the *little everyday aspects* of the people he met, in addition to the official aspects. In reality social life does not take place "above" but "below."

Adolescents in trouble
Nowhere to go when in love

Courtesy New York Times
People watching a marriage ceremony

Modju at work in Austria, 1915
Observe cold, cruel facial expressions of executioners and bystanders; also mild face of victim

me as being extremely instructive; they were, so to speak, sociological schooling in practical life. I did not participate for the purpose of "studying" from an elevated position, but because, as a physician, I was accustomed to making no statements and forming no opinions without having been able to "view the matter from a bedside position." It was truly clinical work in social pathology.

Our society could be greatly improved if leading social economists would form their opinions not at their university offices but at the sickbed of society, on the streets, in the slums, among the unemployed and poverty-stricken. Ethnologists have long learned to rate the scientific results of "field work" more highly than academic investigation. But official sociology is still compiling dead statistics. Accordingly, I would like to suggest that social economists gain their knowledge through six years of practical experience as "social workers," just as physicians gain theirs through six years of hard work in laboratories and clinics. Many "clever," "superior" people viewed my practical course in social economy and mass psychology as "pure madness."

I marched in the ranks of the unemployed but not without a terribly guilty conscience about living in a six-room apartment with two servants. Through my own guilt, I became acquainted with the bad social conscience of economically secure intellectuals, from which stems their active "party fellowship." I compensated for my guilt feelings toward these cruelly mistreated victims of a cruel, disordered society by regular, and occasionally sizable, monetary donations. These people simply had the right to demand money. One would have to have known the unemployed of Vienna at that particular time to understand this; one would have to have personal experience of their marvelous human traits in the face of enormous misery, their childlike hopes, their primitive brutality, the humor they showed in suffering, their physical neglect, their patience and impatience, but above all their decency toward one another. This did not change the fact that they manifested all the characteristics of people in material need. Theft, drunken brawls, and sexual brutality were frequent. In relation to the misery in which they lived, however, they were much more decent, moral, willing to be of assistance, more honest and perceptive than the conceited, overweight, snobbish, good-for-nothing gluttons and cliché-mongers who showed not a trace of humaneness and were sexually far more pathological but less honest about it. One of these reactionary parasites ought to put himself in the place of an individual who has been unemployed for years and attempt to support an entire family on sixty schillings (about twenty dollars) a month, without stealing or robbing *regularly;* never, literally never, being able to be alone with his woman; never having money to spend on sexual necessities; despite sexual vigor, constrained to spend years in abstinence or to masturbate; forced to stand around in bureaucratic employment offices for hours, in the cold, without an overcoat, to receive five schillings; allowing himself to be pushed around by every person in uniform and still having to say "thank you." The beautiful cars, with well-dressed women and fat faces, drive quietly by and the unemployed are expected to stand for this and not smash the windows whatever the consequences may be. Are they to live on potatoes and stale bread and then look into the lighted windows of food stores without stealing what they see, simply taking it, come what may? [Observing the self-control of poverty-stricken people was one of my most profound experiences as a physician. Later I realized that character armor makes this self-control possible.] Thus I understood the "unpaid purchases" in the fully stocked food stores when the winter of hunger, 1929–30, with its vast suffering, closed in on these people. There were 100,000 unemployed literally starving in Vienna. In all of Austria they numbered almost 400,000 in 1930— out of a total population of six million. An overcoat was rarely seen at the demonstrations. Many of the people had holes in their shoes and they had no gloves or woolen clothing. It would have been ridiculous and provoking to appear at a demonstration with a winter overcoat and gloves, so I always marched with them in a leather jacket and slacks.

At first I expected the unemployed to express their demands vigorously and people in the street to stop and be moved to some social reaction. After all, that was the purpose of these demonstrations. The first one ran a pitiful course. There was hope that the second or third would produce results. Neither did.

It is difficult to put clearly into words the futility of these demonstrations by the poor. Starving people in ragged clothing were marching in the streets, not the state politicians' "economic factors." Three or four thousand unemployed in a city of two million inhabitants were demonstrating, not the social economists' "rebelling productive forces." The "conquest" of the city depended upon the *impression* the demonstrations made and this, in turn, viewed from the Marxist standpoint, determined the dialecticians' "immutable course of history." I would like to describe as best I can these demonstrations as they were experienced by the unemployed themselves.

The demonstrations were registered with the police and authorized. There were prescribed places to assemble. There were sometimes "illegal demonstrations" as well, in which a party of unemployed would, for example, call for a "mighty rally against the Fascists and Social Fascists at 3 p.m. in front of City Hall." But the police would already be there at 2:30 and would send the "illegal" demonstrators home one by one. Was all this idiocy? No, it was a surfeit of belief in "the inevitable collapse of capitalism," and "the immutable course of history" as well as the feeling of being "the leaders of the proletariat." [SO: This feeling was illusory, compensating for an emptiness which would lead to a bloody imperialism surpassing that of Peter the Great.] The "legal demonstrations" always followed the same pattern: they marched down Lastenstrasse to Wollzeile and waited for all groups to arrive; then they walked along the Ring to the Votive Church, where the group dispersed. Occasionally cries of "Down with capitalism!" or "Freedom and bread!" were heard. The populace grew accustomed to this and soon hardly even looked their way. Everyone had his own worries. Absolutely everybody was afraid of riots, including the demonstrators. Hotheads were calmed down by the people around them.

These individuals had been mistreated by society and excluded. Although they laid claim to leadership of society, during their demonstrations "against hunger and the system" they felt like the outcasts they really were. The people passing by were indifferent, or pitied them. Some turned their heads away in guilt. Others, in secret meetings, strengthened the defenses against a possible rule of the poor. Employed workers did not participate in these demonstrations. Those who had work were fearful of being identified with those already unemployed. This was obvious at the May Day demonstrations. Hundreds of thousands of industrial workers marched along the Ring. The unemployed workers hailed their "Social Democratic comrades" with "Three loud cheers for the red front," but the Social Democrats did not even look up. It was a tragedy. The Social Democratic members of Parliament stood at the windows watching the demonstration. The unemployed shouted "Down with the Social Fascists!" or "Down with Seitz!" or "Down with Otto Bauer!" or "Give us our unemployment benefits." They shook their fists threateningly, they sang the "Internationale" or "Red Wedding."[8] I felt their rage and sympathized with them. The parliamentary hairsplitting and graft during those times were absolutely exasperating. Police barricades had been erected between the representatives of democratic Socialism and the unemployed. Hundreds of fascistic students stood at the University and sang heckling nationalistic songs during every demonstration of the poor. They sang better, were better dressed, and were not as blue from the cold. They had also occupied the University, the source of the power of knowledge. The workers considered the University the bastion of political reactionaries; the students mocked the workers. There was no trace of the democratic rebel students of 1848. In one such demonstration, the marchers broke through the police cordon when the nationalists began heckling, and stormed the platform. The police cordon broke, several students were severely beaten. But most of the column continued to march by unperturbed. The police began to club the demonstrators right and left. Many ran off and this, in turn, encouraged the police.

[8] Wedding was a workers' district in Berlin.

On this and the following page, Reich's photographs of Austrian workers' demonstrations

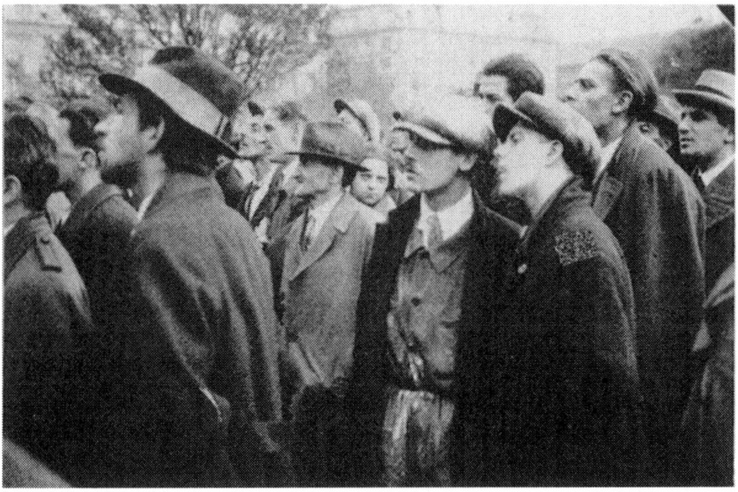

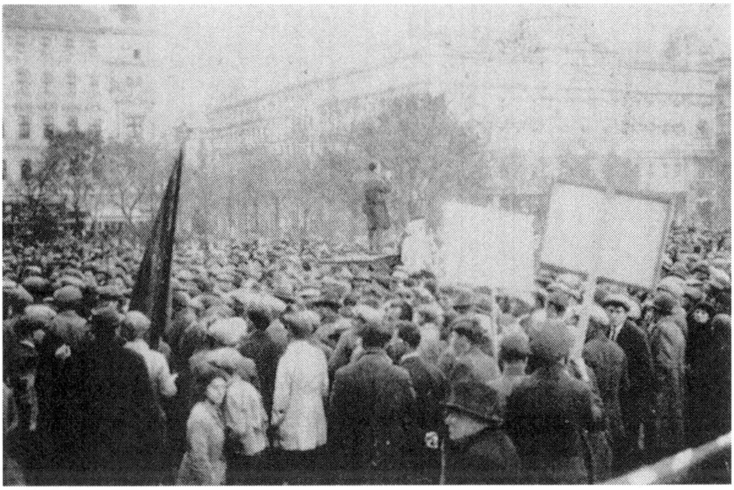

A trivial incident provided me with further insight. I happened to be caught in the midst of a group of men who were brawling. A huge policeman began to club the speaker for the unemployed. The man fell down unconscious and had to be carried away. The policeman then came after me. I stood perfectly still, as there was nothing else I could do, and looked him straight in the eye. The uniformed human animal became embarrassed and did me no harm! The power derived from an identification with the state, through a uniform, suddenly broke down. I have witnessed numerous melees but have never been beaten myself. Bullies feel strong and brutal only toward the weak. If one displays the slightest bit of courage, and does not provoke them, they become human and show sympathy. Human and tyrant, both reside within them and appear according to the circumstances.

This made me realize that by drilling people to hate the police one only strengthens police authority and invests it with mystic power in the eyes of the poor and helpless. The strong are hated but also feared and envied and followed. This fear and envy felt by the "have-nots" accounts for a portion of the political reactionaries' power. One of the main objectives of the rational struggle for freedom is to disarm reactionaries by exposing the illusionary character of their power. This presupposes that, as a freedom fighter, one has stifled all tendencies toward violence and greed for power within oneself and developed no hatred of individuals or social classes but only hostility toward the reactionary conditions which generate social misery.

As a result of these experiences at the demonstrations, I attempted, in the social-hygiene meetings, to present as vivid a picture as possible of police officers as human beings, fathers and husbands at home, no different in their simplest bodily functions from ourselves. In doing so I tried to counteract the helpless masses' fear and irrational hatred of authority which the incorrect propaganda techniques of the Communists had merely intensified. By describing the chief of police or a government leader as a brutal, autocratic, despicable tyrant worthy only of their hate, they simultaneously sowed horror and feelings of inferiority and weakness among the people.

One of the secrets of the success of the National Socialists in Germany lay in the fact that hate for political opponents was derived not from the latter's superiority but from their weaknesses and blunders. This hatred was subsequently implanted in the minds of the opponents' followers; to be ruled by stupid and corrupt weaklings is an insult to human dignity and natural self-respect. This, coupled with a sense of "national greatness," was destined to become an invincible power. In contrast, drawing attention to poverty and need alone could not foster self-esteem and generate power. Man is ashamed of poverty; he feels less secure in shabby clothing than when he is decently dressed—and a uniform awakens his pride in himself. The situation had to be remedied, but no one knew how. One sensed the paltriness of established power in comparison with the high goals of the social revolution, and yet nothing could be done. Hence the Communists and Socialists outshouted each other, developing a *false* sense of power, a *false* heroism, and an annihilating asceticism. This attracted no one.

Solving real problems, whether large or small, is far more radical and convincing than "revolutionary" tirades which foster inferiority feelings in the socially demoralized and generate only scorn, hate, and brutality among the ranks of those better situated.

In practical social work it is unnecessary to give up a single scientific principle. On the contrary, the essence of all practical work is its basic principles; only ideologies and political slogans can be both true and false at the same time. In the social-hygiene meetings everyone saw clearly which social conditions foster human well-being and which ones are socially pathogenic; and it automatically became evident—with little radical dialogue—which conditions needed to be remedied.

Several years later, this type of social approach was so highly developed in Germany that even policemen, government officials, and other custodians of order came to our counseling centers in droves and assisted the unemployed, whom they had previously considered useless rebels. At the same time no secret was made of the fact that there existed both privileged and disadvantaged classes, and that injustice and social murder were rampant. However, emphasis was always placed upon the necessity of despising the pathological conditions rather than the representatives of such conditions.

The course of our work simply compelled my colleagues and me to play off the human qualities which all people held in common against the divisive official poses. This basic principle not only brought about a rush of individuals from every level to the organization, which I directed without presidents, vice-presidents, secretaries, honorary presidents, etc., but also gave birth to one of the most essential tenets of what was later termed "work democracy": "Help yourself and fight for the means to enable you to help yourself. Do not beg for liberty and bread; do not accept them from economic oppressors or political pirates. Achieve them through resolute, rational work, on yourself, on your environment, and on your fellow beings. And above all, do not shift responsibility onto others but learn to bear it yourself."

The systematic distraction of oppressed individuals' hatred away from the representatives of desolate conditions and toward the conditions themselves proved to be a rationally effective measure. This hate on the part of the poor, and the neurotics of all classes, lost its aimless, irrational character and was transformed into logical thought processes and realistic endeavors. This, in turn, awakened the sympathy of many individuals who had previously been indifferent or disdainfully inimical. Senseless shouting and complete lack of responsibility were replaced by purposeful, responsible, cooperative work. The young people, for example, did not submit petitions to parliamentary hygiene commissions, but assisted each other and organized the vital necessities themselves, in a rational manner. Their practical success caused many hygienists to follow of their own accord. It may sound unbelievable but it is true that in Germany it was not the state apparatus but the "freedom parties," to which the youth belonged, which took action against such self-help. That was an

This Is Politics! 99

impressive lesson: The freedom parties themselves thrived on the helplessness of their members.

Frequently, even police officers—who had previously been physically assaulted and, justly or unjustly, were considered homicidal executioners—actually championed the cause of the social outcasts. In numerous social-hygiene meetings police officers were present with orders to break up the meeting as soon as "the power of the state" was verbally attacked. This was routine procedure in political gatherings. But their stern, antagonistic faces grew softer and they displayed active interest when I did not even mention the issue of oppression by law and executive power, but delineated the problems which the unemployed, the factory workers, the youth, the women, etc., had to solve by themselves. (For instance, it was entirely within the realm of possibility for the people themselves to organize children's clinics for the poor, or establish sex-counseling offices, or take various practical measures regarding housing problems.) Then the "human being" that resided in the "custodians of law and order" emerged. And when I began to speak of the misery in the lives of children, in marriages and families, awareness of the presence of "protectors of class interests" vanished completely. It became strikingly obvious to all present that these officers and policemen were themselves employees, despite their uniforms. They had children, wives, marital problems, and housing and child-raising difficulties. Viewed in this way, from a practical, psychological perspective, class boundaries appeared entirely different from the way they were portrayed in purely economistic party programs. [SO: Only much later, in America, did I realize that the police can also be democratic. Naturally, in saying this, I am not overlooking the fact that the emotional plague prevails in America also.]

After establishing the sex-counseling centers, I witnessed the overpowering role played by irrational mechanisms which oppose conscious goals in the masses. These centers formed a focal point for a group of workers who, for a brief period, were important to the movement. I knew that demonstrations and calls of "long live this" or "down with that" could accomplish nothing in themselves. There was a need for constructive work that would set an example. The workers' movement could not lay claim to leadership of society if it did not grasp and attempt to solve, from the very beginning and step by step, all problems created by the splintering of bourgeois society.

Initially, after the upheaval in July 1927, I was not satisfied with my activities. Different organizations—Arbeiterhilfe, Free Thinkers, groups in high schools, universities, and factories—invited me to lecture. I spoke here and there on psychoanalysis, the Oedipus complex, the castration complex, etc. Soon, however, it became apparent that my listeners could not put these ideas to use in daily life or for social change, nor did they need to learn any theories. They needed insight and knowledge to assist them practically in their arduous tasks. I was already aware of some theoretical connections between psychoanalysis and Marxism, but they were of no practical significance. They were more useful among students, especially medical students. I gave my first lecture to a group of Socialist students on "the sexual misery of the masses under capitalism." It was very well received. Since I knew that psychoanalytic theory as it had been formulated was not suited to lectures before active Socialist groups, I shifted my theme to the problems of sexual life among the masses. My experiences in the Psychoanalytic Polyclinic now served me well. Although the psychology of repression and of the unconscious was of no interest, sexual disturbances, the rearing of children, and the question of the family proved to be burning issues. I soon realized that the Oedipus complex was applicable in the context of "the family." After my very first lecture, during the question period, I was confronted with the task of explaining why the family so consistently suppresses the sexual activity of children. This was the same question which had confronted me in my medical practice. No one had the answer as yet. The revolutionary Socialists rejected the family as an instrument of suppression. But their concept of suppression was, in keeping with current views, merely economic—that is, the father, who is economically stronger, subjugates his wife and children. Hence they demanded the "abolition of the family" and gave it no further consideration. [They could not possibly have solved a single problem of family life.]

Socialist theory had confirmed the sociological origin of the family and awaited the collapse of private ownership of property to solve the problem spontaneously. My background was psychoanalysis, where the family per se did not pose a problem but where the emotional relationships within an already existent family constituted the central issue. A bridge between the two viewpoints was yet to be built.

Before a second large student gathering (1928), I spoke on "the relationship of psychoanalysis to Marxism," and attempted to clarify the sociological role of the Oedipus complex. The pro-Communist students had invited a "red professor" from Moscow for the occasion. In the discussion he declared unequivocally (in a manner resembling a party resolution) that the Oedipus complex was un-Marxist, nonsense, and simply nonexistent. Those were his words! Most of the students sided with me, but Moscow's authority was enormous because of the 1917 social revolution, and I had no satisfactory answer to the question of where and how the function of the family is established sociologically. [SO: Since that time, the Communists have never ceased fighting my views, obviously fearing the competition between Marx's economism and psychology.]

My medical and scientific activities were not interrupted in any way by my political activities, although I soon felt the sharp contradiction between science and politics, a contradiction which was ever-present and unavoidable during those times and which I later tried to resolve with the concepts of scientific politics and political science. I must describe the path which led me in my own field of endeavor to a reconciliation of these sharp contrasts. I had no idea then, in 1928, that I would one day recognize social irrationalism in party politics. I was still far from realizing the sharp distinction I later made between what is social and what is political.

[SO: The Sexpol of 1927–37 is dead. Together with all human endeavors based on political thinking, it had no future. It died with the old patterns of life in the Second World War. It was well meant, but wrongly executed, as were all other human hopes in the 1920's. Nobody knew it then. Now we have learned from such mistakes that:

No political arrangement of human problems will ever accomplish anything.

The politician stands, and must stand, against every positive human endeavor, since his existence depends on unsolved problems.

The politician will try to exploit the unsatisfied sexual needs of people in the future as he exploited other needs in the past.

Society must be rebuilt according to human needs, beginning with babies' needs.]

It was considered insane for a respectable physician and scientist to participate in demonstrations of the unemployed, hand out pamphlets on social hygiene in working-class areas, and become involved in clashes with the police. The intellectuals could not understand why I would risk my social position by doing such things. As sociologists, they wrote about problems of society, but in doing so they behaved like a physician who writes a learned book on typhoid without ever having seen a single case. For this reason most sociology textbooks, until now, have not influenced the forward development of society. The same holds true for sexology and sexual reforms. The sexologists at that time based their writings on their experience in private practice. The sexual problems and neuroses of the masses, however, are completely different and pose problems essentially unlike those encountered in private practice, and especially in a psychoanalytic practice. The years shortly before and after July 15, 1927, were characterized, for the psychoanalytic movement, by an influx of Americans who came to Vienna to study. Whereas a Viennese patient or pupil could pay five to ten schillings an hour (only exceptional cases could afford twenty schillings an hour), Americans had to pay at least five dollars (thirty-five schillings) per hour. Many paid ten or fifteen dollars and even more. But one did not need to pity them. Either they were very wealthy or they were learning psychoanalysis and would later receive payment a thousandfold for their own services. Still, the rage for Americans had a basically corrupting influence.

In 1928 a young doctor from New York came to me for training. Today he is a respected psychiatrist and psychoanalyst. One day he saw me in a demonstration march of the unemployed —the one which ended in the riots at the University. The next day he arrived at my office wearing a red tie. I noticed this although he himself seemed unaware of the connection. When I drew his attention to the fact, however, he remembered that he had seen me the day before. He was not a Socialist, but my marching had not particularly upset him; on the contrary, I was able to prove to him that he was not quite able to completely suppress his admiration for me.

I lived in constant fear for my practice, as any move could have destroyed me. Strangely, though, both activities prospered, the medical as well as the political. I did not understand it, for one could clearly see how in my professional circle fear of losing one's practice could inhibit any sincere involvement with social problems.

Among the workers in a party chapter in the twentieth district, where I was active, there was a young married lathe worker with whom I became friendly. His name was Zadniker and he was a splendid person. Through him I learned to know and to appreciate the workers' unique way of thinking. Precisely because of this I never fell prey to the blind idolization of workers seen in many hyperradical intellectuals who hastily join the labor movement [as stooges of red imperialism] and then disappear again just as quickly. Zadniker was simple, straightforward, without manners but also without guile. When he said something he meant it; when he was angry he showed it openly and soon afterward we were good friends again. He possessed great natural dignity which was not at all affected. His handshake was firm. He was able to talk factually about general human sexual problems—not just those of the workers—without a trace of cynicism or prurience. Although he had never read anything by Freud, it was obvious to him that children have sexual desires toward their parents and that hate can develop from this. There was no issue in my sex-economic viewpoint that he did not comprehend automatically, i.e. intuitively, without book knowledge. He was having difficulties with his hysterical wife, spoke about it with reason and clarity, understood the sexual etiology of a neurosis, and knew that people are not neurotic when sexually satisfied. Through him I discovered exceptionally important details about life among the proletariat: the sordid and the sublime, the filth and dirt as well as the beauty in the behavior of these individuals. More and more, he brought me into contact with circles of unpretentious working people who convinced me that knowledge of sex-economic processes and laws is *generally* and *spontaneously* present in the silent, toiling, down-to-earth strata of society.

He was amazed that a bourgeois intellectual could grasp the situation so thoroughly. Then I told him about Freud and my experiences in the Psychoanalytic Polyclinic. His understanding was immediate and direct. With estimable human naturalness he grasped facts which decades of discussion and thousands of articles were unable to teach psychiatrists and *culturati*.

I had attempted, at the time, to make myself useful in the different workers' organizations. I gave lectures on the Oedipus and castration complexes and from this perspective arrived automatically at the question of the family and sexual hygiene. Once Zadniker remarked, "You know, this Oedipus complex seems right to me when you are discussing it, but how are we to use it in our struggle for a better life? After all, we can't analyze everyone in order to make them healthy. First we must change social conditions. We must have something to say before people will listen to us and we can put an end to the misery. We workers would gladly learn even though many of us are lazy and dejected. But you intellectuals must also learn to express yourselves more simply and present scientific issues in a way everyone can understand. Today, only the questions everyone can understand are important." He spoke from the heart. In my first cautious attempts with psychology in the workers' movement, I had seen for myself that little could be done with psychoanalytic concepts. The topics were understood but could not be put to practical use.

The theories that the family is a biological institution, that civilization is based on sexual repression, that mental health can only be achieved through renunciation of the instincts and sublimation, all sounded ridiculous in these circles, really completely ridiculous. I felt stupid trying to tell a strapping machinist or construction worker that he had to sublimate his sexuality in order to become "capable of culture." If he was healthy he embraced his girl lovingly, with no complications. If he was ill he behaved just as any other average person would under similar circumstances. Is it not said that work is based on sublimation of pregenital impulses? I learned how to observe a stonemason. Year in and year out he broke up large stones into smaller ones and fit one against the other to pave the streets. Did this represent instinctual sublimation? If so, what type of sublimation? Anal? Sadistic? Ridiculous! Very soon I realized the mechanical character of this work which had nothing to do with "narcissistic elevation of the ego." The problem seemed, rather, how a manual laborer or a bookkeeper could endure work with no psychic gains for such long periods of time. I personally would not have been able to do it at all, or perhaps only if I had extinguished all life within myself and become a machine. Then, all at once, the missing link appeared: character armor enables the worker to bear the psychic tedium of this kind of activity. Quickly, I grasped even more: Freud's theory of sublimation was correct for research scientists or engineers; it was poorly suited to the average doctor or technician, and altogether unsuitable for work done by the masses.

Zadniker told me that the condition of the unemployed was especially bad. They were always ruined psychically, sooner or later. He did not adhere to the opposing theory of the Comintern, namely that hunger alone—and not sexual repression—was the cause of neurosis. He said that the unemployed were inactive for months and even years, that they were debilitated. Thinking about it, I concluded that this is because the biological energy with no active outlet first causes nervousness and then gradually devitalizes the organism. Zadniker explained, as well, that it was virtually impossible for the unemployed to stay physically healthy and that this led to the destruction of the family and the relationship between man and wife. He became a beggar. When a working-class family is exposed to hunger for a long period of time, all the unconscious sources of hate begin to overflow. Ordinarily, under better economic conditions, they are covered over by conventional attitudes. Zadniker also revealed to me the deepest secret in the function of marriage and the family. He was a politically aware, clearheaded worker; his wife needed him and he needed her as well. However, since he was healthy and she was sexually disturbed, he suffered. He sought out other, healthier women. She was jealous, although she could not give him what he needed, and tried to prevent him from going to meetings where he might easily make the acquaintance of other women. That was undoubtedly her reasoning. He knew it and expressed it in simple terms. And men, he remarked, Communists included, rattle off slogans like "proletarian class-consciousness" and "mutual comradeship between husband and wife," while they still chain their wives to the kitchen stove. They fear, likewise, that their wives may meet other men. He told me much more and I learned to see a great deal that is not described in any political or scientific text. I began to feel acutely the worthlessness of academic science. Much of what I had previously valued began to collapse. To be this kind of scientist meant practicing a subterfuge. How was I to remain a scientist, i.e. work honorably in science, and yet overlook these realities? It appeared to be one of the main functions of many scientists to negate such realities by ignoring them.

The events in Austria were so confusing at the time that academic science seemed unbearably remote from life itself. Communist prognoses seemed to be correct; the Soviet economist Varga warned of a renewed, serious economic crisis in capitalism. This was certain to cause world revolution, which, in turn, would bring rationality into the lives of men. Although I immersed myself even more deeply in politics [which to me meant social work], some presentiment restrained me from following the usual path to a career of a political party functionary. I would have had to give up what to others might seem to be my senseless profession and devote myself entirely to party activity. But I was heart and soul in my scientific work. I sensed the beginnings of a productive criticism of bourgeois psychology without, as yet, being able to formulate it. Leaving an upper-class bourgeois existence behind would be a significant step to take but even the threat of serious consequences had so far never prevented me from taking risks.

During this period I entered a phase which every awakening individual passes through: I began to feel the barrenness of social amusements and conversation. I had already left behind me the "dancing and discussing Goethe" stage. I was still frequently invited to the homes of my colleagues for an evening, but accepted these invitations less and less often. It all seemed such a farce and I had lost the ability to converse in a light vein. On the other hand, my friend Zadniker had inspired me with an idea from which I could not free myself. I was a psychiatrist and sexologist and could exert far less influence as a politician than as a physician. Hence I devoted myself to whatever medical and educational assistance I could give to youth and to the female workers. In January 1929, the leftist newspapers carried the first brief notices about the Socialist Society for Sex-Counseling and Sex-Research, which had opened several sex-counseling centers for workers and salaried employees. After several months of preparation and at considerable personal expense, I had founded this organization with several younger psychoanalytic colleagues who were my pupils, and three gynecologists. The title was rather pompous, but it was customary, at the time, for organizations to equip themselves thoroughly with rubber stamps and letterheads.

We sent out announcements that sexological specialists had formed an organization to provide, in the various districts of Vienna, free counseling on sexual problems, the rearing of children, and general mental hygiene to those seeking advice. Lectures were to furnish information on sexual hygiene and the causes of and possible remedies for emotional difficulties. The society took the position that sexual misery was essentially brought about by social conditions rooted in the bourgeois social order and that it could not be removed entirely but at least could be alleviated by aid to the individual. In addition, information on sexual matters was to be widely circulated among working people. The knowledge underlying this information would be broadened by social work and research on individuals. I reserved the position of scientific director for myself. Six counseling centers were opened immediately, each directed by a physician. Three obstetricians placed themselves at our disposal to assist with problem pregnancies. A lawyer also participated.

[What was new about our counseling centers (sex-hygiene clinics) was that we integrated the problems of the neuroses, sexual disturbances, and everyday conflicts. It was also new to attack the neuroses by *prevention* rather than treatment. This depended basically on the handling of sexuality in children and young people. At this point, *I wish to claim priority and full responsibility for the introduction of the sex-economic view of children's and adolescents' sexuality and the sex-economic view of natural genitality.* No attention had been given previously to this central realm of mental hygiene, and whatever consideration was later given to the neuroses in Germany, in Scandinavia, and finally in America, bypassed the problem of the genitality of children and adolescents with moralizing ideas. Here, it is not only a matter of my claim to priority, it is the advocacy of a social question as forbidden as it is basic, a question which led to the source of the emotional plague.]

The centers immediately became so overcrowded that any doubt as to the significance of our work was promptly removed. During my own counseling hour there were always approximately ten people waiting, so that I had to arrange a second hour. My colleagues were in a similar position, and once the lectures began, the situation intensified. To consider each case with reasonable care required about half an hour. At first, the majority of those who came were girls and women who had become pregnant through clumsiness or ignorance. We sent them to the city birth-control clinics, but we ourselves instructed them in the use of contraception and in the physiological function of the genital embrace. Among them, there was not one single case where advocating a continuation of pregnancy would not have been inhumane, unethical, base, and cowardly. Literally, not one of these women and girls should have been *allowed* to bring a child into the world. In comparison to this reality, all the empty talk about various medical and eugenic indications for abortion (social indications were never mentioned) soon appeared as utter insanity and to the great shame of those individuals who for decades debated whether, and to what extent, a medical evaluation could be viewed as valid and permissible in addition to the consideration of eugenics. No decent physician—or anyone else —would have sanctioned for himself one iota of what he demanded for "the people" to ensure "the safeguarding of morals" and an "increase in population." These issues were treated so extensively in my book *The Sexual Revolution* that I may be brief here. The problem was no longer the indications for the interruption of pregnancy, but the kind of thinking which created the cruel anti-abortion laws and enforced them mercilessly. The immediate problem, however, was the views and thinking of the reformers who did not disclose what I saw and continued to describe, but rather negotiated on various issues with the representatives of the law. [SO: Mothers did not count. Infant misery did not count. What counted was a sick moralism that was to break down only a few years later when "planned parenthood" became a matter of course. How many lives were lost in this instance alone . . .] I was, as yet, unacquainted with their true convictions but was soon to feel the impact of them. They debated whether or not tuberculosis, mental retardation, or flat feet in a family constituted indications for abortion. Only the extreme radicals advocated the woman's "right to her own body." They defended their position with the pacifying arguments that only in this way could women bear their children happily, that the population would increase despite this, as in the Soviet Union, and that the introduction of Socialism would prove that women like to have children but first need to be freed of material need. This was doubtless true, but was only a small part of the problem. Something much more important and encompassing determined my position, namely: even if material provisions were made, and for some women they were at hand, these women whom I was seeing simply should not have children. Aside from all other questions, socioeconomic and medical, I began to see the problem in a new light, that of the emotional state of the expectant mothers. Finding a reason on which to base a medical diagnosis, in the context of current mores, was rare indeed. But to take this as a precedent, to use it as an excuse not to see the main issue, was actual stupidity and a crime against the women. These mothers, and women, and girls, were able to bear a child but incapable of rearing it, caring for it, or keeping it alive. All of them, without exception, were seriously neurotic and had a very poor relationship with their husbands, if any relationship at all. They were frigid, careworn, covertly sadistic or overtly masochistic. They were latent schizophrenics, or morbid depressives; vain little women, or wretched, disinterested work animals. If they were married, they hated their husbands, or they slept indiscriminately with anyone, without feeling. Many lived with from five to eight other people who shared the same room and kitchen. From dawn till dusk they slaved on piecework at home to earn twenty-five schillings a week or even less. They had three to six children of their own and sometimes raised others as well. Drunken husbands beat them and demoralized them. Because the children they already had were causing them nothing but torment and want, they harbored deadly hatred against them and against the unborn child. Idle talk of "holy mother love," in the face of this subhuman misery, could almost have provoked one to draw a gun on the speaker. Even if the worst of the misery had been removed, there would have remained at least as much to be rebuilt if there had been a genuine desire to realize one-hundredth of all the chatter about children and culture. All of these mothers were hysterical or compulsive; their children were either cute little dolls or beaten puppies. Such women should not be allowed to bear children!—quite apart from the inhuman material existence of most.

For these reasons, I advocated, from the beginning, the unquestionable right of every woman who was pregnant against her will to have an abortion, with or without all the various indications. At the time we were able to refer to laws passed in Russia, although I already knew [as early as 1929] they were not genuinely intended; in fact, five years later they were repealed. I sent every woman who had become pregnant unknowingly, or against her will, to doctors who performed the abortion. I knew exactly what I was doing and considered it a matter of course to assume the risk. I always saw before my eyes the well-known hatred of such mothers for their children and did not trouble myself with the concerns of population politicians. I was familiar with their equivocation and the sociological formulations of their attitudes as well. At that time, I had already become involved in a silent argument with the Communists who were against Malthusianism because Marx had not entirely understood Malthus, who contended that the misery would disappear if the birth rate was reduced. Malthus overlooked the origins of the social dilemma. Marx, on the other hand, had discovered these origins and rejected the Malthusian theory because it could easily distract from the real objectives of class struggle and lead to illusions. But since Marx did not clarify this completely, the theory of the necessity for birth-rate restriction led a miserable existence and soon disappeared altogether in the Soviet Union. The solution was: social struggle to eliminate the misery of the masses *and* selective birth control!

For two years I was so overwhelmed by the people's sexual misery that the conflict between the scientist and the politician within me grew even more intense. It increased especially when I came into contact, through sex-counseling, with the average Viennese working teen-ager. Although I had become acquainted with pubertal needs much earlier, the cases in the Polyclinic and my private practice seemed pathological exceptions to the rule, in the light of contemporary psychoanalytic thought, this rule being based on the "normally adjusted adolescent who has overcome his Oedipus complex and complied with the demands of reality." Almost no one reflected upon the concept of a "normal, healthy adolescent," and even less upon compliance "with the demands of reality." The status quo was simply taken for granted and accepted as unchangeable. It was not questioned, in print or elsewhere. But in the sex-counseling centers, and especially afterward in the sex-political youth meetings, the picture changed entirely. Here I was faced with adolescents who were considered healthy; most of them—on the average, between ages fourteen and twenty—came only for advice on contraceptives. Immediately, the question arose whether one should give a fourteen- or fifteen-year-old contraceptives. This question, in turn, led consistently and relentlessly to the whole problem of adolescence. The usual procedure was not to occupy oneself with this age group at all,[9] or to send the youngsters away with the comforting advice to wait until they have matured somewhat. This, of course, was impossible if one wished to prevent neuroses.

Before formulating an answer to the question, I reviewed all the psychic, physical, and social factors. These teen-agers were actually adult individuals. They were employed as apprentices in factories, messenger boys, or domestic help. Many of the young men were members of the Workers' Youth Guard and the great majority of these young people were members of the Social Democratic Youth Association. Either they already had boy friends, or girl friends, or they came to me with the question of how they could "find a way out of their loneliness." My first naïve answer was: "Aren't you in a youth group?" "Yes, but that's—that's not what I mean," came the reply. There was no need for further questioning. The matter was perfectly clear. Gradually I learned to understand, to affirm, and to remove the deep-seated and completely justified mistrust that youth places in everything pertaining to authority and adults. I simply told them they were correct. There was not one who did not immediately grow more confiding after that. They knew the facts and wanted "a happy love life." They did not believe a word of the attempted indoctrination. Many had simply run away from home. There was deep hatred of their parents for suppressing their love life. Those who had partners appeared to consider making love, frequently in doorways or hidden corners, perfectly natural; they also accepted as natural the fact that they were dressed, that they had to be

[9] In the youth organizations the question was not even tolerated; one was too occupied with "high politics."

quick and were afraid of an unwelcome surprise, or of pregnancy. They had no idea of the relationship between their nervous disturbances and this wretched manner of "orderly" adolescent sexuality. The connection between a disorderly genital love life and shattered psychic health was unknown in the political organizations, walled off by false concepts and evasion. There was no eye for the pallor, depression, nervousness, work disturbances, quarrelsomeness, criminal tendencies, and perversions in these young people. Homosexuality flourished, usually in the form of mutual masturbation. Correct understanding existed side by side with the most idiotic subterfuges of bourgeois culture-gibberish or party slogans. However, a brief explanation of the connections was all that was necessary to enable the adolescents to grasp the facts immediately. The false morals and hypocritical concepts disintegrated like decomposing matter. At first I could hardly believe it was possible, especially since the "strict super-ego is so deeply rooted in the biological id."

Changing the basic sexual attitudes from the negative to the positive does not, of course, have any significant effect on the psychic structure. If castration or defloration fears were deeply embedded, the situation remained basically unchanged. Nevertheless, the younger the male or female adolescents were, the faster and more completely their direction was reversed after just a few remarks. It was as if they had been long awaiting the information, as if they had been marching lethargically under a yoke without understanding its meaning. They knew everything about their sexuality; they knew they needed love and stagnated without it. But they were completely unaware of the obstacles which blocked its fulfillment. They led double lives with no idea of the contradiction or of the social prerequisites and conditions for a satisfactory love life. All the girls, regardless of how firmly they demanded their sexual rights, were steeped in conscious or unconscious sexual anxiety. The boys suffered mainly from masturbational guilt feelings, hypochondriacal anxiety, or premature ejaculation.

Within a few short months, I learned more about sexology and sociology than I had in ten years of analytic practice. It was a period of transition for me. I had been taught, and had convinced myself as well, that premature ejaculation is based on urethral-erotic fixation and on the Oedipus complex. That is correct, but in addition I now realized that if sexual intercourse is attempted, or carried out, in haste, with the partners fully clothed, then ejaculation is also premature and occurs before sufficient excitation has been achieved. This leads to neurotic symptoms due to sexual stasis. I researched the genesis of the disturbance and found that these youths had been more or less neurotic at the onset of puberty but that the actual neurosis only developed after several years of pubertal conflict. Fixations created by the sexual taboos of childhood had always been present as a retarding factor, but it was the drastic obstruction of the final step to a healthy love life during the years of maturation which caused a complete regression to infantile conflicts. Hence I felt constrained to make one important correction of psychoanalytic theory. On the one hand, it is true that the revival of the Oedipus complex during puberty causes conflicts, but the conflicts are now much more the result of the social denial of sexual needs at that time. When the forward path toward normal healthy love is blocked, the adolescent reverts to an infantile neurosis which is intensified through increased and simultaneously denied genital desire. Psychoanalysis had completely overlooked this or, better said, *chosen* to overlook it, as was later demonstrated. Other schools of psychiatry did not even dare to mention the problem.

As a youth counselor, I was unable to rattle on about "cultural puberty" nor was I able to comfort the young people with future rewards. This struck me as a medical crime which one could commit only through ignorance or narrow-mindedness or fear for one's livelihood. I had to choose among three possible answers to their questions: I could advise abstinence, recommend masturbation, or simply affirm the adolescent desire for sexual intercourse. There seemed to be no fourth possibility, although I confess I sought one, in my predicament, for quite some time. Fear of public opinion, which was adamant and relentlessly cruel on this issue, prompted this search.

I would like now to relate how this enormous danger to my entire endeavor was overcome. Had I been alone in my scientific work, I would most certainly have been defeated. Perseverance and firmness of conviction were taught to me by young workers struggling for freedom and clarity about their very existence. Young members of the Schutzbund from the Arbeiterjugendwehr[10] came to my counseling center with various difficulties concerning their girl friends, sexual disturbances, etc. There was an immediate rapport, making it unnecessary for me to give them reasons for my advice. They grasped it structurally. I did not wish to evade the issue of the extremely tense political situation, nor could I. On the contrary, it was the intertwining of political life, on a large scale, with the minutiae of personal life which interested me. How often had I seen a labor functionary become politically inactive through entanglement in personal conflicts! From such cases, the political movement drew the false conclusion that politically active workers could have no personal conflicts. I could only view this as pious, wishful thinking comparable, politically speaking, to an ostrich hiding its head from its own kind. The individuals involved shared my views. Many of them came to me with an express desire for help in solving their personal problems in order to be better equipped for the political struggle.

Among these members of the Arbeiterjugendwehr there were two especially outstanding individuals. One was seventeen, the other twenty-one. They told of the unrest among the Social Democratic youth. At this time, emergency legislation had begun to dismantle all the social accomplishments of the Republic, and something had to be done. Schober, the newly elected President, who was concurrently chief of police, had been taking rigorous action. The crisis began to grow in ever-widening circles. The young men told me that the Schutzbund in Ottakring was prepared to do anything at all, and asked me to attend a meeting with them. I went along and spoke with the district Schutzbund leader, an old soldier and labor functionary. No reasonable

---

[10] Workers' Youth Guard. —*Trans.*

worker was in accord with the party platform. Nevertheless, it still represented the unity of the Austrian, as opposed to the German, Socialist movement and no one wanted to sacrifice this at any cost. On most issues the Communists were correct, but the workers would have nothing to do with them. Their shouting was too loud in comparison to the leadership they displayed and the results they produced. [They were not practical enough, and they slandered people so profusely.]

A young married machinist had organized a secret machine-gun division. When the last push of emergency legislation came, he and his men planned to occupy the inner city and shoot everyone down right and left. These people had nothing to lose, they lived only for a better tomorrow, waiting for their great chance to make contact with the movement of social life once again. Society had excluded them and now they were ready to punish it. I understood their arguments so well that no objection to their plans occurred to me, nor did I wish to raise any. Had I been as mistreated as they, my thoughts and desire to act would have resembled their own. It was simple and entirely rational. The workers themselves voiced the correct reservations: The masses would not assist them because their leaders had chosen a course of peaceful infiltration, which actually resulted in fatal compromises. Nevertheless, they wished to hold a large caucus.

Through my efforts, the Schutzbund conferred with the Communists without actually joining them. The convention hall at Stahlehner's in Hernals, which held approximately two thousand people, was rented for the occasion. I contributed the money and at their request gave the main address before an overflowing audience. Those in attendance were, for the most part, active members of the Schutzbund and employed workers. I enumerated past failures and demonstrated the point that the current path would lead unfailingly to disaster. [The events of 1934 confirmed this view. The Social Democratic organization was not destroyed by Hitler in 1938, but by the Christian Socialist Party under Dolfluss in 1934.] There was much shouting; the atmosphere was explosive. The audience was waiting for a positive, productive answer to the question of what could be done. I had no answer except that proposed by the Communist Party: the working class must fight for leadership in society. That was all I could offer, and it was far from satisfactory. Today, in retrospect, it is understandable that the people were not willing to agree with this general formulation. Everyone knew that the Communists were correct in principle, from a Marxist-scientific standpoint. But on practical everyday issues, the Social Democrats seemed to be in the right. And everyone was fearful of the civil war the Communists were fomenting. Now I realize that they were also afraid of the responsibility of social power. The Social Democrats were repeatedly able to prevail with their parliamentary theories. They merely relied on the revolutionaries' fear of revolution.

At this meeting I became acutely aware, for the first time, of the emotional content of party membership. The membership agreed with me, but as soon as the situation began to sound threatening for the Socialist Party, someone who apparently had been assigned this task shouted, "The Communists are only trying to split us and spread discord. All Social Democrats will now leave the room." And with that, the opposing Socialists walked out in a solid bloc. About four hundred Communists who had just come to terms with the Schutzbund, as well as several courageous Social Democratic functionaries and liberals of different organizations, remained behind. Although the meeting was continued, our cause had been lost. At the time we thought that the Social Democrats had once again "betrayed the cause in the service of the bourgeoisie." I was still far from seeing the common principle of all these tangled matters: the helplessness of average people in the face of the political plague. However, I must first lead up to this in a comprehensible manner.

5

The Invasion of Compulsory Sex-Morality into Innately Free Primitive Society

In Berlin my work immediately combined with the great freedom movement. When one is carrying alone the heavy burden of solving a crucial social problem, an opportunity to join such a movement is important. Above all, it protects the psychic apparatus which, due to special experiences in life, has grasped, formulated, and found a solution to the problem. The wider the scope of a concept, the more intricately it is interwoven with the personal life history of its supporter and the greater his responsibility not to allow its structure to contain overly irrational blunders. The most significant index for a concept's reality content is the reaction it produces in its socal environment, whether positive or negative. If a valid idea cannot find an adequate form of expression, this is an indication of insanity or may induce it. In this context I am employing the term "insanity" in the correct sense, i.e. the perceiving of a basic vital problem of life while lacking the ability to withdraw from it, to solve it, or at least to anchor it in rationality. I was well aware of my own personal equation which threatened from within. The suspicion of mental illness did not alarm me, but I was aware that if I did not achieve an adequate degree of success I might become the victim of an old insecurity acquired in childhood, namely the sexual guilt feelings which are destroying the world.

Since I felt firmly convinced that my views were correct and my thoughts logical, although I was not "adjusted" in the usual way of thinking, I felt the need to seek confirmation of the correctness of my approach in my immediate environment. At first, psychoanalysis appeared to yield the confirmation I sought. It became evident that this was partially the case but also that psychoanalysis was unwilling to assume any responsibility for my viewpoint. There was nothing to do but accept this. Then I hoped the Communist Party would accept my position. Its platform contained all the prerequisites and, additionally, some elements I had extracted through a different approach. This explains why I did not set forth my views independently from the very beginning, free from organizational affiliation, but rather pleaded my cause in the name of psychoanalysis or Marxism. When the situation grew serious, the Marxists joined with the reactionaries on this question. For the purpose of agitation, the reactionary world attributes to both Marxism and psychoanalysis ideas they neither accept factually nor advocate on an organizational-political level.

The incorporation of sex-economy into the psychoanalytic and Marxist movements had been a first important step. Now, between 1934 and 1938, the second, more decisive step was undertaken, namely the complete dissolution of ties to both movements. This resulted in a new concept of the relationship between the people and the state. It included the best elements of both parent movements but introduced additional insight which contained the solution to the problem of Fascism.

The problem of "the people and the state" may be subdivided in accordance with its development:

1. Ethnological proof that sex-economy is correct, demonstrated by Trobriand society as investigated by Malinowski.

2. The development of the sex-political (as opposed to sex-reformist) movement in Germany into the independent Sexpol.

3. Confirmation of my sociological and sex-political views,

through new problems raised by German Fascism and Russian Stalinization, while no explanations of these phenomena could be found in the old movements. And finally,

4. Recognition of the natural organization of work as the basis of a cultural movement focused on a practical and socially secure affirmation of sexual happiness for the masses.

In addition to the sex-economic findings and arguments which may be allowed to speak for themselves, the manner in which they evolved is also very important because it proves that nothing could have been "thought up" or contrived, and that it is not a "new system of political psychology" originating within my own brain. My theories only came to life when vague ideas or confused thoughts were suddenly confirmed by events. This caused them to mature, revealing new aspects which, in turn, found confirmation. For example: the ethnologist Malinowski, unexpectedly and with no knowledge of my views, contributed material which could be entirely assimilated into my work; I sensed in 1929 that the Russian sexual revolution was only a doomed first attempt and I was confirmed in this in 1935 by the Soviet Union's total legislative and ideological retrogression; at the first sight of German SA[1] formations, I felt that they represented the usurped German revolution in reactionary terms; I was convinced in 1930 that the battle for the German and Austrian workers' movement was definitely lost because it could not compete with the opposition's mass-psychological methods. Political reaction dominates the working masses and those individuals who are educated to subservience by means of life-negation. The Socialist movement did not advocate an affirmative life attitude for the masses but merely various basic economic prerequisites. There was no organization which dared to formulate the sexual core of life-affirmation, and since the uncomplicated human masses know only their own yearning for happiness but are not interested in the preconditions, political reactionaries everywhere were bound to be victorious.

Their success was based on an ideology which made the stability of society, civilization, and culture directly dependent

[1] Sturm Abteilung; literally, storm troops. —*Trans.*

The Invasion of Compulsory Sex-Morality

upon the abnegation of sexual happiness. I had long since established clinical proof of the opposite. Malinowski's ethnological material signified a major triumph for my scientific position because the political reactionaries founded their line of reasoning on the notion of a chaotic, barbarian state of primitive peoples. The unquestionable conclusion to be drawn from Malinowski's research was that the culture of which the philistines dream is not only in accord with sexual freedom but actually depends on it.

In November 1930, I received for review an English edition of Malinowski's *The Sexual Life of Savages*. It formed a logical continuation of his earlier *Crime and Custom in Savage Society* and *Sex and Repression*. Bachofen had already discovered "free sexual life" and matriarchy in classical myths. Morgan had deduced, through class relationships in the "primal society" of the Iroquois (among whom he had spent decades), that brother and sister were originally natural mates. Thus incest, far from being unnatural, was the very basis of the first human social organizations. It was self-evident that matriarchy was the natural state of human society after the first primitive epoch. Engels had based his political theories on this in his renowned *Der Ursprung der Familie*.[2] If one consolidated the theoretical trend from Bachofen through Morgan and Engels, to Malinowski, a unitary picture of human development emerged. Malinowski had succeeded in actually investigating the relationships of societies which were primarily matriarchal and, through this, in confirming the conclusions of his predecessors. The fact that he himself was unaware of this confirmation increased the value of his documentation which demonstrates irrefutably that common property, matriarchy, a lack of rigid family organization, sexual freedom for children and adolescents, openness and generosity in character structure, are just as interrelated as private property, patriarchy, asceticism in children and adolescents, enslavement of women, rigidity in family and marriage, character armoring, sexual perversion, and mental illness, all of which are the ever-present symptoms of sexual suppression.

After studying the English edition, I obtained the book in

[2] *The Origin of the Family.* —Trans.

German and read it closely twice. Most of his delineations were not new to me. From my experience with numerous youth groups, I was well acquainted with the atmosphere Malinowski was describing. Despite all the moral condemnation voiced in the reports of missionaries and in culturally oriented ethnological pronouncements, I had long sensed the simple naturalness of sexuality, its inherent morality, and the depth of natural sexual experience which makes the very thought of prurience impossible. And yet, I felt an inconsistency in Malinowski's portrayal which I was unable to explain at first. In the midst of Trobriand society, with its obedience to natural law, there lay wedged the demand for moral asceticism. To the extent that this demand was fulfilled, sexual and moralistic misery prevailed and was no different from the conditions in our own capitalistic system. This sector of Trobriand society was governed by different laws and ideologies. They could be grouped under the heading of "moralistic regulation" as opposed to "sex-economic self-regulation." There had to be an extremely important reason for both of these opposing principles to exist in *one and the same* social organization. Careful examination of the findings gradually revealed the historical development of contemporary moralistic compulsion from natural sexual organization. I had found traces of this buried deeply in the neurotic structures of modern individuals. The structure of the "genital character," as it is revealed in successful character analysis, proved to be identical with the average structure of a Trobriand Islander in the sector of society that was still free. The parallels were so striking that I was skeptical for a long time, fearing I had fallen victim to a delusion. My doubts were finally overcome only when Roheim, a strong opponent of Malinowski and myself, unknowingly and involuntarily, by means of a different ethnological approach, confirmed my views that the origin of the sexual suppression of youth is socioeconomic. It has been established through historical development; it is not biologically given. Thus, it is possible to create a culture with free sexuality for children and adolescents.

Three distinct elements impressed me in Malinowski's findings: the demand for sexual abstinence in a certain group of

The Invasion of Compulsory Sex-Morality

children and adolescents, the intricate and seemingly purposeless marital system among the tribal clans, and the rite of dowry.

Children who had been pledged for a certain connubial relationship were strictly prohibited from engaging in sexual activity. Childhood asceticism was to make them capable of marriage. Sexually unrestricted children are unable to meet the strict requirements of lifelong monogamy in its patriarchal form. The same facts were revealed to me through Barash's statistical surveys in the Soviet Union: the earlier adolescents engage in sexual intercourse, the shorter their marital relationships are later.

The connection between the demand for sexual asceticism and the institution of permanent, monogamous marriage was clinically, statistically, and ethnologically verified. It now remained to inquire further into the economic function of the entire issue. From the attitudes of bourgeois ideology toward natural sexuality, one could easily infer that it served the purpose of safeguarding economic interests. The paralysis of will and resolve in great masses of the population, through continuous suppression of physical excitation, had already been known to me for a very long time. However, the relation between this psychic paralysis and the economic interests of those who benefit from it was still obscured. No capitalist has any idea of why he advocates "morality for the masses," nor does the vice squad, the clergy, or the district attorney. Sexual ideology has assumed its own lawfulness and become an independent material power separated from its origin. In addition to this, human beings themselves cling to it and continually reconstruct it due to organic pleasure anxiety. Stated briefly, the economic function of the demand for asceticism cannot be directly grasped in our contemporary social mechanisms. Thus it was all the more gratifying that the developing conditions of economic exploitation in the primitive communists, the Trobriand Islanders, demonstrated this connection directly.

The Trobrianders differentiated between "good" and "bad" marriages. Marriage between the daughters of the sisters and the sons of the brothers—so-called cross-cousin marriage—was considered "good." All other marriages were considered "bad," to a greater or lesser degree. But where did these values originate? They were in such crass disharmony with the Trobrianders' general psychic behavior that they formed part of the foreign wedge (described above). The following diagram will illustrate this.

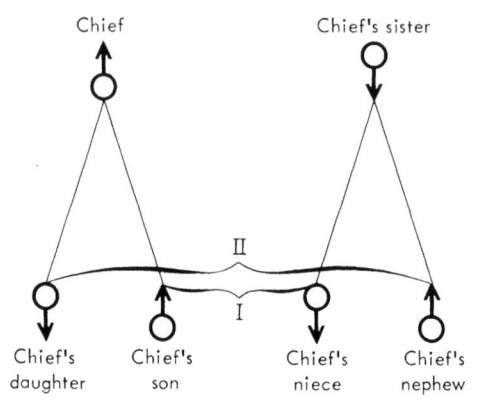

Figure 1. The "legal" marriage (I) and the "illegal" marriage (II), according to Malinowski. I = cross-cousin marriage

Three basic economic mechanisms resulted. Figure 2 shows the course of mandatory dowry in a "good" marriage. It was the brother's obligation to provide this dowry for his sister's husband. If her daughter later marries the brother's son, the girl's family and her brother in particular, namely the nephew of the mother's brother, must again supply a dowry. In this case the dowry (originally bestowed) *returns to the mother's brother,* who—if he is simultaneously a chief and enjoys the right of polygamy—can consequently amass wealth because all the brothers of all his wives must grant him a dowry. In this light, the reason why marriages are considered "good" becomes understandable, as they provide material advantages for the man. The children chosen to secure these advantages, through later marriage, are

[3] All diagrams taken from *The Invasion of Compulsory Sex-Morality.*

The Invasion of Compulsory Sex-Morality

compelled to live ascetically. They are not allowed to engage in sexual play as are the other children. For the first time in history, negative sex-morality invades a human society. For the first time, economic interests begin to form a social ideology and the morality created in the process begins to influence the children's structures. Through the blocking of their sexual energy, they are inwardly and outwardly enslaved.

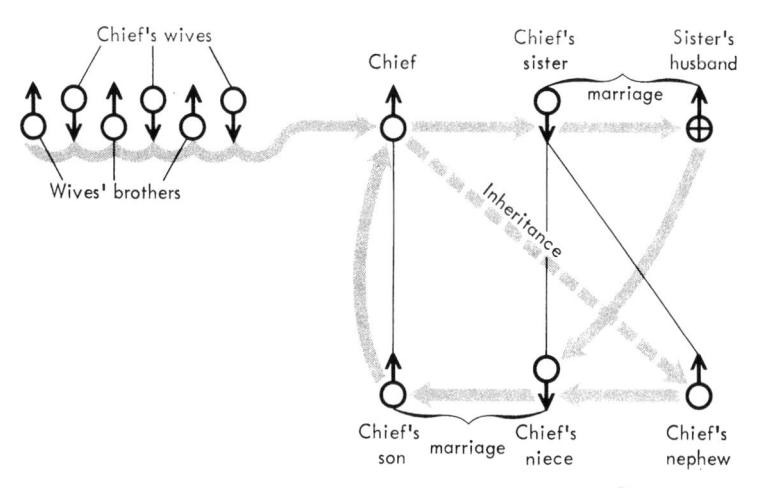

Figure 2. How the cross-cousin marriage benefits the chief by returning to him the marriage tribute he gives his brother-in-law, thus making possible the accumulation of wealth

The two diagrams on page 126 demonstrate the disadvantages of other types of marriage.

A "bad marriage" brings the greatest economic disadvantages. In this, the mother's brother loses wealth on three occasions: First, he must furnish his son with a dowry to care for his sister from an unrelated clan. Second, he must supply the dowry for his own sister who marries a man from a different clan. And finally, he loses the inheritance which passes to his sister's son.

Only the "good" cross-cousin marriage avoids all three dis-

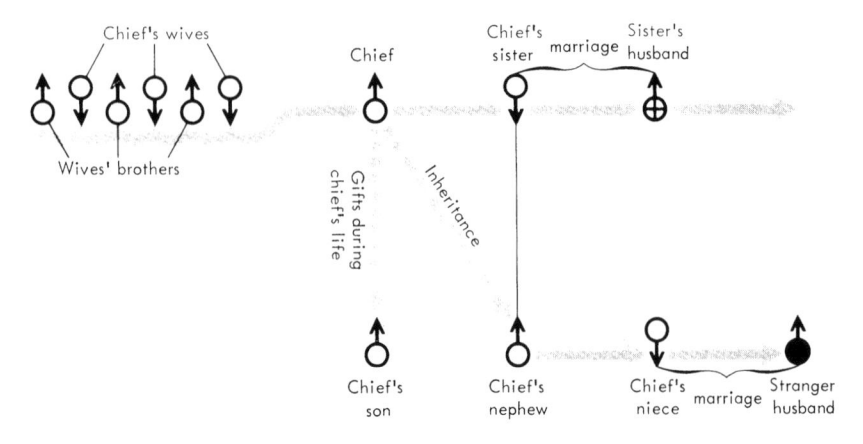

Figure 3. Economic disadvantages for the chief if his niece marries whom she will. (Arrows indicate the flow of the marriage gift)

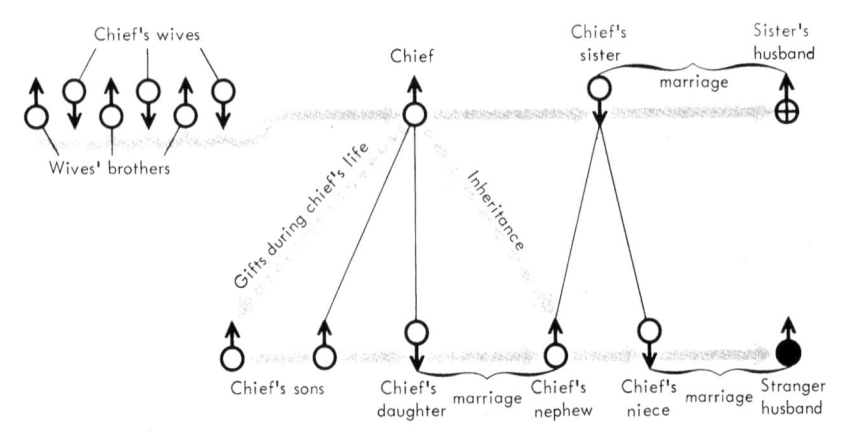

Figure 4. The "bad" marriage (between the chief's daughter and the chief's nephew). The fortunes of the chief's sons, too, leave the chief's line

advantages. The inheritance returns to the nephew and the wealth granted the other clan is temporary and is returned in full.

The institution of the marriage tribute, from the clan of the wife and her family to her husband, soon proved the key to understanding the most important questions of aboriginal society. I am only reporting results. For further information the reader is referred to the explanations in *The Invasion of Compulsory Sex-Morality*.

A survey of ethnological literature showed dowry, and the cross-cousin marriage as well, to be generally accepted phenomena in primitive societies. After difficult calculations I succeeded in constructing a diagram based on the research of Lewis Morgan. In this, the Iroquois's intricate marital system was logically analyzed as nothing more than a complex of "cross-cousin marriages." Iroquois organization was already completely patriarchal. After his return from Australia, I told Roheim of my little discovery. He replied that it was "nothing new," for this marital system had existed in Australia as well. But worthy Roheim did not realize that he had made an unguarded statement; he did not grasp the significance of these facts. If, indeed, a dowry paid by the brother to the sister's husband was a generally accepted phenomenon, then I was correct in assuming that this was *the* social mechanism responsible for transforming matriarchy into patriarchy. Several facts were revealed simultaneously:

1. Dowry granted the sister is an expression of the *duty to provide for her*. This corresponds to the fact that in the naturally organized primal hordes brother and sister were mates and produced children. Logically, the sister's son (i.e. nephew) was the legal heir of her brother. There was certainly no one else to compete with him.

2. The subdivision of matriarchal tribes into clans, with intermarriage between clans and prohibition of marriage within clans, is a universal phenomenon of primitive society. Under these circumstances, the dowry flows from one clan to another within the tribe. The division into clans (each with its own history of rituals and heritage) could only be interpreted as a mani-

festation of a previous merger, into one tribe, of several naturally organized hordes with an incest system (it could not be otherwise). The later clans are the original hordes, each traceable to one primal mother. This led to the inevitable hypothesis that the prohibition of sexual intercourse between brother and sister and the institution of interclan marriage (i.e. between the primal hordes) occurred with the unification of different hordes who were originally hostile and later became friendly. Therefore, the origin of the incest taboo was *social,* and a problem of primitive society found a sociological solution which, until then, had been interpreted biologically or psychologically. Attempts had been made to explain the origin of the incest taboo as an instinct for "natural selection" (Engels), or as guilt following primal patricide (Freud). After the merger of the hordes, the brother still had to support his sister but had to forgo a sexual partnership with her.

3. The dowry was not produced as a necessity, but already had the character of a *commodity.* It was the surplus which the brother and his family had to produce over and above their vital needs. In this manner, the marriage tribute made the brother and his clan economically dependent upon the clan of his sister's husband. Since the first clan to subjugate another retained its advantage in the form of a chieftainship, and since this chief, in turn, was allowed to "marry" several women, a material preponderance was created, first in the clan and subsequently in the family of the chief, in contrast to the rest of the tribe. This forced the lower clans, over the course of centuries, to be subject to the upper clans, especially to the chief's family. The chief simply had to name his son as his heir, instead of his nephew, at a certain level of his material dominance, and the entire organization automatically switched from a matriarchal to a patriarchal system. It then became less attractive, and even a burden, to care for the nephew (the sister's son) if he passed the wealth to a different clan. The cross-cousin marriage led to the legal establishment of a condition long present in dowry practices in tribes subdivided into clans. *The son now became the heir!* The road from chief of a matriarchal tribe—who was not vested with any particular

powers—to a patriarch in a patriarchal tribe—with exclusive power over all members of the tribe—and from there to a "prince" or "king" of a tribe or "nation," is only a sequence of developmental steps clearly described by Engels in his book on the origin of the family.

A naturally organized, or matriarchal society, is still free of sexual negation. During the transition to patriarchy, there arises in society a sexually moralistic sector which proceeds to encompass all of society when patriarchy has been completely established. Whereas the family was previously an economic unit within a clan, and subject to it, it now gains superiority over the blood relationships in the clan, which finally leads to the disappearance of the clan altogether. From the temporary marriage for mating purposes, which characterizes matriarchy, monogamous permanent marriage then develops. This is firmly anchored in economic laws, social mechanisms, and moral precepts.

The transition from free clan society to the bondage of family society also changes human character. A society just a few kilometers from the Trobriand Islands already had strict family organization. In contrast to the openhearted and candid Trobrianders, these people were shy, withdrawn, and plagued by neurosis and perversion. This was absent among the Trobrianders, who despised masturbation and could not understand homosexuality.

Thus the Western European traders and missionaries who invaded the primitive societies encountered natural processes which they could put to their own use. It was so very simple to barter with worthless glass beads in exchange for valuable natural products because genitally structured aborigines act in good faith and are naïvely decent; they have no word for thievery, while hospitality almost literally flows in their veins. This type of character structure cannot help posing a provocation for the degenerate, corrupt, and impotent white trader. Exploitation soon begins, while the missionaries finish off the job by thrashing the children for their innocuous sexual games and sowing the seeds of psychic distress and compulsion until the soil has been prepared for colonization. There is good reason for missionaries always constituting the advance guard of colonial armies. Nowhere is the function of compulsory sex-morality as clear as in this example. Aboriginal peoples are becoming extinct. In earlier days, they inspired great romantic yearnings in white men, but today we record the service they rendered humanity through their demonstration of the laws of natural morality and dignity. There is no room here for cheap romanticism. It must be replaced by the struggle for human organization on a higher technological level, a structure which will never allow itself to forget the process of humanization. This new organization will rectify the misdevelopment of several thousand years and allow us to view the picture of a lecherous, obese, and brutal colonialist, himself a victim of our disgraceful culture, as the nightmare it is.

Ethnological proof of sex-economic regulation of sexual life gave me as much confidence in the conclusions I had drawn from clinical experience as did sex-political work with youth. Clinically, sociologically, and also ethnologically, I now dared to form, in broad strokes, a picture of the genesis of sexual forms of existence.

First, it was necessary to differentiate clearly between *individual* and *social* sex-economy. We now know that regulation of sexual energy in the organism of a single individual depends upon his degree of orgastic potency. This, however, is in turn determined by the social organization of sexual life. Originally, individual and social sexual organization did not conflict; on the contrary, the society of primitive peoples took great care to assure sexual happiness. Affirmation of sexuality prevailed, and not merely tolerance. With the invasion of compulsory sex-morality, however, this affirmation shifted rapidly to sexual negation, and in this way sexual culture embarked on the path to decay. Restraint of natural sexual pleasure created all the phenomena currently termed "sexuality"—neurosis, perversion, enslavement of women and children, and antisocial sexual attitudes—and these can only be considered worthy of condemnation. The process of sexual suppression, which was socially, not biologically, founded, introduced the second social process, which we have already examined, i.e. the division of a united, homogeneous society into

The Invasion of Compulsory Sex-Morality

two classes, the owners of the means of production and the owners of work-power. This ushered in progressive concentration of social power in the hands of the few, such as we encounter in the princes of antiquity and the Middle Ages. Class division maintained and strengthened sexual suppression once again. With the Christian era, sexual suppression was *organized* in a special form.

In the first social revolution of the twentieth century, which took place in Russia, for the first time a shift from sexual negation to affirmation could be observed. Although the process was discontinued after several years, this does not alter the fact that a social movement commenced which represented the exact opposite of the shift in the other direction that occurred at the inception of the patriarchal system.

The principles of economy, namely the system of satisfaction of vital material needs, had been investigated by Marx. There existed, however, no economy of sexual energy because no social movement had yet raised this question. The Russian Revolution was the first social upheaval to broach the question of social sex-economy. Primarily, this took the form of legislation, but numerous obscure issues remained. The problem appeared to me to be divided into three parts:

1. What is the natural metabolism of sexual energy?
2. What is the specific structure of society? Does it correspond to, or contradict, a sex-economic system of sexuality?
3. Which obstacles do conservative ideologies and economic difficulties place in the path of a shift from sexual disorder to sexual order?

The question of sexuality now came forth from the sphere of privacy, where it had led a pitiful existence despite the efforts of various sexologists, and moved into the realm of the full-fledged issues of social politics, assuming a position of primary importance alongside the economic questions. It belonged neither to the "superstructure," as the Marxists contended in consistent misunderstanding, nor to the "conditions of production," i.e. "production of progeny," as Engels had formulated it from an economic perspective. When sexual energy was differentiated from the forms in which it functioned and these, in turn, were separated from human structure and ideologies regarding sex, the following facts became evident: *Human structure is determined by the way the various manifestations of a social organization at any given time influence the biologically determined sexual energy.* Structures thus formed, produced by the social process, themselves *reproduce* moralistic views of sexuality, whence spring all concepts of "good" and "bad." All ethics are basically anti-sexual. This claim has nothing to do with anarchism. Sex-economically organized human structure will necessarily develop essentially different views on sex than the ravaged human structure which is completely unaware of its sexual energy. To prove its existence justified, the reproduced, antisexual morality refers to factors which are responsible for its origin, namely the unnatural, pathologically distorted sexual expressions of patriarchically educated individuals. Sexual suppression preceded compulsory sex-morality, calling it into existence. Likewise, sex-morality preceded that which it attempts to suppress, the secondary drives, and ushered in sexual disorder. For this reason, the removal of moralistic regulation of sexuality, and its gradual replacement by natural regulation, is also the first prerequisite for achieving the goal which compulsory sex-morality justifiably seeks to attain, namely the removal of antisocial sexuality and perversion, sexual violence and degradation.

I soon discovered that I meant something different by "sexuality" than the clergy with whom I had to debate. They meant that which is visible and active today, i.e. sick sexuality, whereas I meant that which lies obscured in the depths of the human organism. I was in agreement with the clergy's condemnation of current sexual manifestations, but did not believe, for one moment, that they would agree with me in affirming natural manifestations of sexuality. [This began to change in the United States around 1950.]

At this point, I was able to integrate the patriarchal-capitalistic mode of sexual regulation into the social process as a whole. Allow me to summarize what is already known:

Sexual suppression supports the power of the Church, which

The Invasion of Compulsory Sex-Morality

has sunk very deep roots into the exploited masses by means of sexual anxiety and guilt. It is also the most important prerequisite for contemporary family and marital structures, which require the atrophy of sexuality for their further existence. At the same time, however, a yearning for sexual satisfaction is created and reflected in those sexual disturbances and perversions which, in turn, undermine marriages and families.

Sexual suppression engenders timidity toward authority and binds children to their parents. This results in adult subservience to state authority and to capitalistic exploitation. [Soviet Russia is a capitalistic, monopolistic state.]

It paralyzes the intellectual critical powers of the oppressed masses because it consumes the greater part of biological energy.

Finally, it paralyzes the resolute development of creative forces and renders impossible the achievement of all aspirations for human freedom.

In this way, the prevailing economic system (in which single individuals can easily rule entire masses) becomes rooted in the psychic structures of the oppressed themselves. When I became aware of this, I had no idea how thoroughly Hitler's dictatorship [and the developments in Russia] would bear out my statement.

All these interrelationships led naturally to the sex-political activities which I then set into motion in Germany. This had to be strictly differentiated from the older sexual-reform movements, which were apolitical. The objective was the integration of the struggle for sexual emancipation into the general struggle for freedom. Furthermore, it was to gather the experiences of the vital struggle in the various practical efforts at that time and constantly readapt them to the situation. And finally it was to combat all factions, whether of the left or the right, which opposed conscious guidance of the process of sexual liberation. [My work was always directed *forward*.]

However, the scientific foundation was still much too inadequate, despite the copious insight already gained. It was not yet clear how deeply, and above all in what manner, human pleasure anxiety is rooted. This would, necessarily, hamper work on the solution, regardless of the intense positive yearning I encountered everywhere. The path from yearning to fulfillment is a long and arduous one. I also felt strongly that I had no proper answer for the arguments and misdeeds of that "school" which claimed to be the "science of genetics." Hitler's racial nonsense was already in the air, and although the Socialists' arguments against it were logical, the issue had no connection with logic and even less with phrenology. However, I could quiet my political conscience; for the moment, there was sufficient, well-founded experience to set the movement on a solid scientific basis. It would have been a mistake to strive for too much at once.

Work in Germany did not proceed according to carefully calculated plans and objectives. The field was too broad for that, and too little practical experience had been gained. I could rely on the fact that sex-politics would be received as before, at every step of the way, so there was no need to "agitate" for it or to resort to indoctrination. It soon became evident that social conditions and the errors of Socialist Party politics themselves elicited the correct answer. It will be the task of the following chapters to elucidate this.

6

Everyone Is "Enraptured"
(1930-33)

In 1933 I was denounced by the Communist Party, and in 1934 I was expelled from the International Psychoanalytic Association. [It should be noted that both organizations had already ceased to exist in Germany.] These were catastrophes which threatened my personal, professional, and social existence and, additionally, called into question the further development of sex-economy. Suddenly I found myself in a vacuum, so to speak, far removed from the life of the people. The slanderous attitude of the Socialists, Communists, and psychoanalysts, which was resolutely directed toward destroying my work and existence, contradicted in a peculiar manner the recognition which the same individuals and organizations had previously given to my theories and achievements. When I first came to Berlin, in 1930, I was still unaware of what was in store for me, despite earlier bad experiences in Vienna. Only after all organizational ties were broken did I have enough leisure time to allow people's attitudes to affect me. Through this, I learned my best lessons about politics. Much would have developed differently had I possessed the necessary foresight at the time. Each change in my scientific position exacted unavoidable and costly sacrifices. They represented indispensable labor pains at the birth of crucial knowledge about mass psychology, and also functioned to produce the iron resolve necessary for me to carry on: never to yield to the pressure of erroneous public opinion.

In Berlin, my first close affiliation with German psychoanalysts was established. They were far more progressive on social issues than the Viennese. The young psychoanalysts could breathe more freely, and my orgasm theory was better received. Marxist sociology was little discussed systematically. Among the analysts, Fromm was the only one considered a Marxist sociologist. At the time, he was publishing his *Analysis of the Christ Dogma*, an exceptionally valuable work, although unrelated to either sex-economic issues or actual politics. In an extensive conversation which we had shortly after my arrival in Berlin, Fromm listened to my sex-economic interpretation and said he realized that only the concept of sexual energy was adequate to explain mass-psychological dynamics. For example, it is true that the mental conception of father and mother was the central content of every religion. Indeed, the sociological character of a religion could be viewed only in the context of its own time. However, the fact that people produce and need religious mysticism at all would remain an enigma without the knowledge of sex-economy. Above all, the emotional content of religious experience, as well as the doctrines of original sin and asceticism, was in need of interpretation from the standpoint of sexual energy.

In my apartment on Schwäbische Strasse, I expounded my basic views to three young analysts, Erich Fromm, Barbara Lantos, and Otto Fenichel, emphasizing especially the method of integrating psychoanalytic theory into Marxist sociology. I often spent hours discussing the basic psychological principles of the social movement with Fenichel, whom I had met before in Vienna. He was not a member of any party, had read little sociological literature, and had never participated in a street demonstration or in social field work. I understood his desire to keep away from this, and he understood and accepted my dialectical-materialistic criticism of psychoanalysis. He gladly agreed to the proposal that he help me organize the younger psychoanalysts for practical social work. He did this for approximately two years, and since I soon had a large work load outside the professional organization, I was glad to leave it in his hands. I was not yet aware of the trap I had set for myself in doing so. Everything appeared to be in order. Only two things displeased me slightly: first, his disinclination to participate in practical social work, which is essential for a true understanding of people, and second, his complete lack of comprehension of the irreconcilable contradiction between materialistic dialectics, [my embryonic functionalism,][1] and abstract logic. Siegfried Bernfeld, who was a Socialist and considered himself a theoretical Marxist, occasionally took part in our discussions. He, too, did not understand the reality of the dialectic process. He felt that dialectical materialism was just one mode of thinking, and that abstract logic was another. I soon gave up trying to convince them.

[SO: In Germany, at that time, Marxism held an academic position similar to "Deweyism" in the United States. Marxism was not yet so badly soiled by its confusion with plain murder of the Dzhugashvili type. The mass murders in the process of the Russian collectivization of farming were just ahead of us. So were the infamous trials in Moscow, the revocation of sexual legislation, and the uniformed, bemedaled marshals of the U.S.S.R.

The fight against the red Fascist political plague in the United States in the 1950's suffered gravely from several gaps in understanding the development of red Fascism and Fascism in general from democratic freedom organizations in the lower strata of the population. Until about 1932, at least in the Central European and Western European countries, no Communist Party member, even if very rabid, would have thought seriously of seizing the government of a country by force against the will of the majority of its citizens. Such tendencies or actions were disclaimed in all Socialist or Communist circles as "Putsch." Whenever such Putsch attempts were made by small and insignificant political groups, the Socialists and Communists would disassociate themselves completely from them. The policy always was to attain power in society by majority vote in Parliament. This was the original idea of the democratic Communist movement.

---

[1] SO: At that time, I ascribed my functionalism to Engels as I had ascribed my sex-economy to Freudian psychoanalysis. My own ideas and thoughts streamed freely into a strange environment which did not and could not absorb them.

Lenin's distribution of land to the Russian peasants, which so sharply differed from the later Stalinist collectivization and nationalization of the agricultural enterprises by force, was a clear-cut manifestation of this policy.

In sharp contradistinction to this democratic Communism with its rule from below, e.g. its elections instead of the appointment of functionaries, etc., stands red Fascism, which has turned every democratic feature of Communism into its opposite:

Sneaking into power by way of terrorism on the part of a minority.

Sneaking into power through conspiracy and underhanded maneuvering instead of by open public choice.

Using force, the strength of the Communist Party, and reliance on the military power of Russia, which by 1936 was a clear-cut, imperialist state having only one thing in common with democratic Communism: the reliance on the people's hope for a better existence. The red Fascists exploited this hope to the nth degree and abused it as never before in history.

These distinctions are sharp as well as indispensable for a successful conquest, with the fewest possible victims, of the red Fascist political plague. The inner dynamics of this change from democratic Communism to red Fascism is the reluctance and inability of the people to govern their own lives.]

The Association of Socialist Physicians invited me to give a lecture on my special field, the prophylaxis of neurosis. In the presence of two hundred physicians and students, I was able to explain successfully the social objectives of serious, psychoanalytic work. They responded with great understanding and even enthusiasm.

Socialist and Communist student groups held a mass meeting on the theme "The Fiasco of Bourgeois Morality." The Fascist student organization was also represented as well as a company of the Rotfrontkämpferbund.[2] After the lecture I had to answer numerous questions of nationalist-oriented students, especially on such issues as "self-control," "dignity," "loyalty," "character," etc. The atmosphere was good and the discussion continued until

[2] Veterans' association of the red front. —*Trans.*

5 a.m. Communists, Socialists, and Fascists discussed the issues heatedly, but never violently. The proletarian participants seemed especially well satisfied because, as I left at 1 a.m., they called out loudly, "*Kräftige Rotfront!*"[3] three times. This was usually not customary, especially following intellectually oriented lectures.

The Marxist Workers' University (MASCH),[4] held courses on "Marxism and Psychology" and "Sexology." In the spring semester of 1931, I gave a course in a school on Gärtnerstrasse, and again in the fall. Attendance rose with each lecture, peaking in the sexology course at 250 individuals from all levels of society. The first course, which was more difficult, was attended by approximately 80 to 100—political functionaries, students, teachers, etc. My writings were distributed throughout the country by the MASCH organization.

After a few weeks, I was speaking at meetings on an average of twice a week. These lectures were highly instructive for me, because I not only felt constrained to present my material in simple terms but also had to learn to answer the numerous, diverse questions and objections correctly. German youth demanded a great deal, above all absolute clarity and simplicity. In these meetings, cultural-political aspects of the subject began to dominate the discussion more and more. Economic policy, as it is commonly discussed, receded, only to return in a *new* and *different* form. Statistics were used for illustration only and questions were posed in a more *personal* manner, e.g. "Are the housing-project designs sufficiently advanced to meet the hygienic needs of the masses as quickly and easily as possible?" The fact that the system of private ownership of houses would never allow for hygienic conditions was too self-evident to require special emphasis. "Will not the already impaired structures of the majority of today's teachers and those in charge of small children oppose the aims of sexually affirmative child education?" "How should the distribution of goods be organized to ensure a firm basis for a steady rise in the cultural level of the working masses?" We were

[3] "Power to the red front." —*Trans.*
[4] Abbreviation for Marxistische Arbeiter Hochschule. —*Trans.*

not speaking of the "principles of socialization." These principles were meant to fulfill a definite purpose, without which they were worthless. They represented the means of ensuring *happiness for all* who create social values! *We approached economic issues from the standpoint of human needs and not, as did the Marxist economists, from historical or economic theory,* which was of no interest to the masses. Such encounters called for scrupulous personal honesty. Any hedging or pompous authoritarianism brought a speedy and blunt rebuttal. A young worker once asked me why I was devoting myself to this social work in the first place, when I occupied a good social position, earned a good living, and had a successful career! Something had to be wrong with that picture. He accused me of trying to make sure of a place for myself after the social revolution. I could only tell him what I felt: Personally, I really do not need to do this, but I am learning a great deal of value for my scientific work. "Then we are just your guinea pigs!," he quipped. To be quite frank, I continued, when I am eating a ham sandwich with butter, it spoils my pleasure to have hungry, grimly envious people watching me. Since the economy is rich enough for everyone, or could be if it did not serve life-destroying purposes such as war, I work gladly to make it possible for everyone to have his own "ham sandwich." Someone said, "That is a primitive idea of class-conscious Socialism." Then from somewhere in the audience came the response, "You know where you can put your historical Socialism! First let's take care of ourselves. Then your Socialism is more likely to come than if you just keep shooting your mouth off all the time!" That was the tone, and gradually, from this, my deep convictions arose regarding correct attitudes toward social matters. It was only after the collapse, in 1933, that I could consolidate them into a larger framework: Necessities first, economic theories later. Develop social views from practical fulfillment of human needs instead of abusing human needs for purposes of political power.

In practical work among the uneducated, and usually politically disinterested, members of these organizations, only one type of approach could possibly lead to success, namely, gaining human confidence through personal warmth, avoiding all theorizing, and awakening an awareness of personal needs, whether large or small. Once this was accomplished, socialistic objectives became a foregone conclusion. From the very beginning I recognized the uselessness of the political brochures of party organizations. I comforted myself, as did many others, with the hope that through the personal approach we would gradually succeed in bringing the lowly party members to the high political levels at which the parties themselves were operating. The illusion was shattered completely by the catastrophe which occurred two years later. Viewed in today's light, the social efforts of that period seem absolutely ludicrous. The party functionaries actually tried to "educate" people through highly political speeches and economic reports. I cannot recall a single group meeting where the members did not have to fight off drowsiness. And these were confirmed Communists. How far removed from this kind of living and thinking must the masses have been!

I remember one enormous meeting in a sports stadium where Thälmann addressed about twenty thousand industrial and white-collar workers. Shortly before, there had been fatalities at a demonstration. The atmosphere was highly charged. The opening by the flag bearers was impressive. Tensely, we waited for the address. Thälmann deflated our high spirits within half an hour; he nullified them by outlining the complicated budget of the German bourgeoisie. It was horrible. The effect of this pseudo-scientific "education to class-consciousness" with the aid of high-flown politics was particularly catastrophic in the youth organizations. [It was always astonishing to witness the respect paid by intellectuals and the bourgeoisie to these weak and empty, fraudulent mass deceptions.]

I concentrated on visiting the most typical youth gatherings —just to listen in and get the feel of them. In the Communist youth cells, there was strict organizational formality; among the Fichte sport groups, it was somewhat better. The youths, accustomed to discipline, bravely bore the hour-long report to show their goodwill. The youth leaders had some contact with working youth on a broader scale, but only on the days of large demonstrations. These leaders were constantly tormenting themselves with the question of how to "approach" youth. They distributed brochures and leaflets from house to house. They painted slogans in red on walls and on paved streets at night, risking the danger of arrest. It was all in vain; the youth stayed away and in the youth groups themselves there was a perpetual turnover of members and functionaries. For a long time, I participated in the enlistment efforts. The lack of success with this manner of recruiting, and even its harmfulness, made an indelible impression on me. Recruiting was usually done on Sunday, even in the most beautiful weather. This reflected the ideology of heroic self-denial. A Communist functionary could have no private life. Officially, there were no sexual issues. In private, an attitude of camaraderie prevailed, with no smug narrow-mindedness. However, strictly ascetic attitudes were also common, and since the sex-political platform of Communist youth was not officially represented, the dried-up ascetics of the "class struggle" could rule the field. In discussions on socialistic morality, there was much talk of new moral attitudes but no mention of the thousands of concrete situations one encounters in daily life. There were no brochures on sex-politics for mass propaganda, only fancy ones on political economics and theory, e.g. "the position of the worker under capitalism," "plant socialization in the Soviet Union," "women in industry," etc. With a stack of such brochures they went from door to door, handed them out, and tried, if at all possible, to strike up a conversation and provide information on the distress of the masses. Communist voters who were known within the groups bought the brochures. Social Democrats furiously slammed their doors at the sight of a Communist brochure, and the indifferent brusquely declined. Sales were poor and depressing; soliciting in rural areas had no less deplorable results. Brochures for these areas were loaded with figures and suggestions for collectivization based on the Russian model. Once, I was selected to speak to a meeting of rural workers and farmers just outside Berlin. I was well acquainted with Russian collectivism and the Soviet agricultural system. I also succeeded in presenting the topic well. When it was over, there was not a single question asked pertaining to the topic, not one positive contribution. Several farmers did ask, however, what would happen to the Church in the event of revolution!

My first deep impression of the gap between politics and practical knowledge was gained while soliciting farmers. A functionary had described the advantages of Soviet agricultural collectivization very well, but received an embarrassingly negative response. One farmer, who had been listening quietly, took a handful of grain out of his pocket, held it under the functionary's nose, and asked him, "What is this?" The functionary had no idea. Recruiting was over for the day.

For rural recruiting, divisions of the Rotfrontkämpferbund were also sent out and they were often quite impressive with their singing and their military appearance. They aroused curiosity, but the feeble curiosity was overwhelmed by a deep-seated fear of the military. The National Socialists were more successful in this because they had their own local groups in the villages; also, they were far more brutal, and in addition clearly represented the reactionary rural ideology, especially the National Socialist "Family and Fatherland" ideology. The latter was so conspicuous that I was amazed at how little attention our people paid it.

In rural political meetings, one saw that the Communist, Social Democrat, and National Socialist speakers all belonged to the same social class and were frequently even in the same trade. I wondered how this could be possible. It was not generally noticed that farmers were called "revolutionary" when they favored the Communists, "reformists" when they spoke up for the Social Democrats, and "reactionaries" when they leaned toward National Socialism. Any opinion (and most of them changed opinions rapidly) was sufficient to classify the person advocating it. But how was it possible for individuals at the same social level to be split into such different political factions, all of which were advocated with equal zeal?

Demonstrations in Berlin were much more tightly organized than in Vienna. One marched in military formation and sang revolutionary songs lustily. Attempts were made to attract people's attention by shouting "*Rotfront!*" or some other slogan. However, the populace had grown accustomed to this. Since I participated in all the larger demonstrations, I was able to see that they served the purpose of encouraging the demonstrators rather than gaining the favor of the people. Each one showed his own courage and even his honest resolution to die for the cause, but the masses were indifferent. A few thousand demonstrators made no particular impression in a city like Berlin. Also, defamation through the expression "Communist" had its effect.

The large May Day demonstrations were better. The Communist Party of Germany was able to muster about eighty to a hundred thousand at the Lustgarten, and the Socialist Party somewhat more. The routes which the demonstration march was allowed to take were strictly marked. The police were tense. On May 1, 1931, I volunteered for monitor duty. The monitors wore identifying red armbands and were assigned the task of flanking the marching columns and protecting them from police attacks. My troop and I accompanied a children's column. The children simply sang forth happily and brightly without considering whether this was permitted or not. Some songs were strictly prohibited, such as "Red Wedding" by Erich Weinert. When this song rang out, dozens of policemen suddenly sprang from their cars and struck blindly into the children's group. At the last minute, we succeeded in locking arms so tightly that all the police were not able to break through. We tried to talk with them. I was amazed at the machine-like quality of these police assaults. On such occasions, I repeatedly had the impression that an automatic reaction functioned, in place of living thoughts and feelings: Forbidden song—reach for the club!

The gun of each policeman hung loosely in its holster. There was hardly a meeting at which shots were not fired. I never saw the participants at the meetings attack the police, although it did indeed happen that Socialist youths called them ugly names. I thought I noticed that the police grew nervous when referred to as "capitalist lackeys." Still, there were frequent clashes when a typically Prussian police lieutenant began to order his men around just to flaunt his power. The mounted police took particu-

Everyone Is "Enraptured" 145

lar pleasure in demonstrating its official authority by riding through a crowd and demanding that the people move aside. Again and again, this emphasis on official authority and the training of its subordinates! These were provocative actions and the participants of the meetings were conscious of them to no small degree.

Arrogant police lieutenants were greatly despised, but hate for their troops was no less intense. No one gave thought to the fact that they were the sons of workers and farmers. They fired their weapons and used their clubs and therefore they were hated. Again, it was not capitalists versus workers, but rather uniformed workers versus workers out of uniform.

Whereas practical social work in Vienna had already provided the foundation for an empirical mass psychology, Berlin now offered me splendid opportunities, not only to define my concepts more precisely, but also to complete their restructuring in my personal thoughts and feelings. The atmosphere of sterile academic book knowledge finally became unbearable. It was even more painful when encountered in the midst of organizations whose goal it was to establish a new foundation for German society. I was asked to join the circle responsible for the scientific organization of the party, headed at the time by Karl August Wittfogel, a clever and academically very productive man. There were several economists and a great many (too many) philosophers. In the discussions, a certain fear of expressing one's thoughts candidly was evident. There was disagreement, but always within the strict intellectual framework demanded by the party. It was dangerous to overstep the "party line." The party was indeed capable of indicating a general trend of thought, but it could do no more. There could not be a party answer to specialized questions in all instances. This depended entirely upon the presiding functionary. If he was not opposed to psychology, then the problems of psychology in the socialistic movement could be discussed under his tenure. A different functionary might have been uninformed in this field and consequently hostile to it, as though psychology played no role in politics. I soon understood that this attitude was not merely stubborn narrow-mindedness. If a people's party is confronted with issues such as those that rocked Germany at the time, and does not have sufficient independent scientific minds and the necessary free thinkers at its disposal, and if the few intellectually trained individuals waste their mental powers in trivial academic issues while the masses are clamoring for answers that no one can supply, it is understandable that a small group of pioneers fighting for a difficult cause would cling to a "party line" as they would to a life raft. Obviously, however, one can never learn to swim freely in this way. Therefore it would appear better to solve a small number of problems reasonably well than to allow clear thinking to fall prey to intellectual acrobatics. I consciously used the word "appear," because without serious and extensively organized, radically inclined scientific research, the thousands of problems which a people's movement poses cannot be properly mastered. Although this must be admitted, the manner in which the party attempted to overcome its difficulties could only lead to ruin. It did not have a choice between a "line" and intellectual acrobatics, but had the task of allowing the masses themselves to ask the questions. The correct answers would then have been found, because the honest young scientifically trained minds would have come forth, joined the movement, and perhaps saved it from destruction. The party did not allow the masses to speak, and that was the reason it disintegrated. I experienced its downfall, and the reason for it, step by step, over the course of two and a half years. During the struggle against this fear of the masses, I evolved not only my subsequent *Mass Psychology of Fascism*, but also many of the practical organizational principles which I am presenting to the world only now, many years later.

In the academic section of the party, I encountered again all the worst qualities of academicism, only this time glorified as "revolutionary." There was one philosopher, Kurt Sauerland, who later published a book on "dialectical materialism." In it he represented Stalin as the greatest contemporary philosopher. This individual contaminated and dominated the entire party intelligentsia with dogmas which he claimed were dialectical-materialistic philosophy. In his ignorance, he actually confused the slogans of the day with the results of scientific research. Several young economists struck upon the idea of visually portraying the Marxist value theory, thus making it accessible to the uneducated. I was among those to preview the film; we found it splendid. But the top-level philosophers would not allow it to be shown in public (although the rank and file praised it) because it supposedly contradicted some word, here or there, in Marx's theory. In such "top level" discussions, one could observe, in action, all the irrationalisms which distort people. Uprooted individuals heatedly gave full vent to their conceit, but always within the framework of the "party line," which they never overstepped. Frequently this was seriously discussed among friends of mine. With horror we watched all initiative being suffocated. My friend Neugebauer, the parliamentary delegate of the Communist faction, a brilliant, scientifically trained sociologist and a decent fellow, once remarked, "What shall we do? Actually, they should be thrown out, but will those who replace them be any better? What we lack is trained intelligentsia. For the moment we can only grit our teeth and bear it."

I could still work unhampered alongside the philosophers. It was only when my book on youth[5] came up for discussion that a conflict ensued.

None of the notable party members had read Hitler's *Mein Kampf*. Only a few, Wittfogel and Duncker among others, were concerned with analyzing the works of opponents. The SA was already marching the streets in ominous groups. No one noticed that these were the same types who had formed our own militant troops—laborers and employees whom we now considered reactionary mercenaries.

In July 1931, the gigantic bank crash occurred in Germany. Everyone waited for the Communists to speak a decisive word. The first comments came eight days later. From that time onward, the serious workers in the party knew the cause was lost. Only now did the National Socialists, whose numbers had increased in 1930 from eight hundred thousand to approximately eight million voters, become really active. "Marches on Berlin"

[5] *Der sexuelle Kampf der Jugend* (*The Sexual Struggle of Youth*).

became increasingly frequent. In the cells, groups of protective guards had been formed, together with members of the Arbeiterwehr. I was appointed to the so-called Red Housing Block on Wilmersdorferstrasse. Rage over the casualties we had suffered, and deep-seated conviction about the good cause we were advocating, together with our inability to slow the momentum of the reactionary landslide, often led to grotesque but courageous behavior. The SA had announced another practice march in July 1931. Afterward, it was rumored that Berlin was to be occupied. The party mobilized. Our group, about thirty individuals, among them women and girls, stayed in the cell quarters. This was supposed to ward off a possible attack on the apartments. There were three pistols in the group and only four men with combat experience. The rest were brave in distributing leaflets and pasting them onto walls, i.e. brave in spirit. But now it was a question of dealing with violence. We filled bottles with water and stood them by the hundreds along the window and door ledges, ready to drop them on the heads of the SA below. This will provide just one picture, among many, of the "situations surrounding the class struggle." Fortunately, nothing happened that night. Had the SA really attacked, the result would have been a stupid slaughter between individuals living under the same working conditions, in the same material situation, and even sharing the same determination to "do away with the capitalistic machine."

Newspapers and books were full of stories about inimical political groups, programs, capitalist and anti-capitalist interests. In the cells, on the streets, demonstrating or pasting up posters at night, it was a different story. *Class struggle was taking place among members of the same class.* When I discussed this with friends in the youth organizations, they understood. "How is it possible," I asked, "that laborers, employees, small merchants, housewives, domestic help, split into such diverse groups and develop such contrary political sympathies, despite sharing the same economic status?" The answer came: "We have not yet convinced them of the correctness of the class perspective. We have not yet won them over; they are still held in ignorance by the capitalists." In my cell, there was a mechanic who also worked as a chauffeur. He participated vigorously in the discussions, was inquisitive, and wanted to increase our activities, but he was not satisfied with the difficult theoretical answers he received and subsequently joined the Nazis. During the presidential election in 1932, his former cell comrades spat in his face. He was a "traitor." But how? Why? He was not especially different from the others.

It was not possible to present, in party circles, the answer which experience in practical work had given me. Several hesitant attempts to do so had convinced me that I would only make myself disliked. (I do not mean among friends, in private, but in the official cell meetings.) Finally, I gave up trying to persuade people, and concentrated on sex-political work with the masses. This had developed rapidly from the first months of 1931. I became convinced that mass psychology and sex-politics contained the answer to the question which Fascism posed to German society.

ORGANIZING THE SEXPOL IN GERMANY

Developments in sex-political work between 1931 and 1932 demanded an analysis of fascistic ideology. I had not sought a connection between the two, nor had I started a movement with the direct aim of "destroying," or "ideologically mastering," Fascism. The problems I encountered in Germany, and earlier in Austria, were the same as those on which fascistic mass manipulation centered, namely marriage, family, race, morality, honor. From the very beginning, numerous members of the middle class, semi-intellectuals and high school students, joined my groups, bringing with them the great interest of the middle classes in precisely these problems. This, in turn, broadened the scope of my endeavors, which then encompassed youth, the existing sexual-reform organizations, the free-thinker and culture organizations, children's organizations, and the women's groups.

For several months I visited the youth groups in various

districts of Berlin to absorb the general atmosphere. I declined to lecture, saying that I knew these young people too little and they knew nothing of my theories.

Based on experience gained in Vienna, I drafted a "sex-political platform" containing, essentially, the themes of my lecture at the convention of the World League for Sexual Reform in 1930. The cultural adviser of the Communist Party Central Committee approved it and I then presented it for approval to the World League commission in Berlin. J. H. Leunbach, later a leading pioneer of Sexpol, was also present at the meeting where the decision was to be made. All present—the chairman of the Association for Birth Control, the secretary of the World League, and Leunbach—vetoed the platform. They felt it was "communistic" and that the sex-political organizations wanted nothing to do with Communist views. Although they did admit that my views were correct, they did not wish to "provoke" anyone. The organizations, they said, had to remain "apolitical" and could not incorporate into any specific party. Later, it was revealed that this was as wrong in principle as it was correct in practice. Afterward I was also obliged to assume a nonparty (although not an apolitical) stand, because the affiliation of the cause with party interests had ended in a fiasco. [Unfortunately, at that time, I had not yet distinguished between "social" and "political."]

In 1930, there existed approximately eighty sex-political organizations in Germany. Each was structured differently, under independent leadership, and there was frequent antagonism among them. Their total membership of about three hundred and fifty thousand was greater than that of any of the large parties. To be sure, most of the functionaries in these organizations were simultaneously members of the Christian, Social Democrat, or Communist Party. However, there was no connection between their roles as functionaries in the sex-political groups and membership in their political parties. Many of those who were enthusiastic about their own party opposed the incorporation of these groups into the party organizations. The parties also paid no attention to the sex-political organizations, even though they published announcements of the meetings in their newspapers.

Each sex-political organization had its own newsletter, and many of these were illustrated to attract the public, in keeping with the current trend. They were not pornographic, but they were not clearly enough separated from pornography. They contained no basic views on sexuality, and even less on socio-political orientation. Still they advocated unrestricted birth control and legalized abortion and spoke out against compulsory child bearing and against penalization for sexual deviations, especially homosexuality. They tried to protect marriage more than did the bourgeoisie themselves. There was no mention of youth problems; these were avoided instinctively. Magnus Hirschfeld's incorrect views dominated both theory and practice. Many valuable details were elaborated, but all measures to ensure consolidation and the achievement of goals were scrupulously avoided.

Over the course of decades, thanks to the self-sacrificing efforts of people like Helene Stöcker (who directed the Bund für Mutterschutz[6] and also published the newspaper *Neue Generation*[7]), Germany was covered by a network of birth-control centers. Although they did not reach even a tenth of the population, they did constitute a powerful voice for social hygiene. Those accused in abortion trials were given legal and moral support. Regular lectures acquainted members with the social implications of sexuality, although the information provided was often incorrect and overburdened with questions of eugenics and population politics. The dealers, who infiltrated the groups and made their profits from the demand for contraceptives, constituted one of the greatest evils. There were numerous bad characters among them; but this could not be held against the organizations. They were dependent upon them because official government agencies took no interest in this facet of the problem and only caused difficulty.

My plan was to form a united association from these separate organizations. Through the introduction of consciously directed effort and affiliation with the Communist Party, the individual sex-reform factions were to be welded together to

[6] Association for the Protection of Mothers. —*Trans.*
[7] *New Generation.* —*Trans.*

form a unified sex-political association. Following consultation in the physicians' division, the medical program was turned over to the IFA for preliminary strategy. The IFA was an organization which comprised all cultural subgroups in the party. Three doctors (myself among them), a parliamentary delegate, and two leaders of the IFA were elected to lead the national sex-political program. The latter two were assigned the organizational and party-political leadership and I was allotted the sex-political program on a nationwide level. Opinion on the usefulness of my platform was unanimously favorable and everyone expected positive results. A sex-reform group in Düsseldorf printed the platform and this immediately brought it to public attention. Thus the work in West Germany began quite spontaneously.

In 1931, the first West German congress was held in Düsseldorf. Surprisingly, it mobilized about twenty thousand members from approximately eight different groups. I delivered the main address, merely elaborating upon what the platform contained in brief. Not a single nonpolitical group present was in disagreement. In Berlin and vicinity, various local groups were founded where none had previously existed, or existing organizations were consolidated. Here, unification was more difficult. Until that time, the Communist Party had had no organizations for sexual reform, and also had taken no stand on sex-politics, except toward Soviet legislation. Hence, I enjoyed great recognition from the party leadership. In the course of a year, unified organizations were also founded in Leipzig, Dresden, Stettin, etc. The movement spread rapidly. Within a few months it had doubled in size, comprising approximately forty thousand members.

As the movement grew, the demands placed upon us also increased. Three clearly delineated, extremely difficult problems arose. I could not neglect them because they had developed logically in the course of the work. On the other hand, I was also unable to solve them, as any practical solution would have required going against the party leadership and that was impossible. The three problems were:

1. *Practical training of the leaders of the movement.* In the party there existed no theory of sexuality, or only incorrect

views. The groups and masses which were now included had no trained personnel to contribute. As simple as sex-economic principles were, there was no hope of being able to train, even hastily, a sufficient number of functionaries. Today the situation has improved, but at the time the problem remained unsolved.

2. *The inclusion of youth.* The sex-reform groups had avoided the question of adolescent sexuality so meticulously that they had no contact with middle-class or working-class youth. The groups consisted predominantly of the middle-aged. In 1931, Communist youth numbered approximately forty thousand, Social Democrat youth about fifty thousand, and National Socialist youth also about forty to fifty thousand. The Christian Center Party had almost two million young people in its organizations. This party, in contrast to the others, had consistently pursued sex-politics and, as a result, was largest in number, indicating that only youth could carry on the sex-political movement.

3. *The inescapable transformation of views on all politics, which resulted from the inclusion of psychology and sexual issues.* Although I saw the beginning of this transformation everywhere, I deliberately avoided setting it in motion. First of all, one could only take the position that sex-politics had to be included in the overall political efforts of revolutionary Socialism. No party functionary could oppose this, despite the fact that the effects of sex-political work among the people were so strong that the party leadership could only view them helplessly and uncomprehendingly. My cautious formulation was useless. Instinctively the functionaries sensed "danger" for party politics and doggedly claimed I was attempting to "replace economic politics with sexual politics."

I shall now attempt to illustrate the three basic problems of the sex-political movement with separate, typical examples which are still valid today and will remain so for a long time to come.

The lack of training was manifested as follows: As long as I was present in the Ruhr district, the meetings went smoothly. Several months after my departure, however, the functionaries began to complain that sex alone was being discussed, and that interest in the questions of class struggle was decreasing. Some women had spoken out against this trend. The united front politics could not be maintained in some organizations. What had happened? The platform and the reports presented at the first congress had aroused people and had immediately stimulated thousands of questions in need of answers. The party functionaries who, until that time, had worked with slogans, and who were far removed from the actual class struggle, were helpless in the face of the demands. In addition to this, women from the National Socialist and Christian parties had joined the organizations in droves, and the functionaries had never learned how to handle them, how to make human contact, and how to deal with their complicated emotional reactions. The "population politics" they had expounded until then had now become even less interesting. The people simply wanted practical advice and help with their marital and child-raising problems, their sexual disturbances, and their moral pangs of conscience. Then the clergy put in its appearance, but their old arguments were useless now that they were confronted face to face. The functionaries interpreted manifestations of sexual anxiety as proof of the harmfulness of sex-political work. They were unable to grasp the fact that the masses had finally been successfully stirred into action. They became afraid!

It was impossible to explain this to all the psychologically untrained party members. I tried as best I could to maintain my position; for example, by taking younger youth functionaries and teachers along to my evening youth session and demonstrating, in a practical way, how overwhelmingly interested the young people were and how easy it was to approach the great social issues. Fear of the movement and of the people's demands spread to Berlin. When the IFA leaders, Bischoff and Schneider, began to sabotage our efforts, I quietly resigned from the national control board and arranged training courses in various districts of the city. And with great success! In Charlottenburg, I concentrated my best efforts on forming a model group, and informed the party leadership of this. All other groups were to profit from the experiences of this one, which was under my direction. I was sure that, gradually, the uncomplicated prin-

Everyone Is "Enraptured" 155

ciples of the movement, together with their practical application, would gain ground. But the rush of demands was overpowering and there was simply no time for quiet, thorough work. Meanwhile, the nervousness of the untrained functionaries increased with the growing strength of the movement. Instead of educating themselves, and preparing on a long-term basis, they began to arrange "unification conventions" and wanted to quickly consolidate all the sex-reform groups in Germany. This was taken as provocation by all the opponents in these groups, and resulted in a total fiasco. The movement for a unified group became deadlocked in discussions on fundamental politics and organization. In addition to this, the police began to intervene. On May 23, 1932, they broke up the Workers' Cultural Congress, and on May 24 the unification convention of our organization. I simply allowed matters to run their course and took no further part in the negotiations. Instead, I continued work in the organizations at lower levels, particularly through training. I selected the best students from my current course at MASCH and distributed them among the organizations. This enabled me to maintain my position when the party bureaucracy lashed out against me. I believe I experienced, on a small scale, the later general course of events in the Soviet Union: *The contradiction between the demands springing from the people and the organizations' incapacity to resolve the problems causes a hierarchically structured machine to resort to acts of terrorism against the very individuals who had encouraged the masses to question.*

In the meantime, through my medical activities, I had met numerous young people from various circles. All of them encouraged me to write a book for youth. I prepared a manuscript in several weeks and distributed copies of it. They were returned to me full of comments and suggestions, which I then incorporated into the final version, which was presented to the Central Youth Committee, accepted, and sent to the youth committee in Moscow. The Youth Publishers there were to print it. From Moscow came the reply that the book was indeed good, but that it "would be better not to assume responsibility for it." It was to be printed by the Workers' Cultural Press, which was less official. However, the director of this press sabotaged it for a whole year. I had presented the book, *The Sexual Struggle of Youth*, in the summer of 1931 and it had not yet been published by March 1932. I then founded my own publishing house for sex-politics, Verlag für Sexualpolitik, which subsequently published this book and *The Invasion of Compulsory Sex-Morality*. [It was crucial to be completely independent of these petty politicians.]

Following a suggestion by me, one sex-political pedagogical team had drawn up a small children's book, *Das Kreidedreieck*,[8] as well as a brochure for mothers entitled *Wenn dein Kind dich fragt*.[9] I financed the printing of both. These two small works had been studied and discussed earlier in children's and women's groups—the first one mainly in a Fichte children's group in Charlottenburg. It was read by my wife to an audience of eight- to twelve-year-olds. Whereas the group meetings were ordinarily attended by about thirty children, this time approximately eighty youngsters sat there with beaming faces. And *what* questions and demands were heard! "You've got to write more about parents!" "Let our teachers have it too!" "Why didn't you say anything about the whores we see walking our streets?" The leader of the Fichte group was both pleased and perplexed. He had never seen the children like that before, and remarked, "We'll take this to the Christian Party. They always talk such nonsense. They should really hear something for a change." My daughter attended a school in the northern part of Berlin. After several weeks, the school was in an uproar. Children who ordinarily discussed sex among themselves and kept it a secret from adults out of fear, now felt in league with the adults. It was no longer a taboo subject and had taken on new directions. We were enormously successful with functionaries who were in direct contact with children. They were now able to share, in confidence, the children's best-kept secrets. The book for working mothers, on explanations for children, was equally successful. My cleaning lady distributed dozens of copies among the women of her milieu. Thousands of copies were literally snatched from my hands. The

[8] *The Chalk Triangle*. —Trans.
[9] *When Your Child Asks Questions*. —Trans.

youth book was printed in an edition of ten thousand copies, and four thousand were sold within six weeks. It cleared the path for our youth to reach the youth of all circles—high school students, Social Democrat, Christian, and National Socialist youth included. From these experiences I drew the strength to persevere later, and to resist the impressive rhetoric of the party Socialists.

7

Irrationalism in Politics and Society

THE INCONSISTENCY OF NATIONAL SOCIALISM

Much that sounds commonplace today—1938—was new territory and difficult to comprehend in 1930, e.g. the subjective Socialist character of the SA, and the resultant schism in National Socialism; the strength it derived from the latent determination of the masses; the novelty of this determination and the power of the mystical devotion to a leader. The average politician could not understand the Führer's power over the manifest will of his followers. The deep cleavage separating the hopes of Germany's people from the reality of Hitler's barbarism confused people's thinking. The collapse of bourgeois democracy shattered liberalistic ideas. The measures which Hitler no doubt intended "socialistically" bewildered anti-Fascists. They did not comprehend the welding of these measures with an equally intentional, predatory, imperialistic expansion; nor did they grasp the similarities between the Soviet Russian and the National Socialist ideology and mass leadership. In December 1932, when the German National Socialists, together with the Communists and Social Democrats, called a strike of the Berlin transportation workers, it was labeled a "maneuver." In 1930, I saw Berlin SA columns marching through the streets; their bearing, facial expressions, and singing were no different from the Communist Rotfrontkämpfer divisions. Leading representatives of the Communist Party declared it "counterrevolutionary" to claim that the SA was a troop composed of laborers and white-collar workers. German Fascism was considered a "political reaction," as was Horthy's dictatorship in Hungary and that of Dollfuss later in Austria. Even long after 1933, it was impossible to convince a member of the Communist or Socialist Party that German Fascism was essentially different from all other political reactions because of the mass support which bore it to power. Everyone knew that conditions in Germany were intolerable. Everyone wanted change, but no one knew what needed changing. The National Socialists alone had a program everyone could easily understand, namely revision of the Treaty of Versailles, at any cost and by any available means. Hitler's reactionary and imperialistic aims were unequivocally set forth in *Mein Kampf* and still each new election brought him the support of additional millions. When the Communists realized that their revolutionary slogans were losing appeal, they began to compete with Hitler in advocating "national and social liberation." [They later surpassed Hitler.] In 1932, in league with the National Socialists, they took action against Braun's government in Prussia. But as early as July 1931, after the great bank crash, many individuals in the party knew that the cause was lost. Those with the most insight sensed that the subjectively aroused, revolutionary masses were, for the most part, following Hitler because they wanted an upheaval but, at the same time, feared genuine revolution. Hitler freed them from the responsibility for their own fate with which they had been burdened by the German revolutionary movement. "Hitler can—and will—do everything for us," they said. He was able to do everything, and accomplished unbelievable feats, because he was aided by mass fear of revolution. Simultaneously, he provided illusory satisfaction for the people's revolutionary, anti-capitalistic, and socialistic yearnings. It was impossible for German Socialists to see such contradictions. They believed that if economic exigency alone motivated the desires and actions of the working class, then the people could not help but want social revolution and could not simultaneously fear it. In this case, Hitler's attraction could only be attributed to "mystification" and "demagogy." In the precipitating events between 1930 and 1933, it was inconceivable that people could imagine themselves to be leaders of a better Germany without, for one moment, being disquieted by the fact that "mere mystification and demagogy" could have such an effect. Although they stood at the edge of an abyss, they didn't want to think about it, and we shall soon understand why. Even in 1938, I ran across "representatives of labor" who still were talking about mystification and demagogy, just as in 1930. Their comfort then, as before, was the fact that the price of butter had just gone up and that here and there "criticism was already being voiced in the factories." Reviewing those last eight years from the standpoint of present-day events, one must marvel at the kind of mentality in which millions of people once placed their trust! This highly naïve and extremely dignified mentality attempted to reduce the gargantuan problems of German society to the rising price of butter and the comments of a few discontented individuals in the factories. Not only that, but they wanted to attribute the problems to these phenomena and, moreover, refused to tolerate any other explanation.

None of the "leaders of the workers" I knew had seriously studied Hitler's *Mein Kampf* and other writings for the masses. None had asked themselves how this arch-reactionary hoax perpetrated by a group of bandits could seize and poison millions of warm, honest German hearts. The race theory, they said, was "nonsense," merely "imperialistic chatter" and "nothing new" in principle. The attack against the Jews was just "an old technique for diverting attention from the class struggle." At one time Socialism had prided itself on being the first social movement to function on a serious scientific basis. But no one seemed able to ask himself the simple question of why millions of individuals allowed themselves to be so influenced by nonsense and idle chatter. They even flew into a rage when such questions were posed. In order to defeat a strong opponent, one must examine his methods and motives most carefully. Recognizing them as facts is a far cry from agreeing with them. However, it was considered preposterous to take Hitler's mass-psychological adeptness seriously. Members of the Socialist Party in Germany took it as a personal affront if one contended that essential, unrecognized processes in the masses had to exist in order for Hitler to be so successful.

Prior to 1933, there could be no mention of coping seriously with the problem of Fascism. Even the most basic inquiries were pointedly rejected and, consequently, no answer to the questions could be found. As was later demonstrated, these answers were so horrifying, far-reaching, and, in a sense, revolutionary that at first they only increased one's powerlessness in the face of onrushing events. Fear of this sensation of helplessness accounts for part of the adherence to empty phrases which still gives the workers' movement the illusion of security today. It is simpler to place one's faith in the healing powers of useless medication than to admit that one is caring for a dying patient who is beyond help, even though one is beginning to grasp the reasons for his death.

The main statements of Fascism's opponents were correct in principle. Fascism threatened "democratic freedom of speech," but millions endorsed this threat to free expression of their opinions. Fascism spoke candidly of war, even clothing wholesale murder in portentous words such as "duty," "sacrifice," and "obedience," yet millions rallied to duty, obedience, and sacrifice with life and limb. It divided human beings into "natural leaders" and those "born to be led," and again millions rallied to the class of *Untermenschen*.[1] Fascism promised capitalists it would secure their control of industry and promised the workers they would share this control—and both accepted. Complete military mobilization of the people was announced, and the people affirmed it. In short, every political attitude in Fascism should have caused flaming rebellion, but had the opposite effect. Many Socialists fled from the insanity of the situation, renouncing their belief in the value of mass will and mankind's ability to think. Many were willing to proclaim the old basic thoughts of the freedom movement invalid, insofar as they were not party

---

[1] Subhumans. —*Trans.*

employees who were literally forced by circumstances to give lip service to "freedom." Their advocacy of freedom in the face of the unrestrained brutality of Fascism, which concurrently promised the longed-for national independence, was extremely sad, harmful, and degrading. Freedom's enemy struck wherever he could, and freedom's advocates complained about his blows to the police. But the enemy's function was to strike, and to complain was senseless. So they imitated his slogans while simultaneously preaching a people's democracy long since inoperative due to misuse. Hitler's strength lay in the people's disappointment in "scientific Socialism" and in the futility of parliamentary-democratic and reformist-socialistic ideology. Neither the freedom offered by Socialism nor the freedom they had experienced under bourgeois democracy was enticing, and we must bear in mind that these working masses included almost seven million unemployed. As the year 1933 demonstrated, not only were people unwilling to defend their established liberty but, on the contrary, the masses willingly and enthusiastically submitted to the authoritarian yoke of Fascism, which negated all liberty. Granted, the concept of freedom offered by Hitler's opponents was barren, but this mass reaction posed the question whether people desired freedom at all, or whether they simply preferred to exchange personal freedom for freedom from responsibility. The people's confidence in democratic and socialistic leadership had sunk to zero, if indeed it had ever existed. The Communists arranged "spontaneous mass demonstrations" in which their own party groups were enjoined to participate. On the decisive election day (March 5, 1933), forty thousand workers, some armed, waited in Berlin's working-class districts for the "spontaneous mass demonstrations," hoping thus to prevent Hitler from seizing power. No one stirred. No one seemed eager to defend his own liberty. In Germany, with its very strong tradition of Socialism and trade unions, this was incomprehensible to the rationalistic thinking of that time: "The economic crisis is pauperizing the population; therefore it desires Socialism and socialization of the means of production. Hitler is a representative of big business; therefore the people will oppose him." Exactly the opposite occurred. The

Irrationalism in Politics and Society 163

entire body of Socialist theory, the work of generations of brilliant intellects and pioneers, seemed to collapse at one stroke.

Expressed in most concise terms: Marxist theory, which directed the German workers' movement, demanded, as the result of a deep and enduring economic crisis, a revolutionizing of the people's sentiments. In reality, the German crisis had caused not only mass paralysis but a clear popular swing to the right as well. Thus a split occurred between economic and ideological developments, or, better said, the latter was in direct contradiction to the former. One could not bemoan this; it had to be understood. Only then could a practical solution be found. Once again, scientific, unsentimental thinking proved its consistency. While party representatives of Marxism hid behind thick clouds of illusion, political psychology logically combined staggering facts to form a composite view. I felt more like the transmitter of a certain logic than like a wise thinker drawing scientific conclusions in a "superior" manner. The consolidation of all problems into one basic question took place for me through the experience of the reverse mass reaction to "freedom" propaganda, although I had been prepared for this by long years of practice in handling the problem of freedom and witnessing man caught up in the political machine. I was well acquainted with the mechanisms of irrational, unconscious emotions discovered by Freud. My own experience in correctly integrating mass-psychological questions into the social processes enabled me to give close attention to one decisive, basic issue: If the events in Germany during those years were possible, then, within the emotional life of the masses, there had to be important processes at work which were unrecognized or misinterpreted by the participants. "What is occurring among the masses? How do they experience the social process to which they are subjected and which they themselves determine by their reactions?" Questions such as these suddenly became so crucial that I became more and more amazed at how inaccessible they were to the leaders of the masses. Hitler's *Mein Kampf* showed that the National Socialist movement had come closest to understanding (even if unconsciously) the psychic reactions of people in 1930. Marxists presumed a fully developed "class-consciousness" in the working masses, one which needed only to be organized. In day-to-day political life, I had seen people in a different light. Their feeling for justice, for capitalistic contradictions, and for life in general was infinitely more diverse and richer than, and above all different from, that embraced by Marxist concepts. Therefore, two kinds of "class-consciousness" existed, namely "consciousness" of social exigency and "consciousness" of what is required to change it. The one, held by the leaders, included intellectual knowledge of large historical perspectives and economic processes; the other, that of the people, understood nothing of these issues and did not wish to understand, but was full of the details of daily life, primarily sexual and cultural worries—where actual hunger did not suffocate all else. In Germany, an estimated two million people were actually starving. Approximately sixty million suffered from the general pressure of social disorder. A youth group leader from Neukölln impressed upon me briefly and factually what this meant: As soon as the average teen-ager has even partially satisfied his hunger, he immediately begins to think of his girl friend, if he has one, and the amount of money they need in order to go out and enjoy themselves. If he has no girl friend, he wants personal independence and the means to find a girl and make her happy. Cinema, theater, books, decent clothing, and a room for oneself are elementary desires of every human being from adolescence to middle age. The driving factor here is yearning for sexual happiness, both in the narrow, sensual sense and in the broadest cultural sense. Future historians will comb the Socialist Party literature of those decades in vain for references to this overpoweringly obvious fact. To the extent that they were not depraved or demoralized, people desired a social system in which the needs of all would determine economic production. Contrary to this, a high party representative told me that such views were "reactionary" and that the "development of the means of production" was the sole concern!

The average individual was suffering from a contradiction: he wanted the world changed but the change was to be imposed upon him suddenly from above, just as the exploitation and suppression had been imposed upon him. With the exception of very knowledgeable workers, the masses could not conceive of a change in their lives different from that which they had previously experienced, i.e. by force. No leaders entertained the thought of telling them the truth, namely that they had to think and act in a responsible manner for their freedom. On the contrary, the Communists, for example, did everything in their power to make the masses subservient. The events that occurred later in the Soviet Union and in Spain proved the truth of this statement. Therefore, Hitler had to succeed. He resolved this contradiction. He replaced the hazy, inconceivable freedom to determine social life with the age-old, easily conceivable illusion of national freedom. He demanded no responsibility; on the contrary, he promised that everything would come from above and that he would alter the system single-handed. And the upheaval took place, induced almost single-handed by an ignoramus like Hitler. The greater the scope of the problem, the more successfully the passivity of the masses could be exploited.

It was not Hitler's economic program which gained him the masses. In his daily propaganda, it was the strengthening of German self-esteem through intense race propaganda, the war he proclaimed against "world Jewry," and the strong advocacy of the authoritarian family which brought him victory. At first sight this was incomprehensible, and even today Marxists do not understand it. The masses of workers are not anti-Semitic, and yet hatred of Jews was effective. The masses are never proud of their race; on the contrary, they are decidedly cosmopolitan and inclined toward international humanism. Yet race propaganda was effective. The vigorous family and clan propaganda was not essential, because people were already for the authoritarian family, yet it too was extremely effective. Each of these three pillars of National Socialist mass propaganda had its own special mechanism. Starting in 1930, I followed every important step the National Socialists took, and by 1932 I could claim complete understanding of their methods. In my book *The Mass Psychology of Fascism*, written between 1931 and 1933, I established the most important facts in such detail that I shall be brief here.

The concept of "race" influenced the unconscious emotional

life of human beings through its similarity to the word *rassig*, i.e. purebred, powerful, strong, unique. This concept brilliantly compensated for the people's deplorable sexual and general self-image stemming from the world crisis. Since everyone, without exception, suffers more or less consciously from hypochondriacal fear of syphilis, and since syphilis implies poisoning of the blood, the promise to protect "purity of blood" struck a deep chord. Hitler's description of syphilis in his book *Mein Kampf* is quite explicit. The concept of the *Untermensch* is inseparably connected with the "underworld" and this, in turn, with "proletarian," "ragged peasant," and "criminal." The unconscious, however, must equate "crime" with sexual crime. No one wishes to be an *Untermensch*, proletarian, criminal, sexual criminal, or Negro, in this sense of the word, or even a "Frenchman" for that matter. Fear of the "French disease"[2] is too deeply rooted in vulgar imagery, even among proletarians. For this reason the average worker does not enjoy being called a *Prolet*. Despite all well-meant interpretations and explanations, it still simply connotes "depraved," i.e. "syphilitic." If we consider, in addition to this, the raising of self-esteem which, through illusion, assists in overcoming real misery, the circle of necessary emotional reactions is closed. Hitler revealed the social impact of fantasy.

The race problem connects logically with the "Jewish problem." Jews were viewed in general, and especially under pressure of the relentless propaganda of a pervert like Streicher, as "kosher butchers," i.e. people with long knives who butcher Christian and German children at Passover. Because of the practice of circumcision, fear of Jews is intensified through age-old castration fear which is universally present. Only a person desiring to steal all pleasure for himself (especially sexual pleasure) could engage in such practices. Thus Jews, having castrated the men, proceed to rob the Aryans of their women. Jews are always taking something away. Since, in addition, they suffered the misfortune of having to practice trade, due to previous persecutions, they are robbers

[2] *Französische Krankheit,* a slightly obsolete German expression for syphilis. —*Trans.*

Irrationalism in Politics and Society 167

of money. Carried just one step further, they become the prototype of the "capitalist." Thus, through highly skillful use of the sexual fear of the "kosher butcher," the entire emotional mass hatred for usurers, in other words "capitalists," can be transferred onto the Jews. Thus Jews become the object of both socialistic hatred of capitalists and ingrained sexual anxiety. Marxists, and Jewish Marxists as well, frequently oppose this logical train of unconscious conclusions, but in vain. It explains all the irrational phenomena which left their stamp upon Germany since the beginning of Nazi rule. The fact that this diverts all energies from the real mastery of difficult life problems only completes the picture and the effect of the emotional plague in Germany. A thousand-year-old, degenerate human character structure serves as its background.

The problem of the family is somewhat different. Here, bourgeois and Marxist mass education not only missed the mark completely, but actually paved the road for Fascism. In a different context, *The Sexual Revolution,* I have already described the family problem in great detail and shall thus limit myself here to establishing the relationship of the family problem to Fascism.

The problem of race and the Jews was nothing other than an eruptive human reaction, incomprehensible to the average person. It was determined by irrationalism and sexual anxiety and resulted from sexual depravity in human structure. Primitive sex-economy, its transformation into a patriarchal form, and its further development into the form of an absolute state, first explained the social basis upon which the grotesque manifestations of human irrationalism could prosper. The family, as we already know, constitutes the central element of social sex-economy. Even the pre-Fascist period had left no doubts as to its function, social sources, and structural consequences. The strict clan ideology which was introduced by Fascist family politics was, in itself, no innovation but merely a culmination of age-old factors, intensified to the highest degree. The patriarchal state is reproduced in the patriarchal family. Therefore an absolute state, or a total dictatorship, must affirm family ideology and defend it rigorously. It is the most important transmission belt between the demands of dictatorship and the sources of structure formation. This holds true wherever we encounter dictatorship which, in addition to the terror it employs, is supported by powerful emotional forces within the people. Bourgeois sex-economy, and prior to that, patriarchal sex-economy, transformed natural sexual impulses into grotesque, distorted, socially intolerable secondary drives. Sexuality became a horrifying apparition, the actual content of social chaos. Social revolution contemplates regaining sexual freedom within the framework of a general reordering of existence, but neither the advocates of revolution nor the people themselves are capable of imagining the true nature of this freedom. They fear it, irrationally and intensely. As a result, fascistic "preservation of family and state" from "bolshevistic cultural chaos" strikes a responsive chord within the masses, and two birds are killed with one stone: first, revolutionary thinking is destroyed, and second, Fascism's own tyranny receives massive support. "Pollution and contamination of emotional life" are realities, not fantasies. No organization had opposed them prior to that time. The doors were wide open for rampant pornography, perversion, and sexual prostitution; no one had attempted to stamp out the "sexual plague"; and no one conceived of a sharp distinction between natural and pathological sexuality as a positive solution to the problem. Science strictly avoided the issue and the parties had no idea of what was going on. Outside of a limited social circle, the birth-control programs of the Communists and sexual-reform groups were considered within the framework of the general plague and could serve only as a brilliant excuse for a "purification." Thus the flight from the sexual "bolshevist plague" joined with a sexually emphasized enthusiasm for Hitler, uniforms, marches, and liberation of German girls and women from the sensual Jewish swine. National Socialism drew its greatest strength from this source. These general reactions were prepared by the family. In addition, many very healthy manifestations and premonitions of the force of natural sexuality appeared in the flight from the sexual plague. In National Socialist youth circles, views emerged to which there could be no objection, not even from the most strict sex-economic standpoint. Even though these views were smothered in a mystical veiling of healthy sexual attitudes, they aroused the concern of government leaders, and occasionally led to conflicts and to the prohibition of mixed-group youth outings. The tables were turned when the National Socialists, who had set out to eliminate the sexual plague, coined the expression "Bubi drück mich"[3] for the BDM.[4] Social Democrats, Communists, and Christian Democrats joined in accusing National Socialism of immorality. In 1935, the French Communists claimed they could save the family far more effectively than the National Socialists. In short, there existed a tangled chaos of events and ideologies. Fascism built itself a firm foundation through rigid family ideology while simultaneously abetting the young in their demands upon the older generation, thus drawing masses of youth away from home and collectivizing their lives and, consequently, their sexuality. All this was done without the slightest knowledge of the processes it set into motion and without any concept of the positive precautionary measures necessary to control the development of such a tumultuous movement. I contend that the same forces which elevated Fascism to its power over the people had to lead to its downfall. Fascism is anti-sexual, although it thrives on the masked sexual yearning of the population. Its authoritarian family ideology, and its encouragement of pronounced expressions of life-affirmation, are incompatible. In this, Fascism involuntarily made valuable contributions to future developments, contributions which will be felt long after its own downfall. It destroyed democratic illusions, awakened vital, vegetative longing for life, emancipated youth, and overthrew the exploiters of sexual misery. However, it lacks the means to harvest even a single fruit of the seeds it sowed because it is undermined by its own political, social, and psychic structure. It would be impossible to intensify the organization of human life around the family beyond the present fascistic level

---

[3] "Hug me, honey." —*Trans.*
[4] Bund deutscher Mädchen, the National Socialist organization for girls. —*Trans.*

because the vital contradictions contained within the family have already reached their peak. Suppression of spontaneous manifestations of life has reached a point where it can only boomerang—and precisely with the help of the same anti-capitalistic, sexual, cosmic yearning which bore Fascism to power and which Fascism could never understand or satisfy.

Many people grasped these grotesque contradictions in 1938. Hitler's opponents, however, overlooked them in directing propaganda to the masses. They not only considered these contradictions irrelevant nonsense, but advocated the same principles although in a milder and less stimulating form. Viewed factually and unsentimentally, these individuals were not Hitler's opponents but the forerunners who paved the way for him. Race theories and mystical genetics were already regnant schools of thought before Hitler, even among Communists, including those in the Soviet Union. German geneticists were later enraged at Hitler's race practices because these ruined their own concepts of race and aroused justified hatred for the expression "'hereditary." All this simply fit logically into the current course of events.

Between 1930 and 1933, not all aspects of these processes were visible yet. I had no premonition that my politico-psychological views would be confirmed as they were in subsequent years. Nevertheless, sex-political work among various classes of the population allowed occasional insight into relationships which, despite all the misery, offered a glimpse of freedom. Until Hitler's time, Socialism had been dealing with an approximately three-hundred-year-old problem, namely the capitalistic phase of patriarchalism in its economic function alone. Hitler forced a general consideration of the problem—thousands of years old—of suppression of human life through patriarchy. This could no longer be avoided and Hitler represented the grotesque climax of this development. He forced the relationship between psychic and socio-political processes to be accounted for. Never again would the thoughts and emotions of the masses be neglected and overlooked as they were before his time. Until Hitler, the people in general had always merely tolerated tyranny. During his time they stepped forth irrationally, in active support of tyranny,

Irrationalism in Politics and Society

against their own vital interests. For the first time in history, the hitherto unknown significance of irrationalism in the social process was revealed. In order to gain support from the damaged human structure, National Socialism had to imbue the masses with so much new vitality, and elicit such great energies, that the reactionary content of the movement clashed with its own revolutionary spirit in a conflict which defied solution. All further developments depended upon which forces would emerge to comprehend this gigantic process, to direct it, to supply the clarity necessary to allow it to follow the path it was urgently pursuing, unbeknown to all. It was already clear in 1932 that any movement to defeat Hitler could only spring from within the ranks of National Socialism itself, through the factual solution of those crucial questions which Hitler had unwittingly raised. Such insight shielded one from the illusion that Chamberlain and Daladier could "save" Germany.

Observations of fascistic mass propaganda thus confirmed the assertions of the young discipline of political psychology at every step. Briefly summarized:

1. Objective social processes, and the subjective experience of those processes, must be carefully differentiated. Each follows its own laws and has separate sources of energy.

2. Leaders are always an expression of the popular will, i.e. a reflection of average human structure. Their thoughts and actions are self-contradictory and correspond exactly to the contradictions in the average human being, whose structure is simultaneously progressive and reactionary. This structure is prepared within the family and continues its effect in the structure of the state. Therefore, the problem of the family, i.e. of sexual conditions, is older and more significant in every respect than the problem of technology. This is still true despite the fact that a change in family organization is entirely dependent upon a change in human technological mastery of the world.

3. Economy and ideology do not bear a simple, direct relationship to one another. In principle, the former can determine the latter, or vice versa. Furthermore, they can be in contradiction to one another in their development (divergence).

4. Considered technically, the moving force of history is vegetative energy,[5] which is expressed as sexual feeling and as the desire for happiness. These expressions are subject to the limitations of political, social, and economic conditions.

5. If a community's bio-energetic expressions exceed the limits set by these conditions, then regression, as seen in Russia, is inevitable. In Fascism, the vital energy of the masses regressed to abject spiritual and material misery because it was unaware of its own intentions and objectives. Thus an ancient statement is confirmed, namely that a society can only accomplish those tasks it has consciously set for itself and those which it is able to complete within the framework of the available resources of its own social organization.

6. Despite their lack of awareness of *progressive* processes within German society, both conservatism and political reaction were brilliantly aware of how to harness the energy of the masses and direct it in their own interests. This, and only this, constitutes "Fascism." It follows that Fascism can only be overcome through the conscious guidance of the same processes it has set into motion.

ALL POLITICIANS UNITE AGAINST SOCIAL PSYCHIATRY

I can only hope I have succeeded in demonstrating the importance of the sexual life of the masses. It is a general human, and consequently social, issue. The sexualization of political life in our time ought to be replaced by the politicization of sexual life based upon the scientific mastery of the deterioration in private life. Communists, Social Democrats, National Socialists, psychoanalysts, and the police all, in turn, claimed to be able to bring about a new social order. Let us observe the experiences encountered in our work when it was no longer applied merely in academic and private circles but put to purposeful and meaning-

---

[5] With the discovery of the specific life energy in bions and the atmosphere (1939–40), the term "vegetative energy" was replaced by the terms "bio-energy" and "orgone energy."

Irrationalism in Politics and Society   173

ful use, namely among the people themselves, who, in the last analysis, determine the further development of society. These experiences made me think of a stage set, with Fascism holding its victory march. This set contained not only the magnificent trappings of Fascism's ideological power but also the confusion and rubbish which the brilliance of the stage obscured. And in the midst of the rubbish there were simple, uncomplicated people with uncomplicated, natural desires. For example, there was a fourteen-year-old girl who had come from the Hitlerjugend[6] to join a youth group under my supervision. She had become pregnant and had heard that "the reds" had reasonable doctors who understood such matters. She came seeking help, and I provided it.[7] On that evening I had explained to the youth group the social conditions which threatened to plunge that girl into dire misery. Had she not, by chance, come to me but to the usual kind of physician, she would have been sent to an institution which would have destroyed her. I shall never forget the burning expression in that girl's eyes. Her thoughts and emotions were those of a million others like her.

After the meeting a girl about ten years old approached me. For a long time she simply stood there thinking. Then, with tears in her eyes, she stroked my arm silently. Although no word was spoken we knew what we both wanted. We understood how close, how desperately and precariously close our sentiments and work were to the filthiest, most abject realms of contemporary human experiences. But we also both understood that one cannot remove a dunghill if one fearfully avoids contact with the dung.

During those years, among young people and adults of various parties and political persuasions, it became clear that my work in the "lower regions" of society was gradually providing an answer to National Socialist ideology, an answer to the problem of "mankind, culture, and nature." I zealously avoided indulging in philosophical thinking on the subject. It required ten times the Hitlerian grace of the gods for me to even stick it out. What

[6] The Hitler Youth.—*Trans.*
[7] I later enabled her to give birth under proper conditions and without fear.

happened to me and to my work in the following six years could be borne only by keeping before me the mental picture of these people whenever a situation arose which seemed to indicate defeat. I am not shrewd by nature; quite the contrary. But the picture of these people taught me shrewdness. I could have withdrawn from politics, as many others had done, but the crimes committed everywhere against children and adolescents restrained me and made any other path impossible.

In 1937, while I was in exile in a foreign country, I was visited by some young members of the Hitlerjugend who had come to fetch several expurgated copies of my youth book for their comrades. It had been necessary to delete only those portions of the book which bureaucratic party members had influenced me to insert. Logically, after a five-year span, everything the dehumanized party line had considered correct had been falsified and was useless. Everything capable of offering adolescents an answer to their existential questions had remained valid.

It is audacious to lay claim to having answers to the entire problem of National Socialist ideology. Thus I shall have to describe how the events between 1932 and 1938 confirmed my views and how my opponents' objections at the time were nullified and the views which they opposed successfully put to the test, independent of me. It is imperative to do so because this confirmation was possible only under the pressure of Fascism, which was pauperizing the world and which these opponents did not understand, did not want to understand, and carried within themselves as a basic attitude. Fascism had placed three great questions before the world, to which I gave the following answers:

1. *How is sexual misery to be eliminated?* The answer was, in principle: through restoration of natural sexual life and differentiation between this and the distorted sexual manifestations of the present, which were opposed by everyone.

2. *How is man's borrowed, false, and illusional self-esteem to be replaced with natural self-confidence stemming from a satisfying life?* The answer was provided by clinical and mass-psychological experience. It would be necessary to create un-

armored, unrestricted, productive, sexually affirmative character structures.

3. *How is dictatorship of the masses by an individual to be prevented?* By establishing man's capacity to determine and govern his own life, i.e. by genuine social democracy.

Socialists, Social Democrats, and Communists, on the other hand, offered these answers:

On December 5, 1932, two months before the great bank crash, the newspaper *Rot Sport*,[8] sponsored by the Fichte organization, published a notice strictly prohibiting further distribution and sale of my publications. Among them were *The Invasion of Compulsory Sex-Morality, The Sexual Struggle of Youth, When Your Child Asks Questions,* and *The Chalk Triangle.*

Stop Distribution!

All brochures by Reich, handled by the literature distribution division of the KG for the Verlag für Sexualpolitik, are to be withdrawn and further distribution is to cease.

Distribution activities were assumed due to a misunderstanding. Reich's brochures treat the issues in a manner contradictory to the revolutionary education of children and youth. (Detailed commentary to follow in the next edition). [It never followed!]

Thereupon, my sex-political organization spontaneously demanded a meeting of functionaries from Greater Berlin. This and all further actions which were undertaken under difficult circumstances in behalf of my work were always spontaneous. I made it a principle never to "lead" or "start campaigns." If the issue was valid, it first had to prove itself independently through the verbal support and actions of those concerned. This was their only means of having the bitter experience of steering their own course, despite their meager or nonexistent factual training. A letter from the Charlottenburg group to the party leadership (dated December 10, 1932) stated: "The directors of the cultural division have sabotaged, through the basest intrigues, the distri-

[8] *Red Sport. —Trans.*

bution of literature necessary for our movement, and are still attempting to suppress this literature, contrary to the resolutions of the Greater Berlin faction of the organization." The organization proposed a motion to remove the leaders of the German cultural division of the Communist Party. In December 1932, shortly after the banning of my writings, representative Grube, director of the Berlin-Brandenburg Fichte sports organization, called a conference of functionaries. He justified and defended the ban with the worst kind of distortions and sharply worded threats, saying it was simply "counterrevolutionary" to expose youth to such trash and that it weakened their fighting spirit and was irrelevant to "proletarian class morality." He stated further that adolescents had recently approached the leaders of the Fichte sports organization and demanded that the organization supply clean rooms so that they could have undisturbed sexual intercourse. Supposedly they had claimed that such deficiencies were damaging to the organization and had "referred to Reich." Reich, he continued, had written to the directors of Fichte when he heard of the "scandal" and claimed that the youths were absolutely correct but had simply written to the wrong address; society was responsible and not a sports organization. Unheard of!

Afterward a friend of my work visited me and told me that 80 percent of all functionaries—otherwise faithful, obedient party followers—had opposed the director of the organization and that there had been great commotion. The following day I was visited by some young workers who informed me that my publications would continue to be distributed despite the ban. And so it went!

One day there was excitement in the Communist parliamentary faction. In Dresden, a resolution of the socialistic youth organizations, dated October 16, 1932, was being circulated among adolescents of every political affiliation. This resolution was, in their opinion, a gigantic scandal which jeopardized the "party image" and sullied its greater political objectives. It was shameful; the opponents could "capitalize on it politically" at any moment. They felt that the slogan "A room of his own for every adolescent" was "incredible" and that they were losing every

Irrationalism in Politics and Society 177

opportunity to "conquer the Christian Democrats." (In 1936 they *allied* with the Christian Democrats!) The instigator of the resolution was to be immediately expelled from the party. When they discovered that the resolution had been drawn up following a youth conference to which I had been invited, there was great embarrassment. They could not expel me at the time. The Communist, Social Democrat, and bourgeois youth organizations had already distributed thousands of copies of my writings. There would have been outright rebellion. Shortly before this, the Berlin Communist youth organization had succeeded in holding a meeting, together with Socialist youth, for the first time since the inception of the unification movement. Their objective in this was to discuss the personal and, subsequently, the general social state of youth. I had spoken at this meeting and had been received enthusiastically. They had finally overcome their differences and found common ground to work on. In addition to this, the organization had originally requested me to write my book[9] and had officially accepted it. It was not a pretty picture! An earlier adamant opponent of my work with young people had attended a meeting in Neukölln and was extremely surprised at the interest young people showed, at their active participation in the discussion, and at the fact that even "highly political" issues were brought up. The work had spoken for itself. The former opponent was transformed into a friend. The text of the Dresden resolution of combined revolutionary and other young groups read as follows:

Resolution

passed at the Conference of Representatives of Proletarian-Revolutionary Youth Organizations of the U.B. Dresden, October 16, 1932.

The assembled representatives of the proletarian youth organizations (KJV, IAH, SJV[10]) have resolved to incorporate all endeavors in the field of sex-politics into the general endeavor to defeat capitalism, and to do so for the purpose of the broadest possible mobiliza-

[9] *The Sexual Struggle of Youth.*
[10] Kommunistischer Jugend Verband, Internationaler Arbeiter Hilfsverein, and Sozialistischer Jugend Verband. —*Trans.*

tion of working youth. They have arrived at clear recognition and are unanimously of the opinion that the neglect of youth's sexual problems until this time has had an extremely adverse effect upon the revolutionary work of the youth organizations. The dissolution of groups, great fluctuation in membership, political passivity, etc., are intimately related to disturbed and unclarified sexual life. This confusion and obscurity in the question of adolescent sexual activity is, in itself, a result of the kind of sexuality that exists in the capitalistic system. It serves the purpose of the Church and the ruling classes through intellectual subjugation of all youth. Sex-political work, as an essential element of all revolutionary endeavors, must first concentrate on the following issues:

1. Clarification of the question in the party itself, and within its organizations; correlation, and not separation, of personal and political questions, i.e. *complete politicization of all sexual activity*.

2. Abolition of the one-sided truce between bourgeoisie and proletariat still prevailing in this domain (only the bourgeoisie is fighting for its own interests in all areas of sexuality). This entails declaration of war on the bourgeoisie by means of proletarian strategy in this area as well (e.g. action against laws governing morality such as that proposed by Bracht, etc.).

3. The mobilization of youth of all political convictions on the basis of a clear, affirmative attitude toward adolescent sexuality, while proving the impossibility of creating the prerequisites for healthy sexuality under capitalism. Penetration of the Christian, National Socialist, and Social Democrat organizations through complete exposure of the contradictions between the members of these organizations and their leadership.

4. The precondition for the above is ideological clarification of the difficulties in the youth organizations (ratio of boys to girls, enlistment of indifferent adolescents from dance halls with the aid of sexual issues, etc.).

The conference is aware of the enormous difficulties which must be overcome in this field, but is equally convinced that the question of adolescent sexuality is one of the most significant issues of class struggle in regard to mobilization of youth for overthrowing capitalism. Youth is not only allowed to starve, but is also downtrodden through deprivation of its right to a sexual life, by means of legislation, persecution, and education. Reactionary bourgeois sex-politics of every hue, by which working youth is enslaved to capitalism (e.g. the Center

Party with its one and a half million youth), must be opposed by clear, sex-affirmative, revolutionary sex-politics in order to reinforce powerfully the proletarian struggle against the bourgeoisie. Its defeat and the institution of a workers'-council government will subsequently solve the burning question of adolescent sexuality within the general framework of the social revolution.

Long live the proletarian revolution!

"Well-meaning friends" had always advised me to "act tactfully and less aggressively." In the Dresden region, operations were directed by a twenty-one-year-old friend of the cause who hardly knew me. Several excerpts from the reports in his letters are quoted below:

I would like to relate some of my experiences and point out the difficulties which may arise in treating these questions in youth groups. . . . Of all places, in the youth group the secretariat is giving me trouble about discussing these questions, and intends to prohibit me from speaking. I treated the questions clearly and factually and was even understood by the boys, with the exception of a certain few, namely those standing at the political head of the organization who should have been able to grasp what was happening in the organization; they were the very ones who opposed me. I can only tell you it was a joy for me to see youth defending its rights. I had the impression, figuratively speaking, that those young people were struggling against the suppression of their own bodies. Thirty-eight of the forty present agreed with me . . . just those two, the political youth director and another director, took a different stand. . . . I wanted to withdraw but the youths refused to have anyone else discuss these questions and insisted that I return. I now have to face the question of whether to fight my way through on valid issues and discredit the political leaders, or submit. It is a very difficult decision. . . .

The moral is: it is impossible for today's human beings, even adolescents, to hold a political position without becoming sexually intimidated. Contemporary organizations demand "dignity" from their leaders. *Rigid dignity and sexual health are incompat-*

ible. Therefore man's existential questions cannot be solved with these leaders. Bureaucracy and life are deadly enemies. We shall encounter the deep significance of this issue repeatedly, as it constitutes the essential problem in all serious impulses for innovation. It is sustained by the masses' need for authority. They wish a simple sexual life for themselves while demanding that their leaders be authoritarian, i.e. bureaucratic, which implies "chaste." The leaders who are forced into chastity, in turn, take revenge upon the masses by likewise demanding chastity, morality, and good conduct from them instead of finding a positive answer to the question of sexuality. This is wrong! A forthright leader will tell people, "I am only a human being and thus must also love and embrace women (or men, respectively) like everyone else. Anyone who is incapable of understanding this is equally incapable of understanding revolution in our lives. How am I to grasp life if I am immobilized or am forced to satisfy my desire for love on the back steps?" This is the way genuine leaders of social groups speak. All else is Hitlerism, i.e. divine impotence! Thus Hitlerism was embedded in the party leadership which strove to secure a "new, better, and freer future for Germany."

On January 29, 1933, four weeks before the impending catastrophe, a conference of the German National Association took place in Berlin. It proved Hitler incorrect in accusing the Communists of "cultural bolshevism." A physician, Dr. Friedländer, who had warmly recommended my youth book when everyone else had favored it, led a dull discussion on the subject, "The Political Situation and Our Objectives." The following excerpts were taken from the stenographic minutes:

Sexual pleasure is not, as Reich claims, a moving force in history. . . .
    Reich's theory is a concession to the petty bourgeoisie . . . [who were at the moment flocking to Hitler with colors flying and hearts aflame!].

The leader of the Communist culture organization of Germany:

Irrationalism in Politics and Society 181

Why, then, are only hunger and sexuality considered moving forces in history? One might just as well also say that the need to breathe is a decisive historical factor. All this nonsense only distracts the masses from the struggle against the economic basis.

(The good fellow, who alas was hindered in becoming a future protector of culture, could have had no idea of what he was saying when he mentioned the masses' need to breathe. I myself was only able to confirm this sentence clinically three years later.)

Reich's contention that sexual repression includes both classes is equally outrageous. This denies the existence of class antagonism. Worst of all, however, is his claim in *The Sexual Struggle of Youth* that there is antagonism between the generations. This implies that the class struggle is shifted to the family sphere instead of all forces being concentrated upon the political struggle against exploitation and misery.

E., the director of the German sex-political association:

The great majority of our members do not come to us with sexual problems. Our organizational statistics prove that most of them are unemployed. [Logical!]

A functionary from Essen:

We have observed that one can enlist the interest of otherwise inaccessible individuals with sexual issues—not merely the Christian Democrat or Christian Party women, but National Socialists as well. We have even been successful in getting them to participate in demonstrations.

D., directress of the West German organization:

We too have established the fact that one can approach otherwise inaccessible strata of the population through sexual topics. A first meeting [on sex-politics] in a strategic defense plant which we had not yet infiltrated was attended by sixty women. We now have groups in that plant advocating "special social-hygiene demands." [But of what importance was this to these organizations?]

A Communist physician:

Reich is trying to turn our organizations into "fucking clubs"! This is a crime against youth, and the future lies in their hands! [Protests from the majority of those attending the conference.] I have never in ten years had difficulties with sex-political work. [How very much I envied this cheerful class warrior!]

The situation could not be smoothed over. A vote taken among the national functionaries on a resolution against my work, resulted in thirty-nine votes cast for the party representative and thirty-two cast for me. (I must add that the party leadership had been preparing for weeks, whereas I had not so much as raised a finger to solicit votes for myself, due to my continuing conviction that persuasion and suggestive measures are senseless. Only individuals who defended their own standpoint were useful in this struggle. Proceedings continued on February 18 and 19, 1933. This time "the party" itself spoke through its cultural representative, B., in "A Political Report and Our Objectives."

Reich's publications are intentionally or unintentionally—for the moment I shall assume the latter—counterrevolutionary. . . . The Central Committee of the Communist Party has confirmed our views completely. A detailed examination of Reich's falsification of Marxism will follow. [This never appeared.] The Berlin faction's decision to distribute Reich's works runs contrary to the decision of the National Directors. . . . Reich's writings constitute an attempt to discredit Marxism. Anyone who believes that he can pursue sex-politics in our organizations [N.B.: sex-political organizations] is mistaken. We are pursuing politics, not sex-politics!

At this, the same female functionary who had previously boasted of her positive experiences in sex-political work suddenly reversed her position:

Irrationalism in Politics and Society

One should not report anatomical details and "unaesthetic trivialities." It was wrong to give precedence to sexual issues in the training of functionaries. [Then why have sex-political groups at all?] Our members show greater interest in the strategy and tactics of the class struggle.

The party representative of Marxism, B.:

Reich's claim in *The Invasion of Compulsory Sex-Morality* that the productive force, work-power, is sublimated sexual energy, is monstrous. This is an outright contention that dialectical materialism is false. According to this, Marx's *Capital* is also sublimated sexual energy. [What a shame for "Communists"!]

The Communist physician Marta Ruben-Wolff stated that no orgasm disturbances existed in the proletariat. Such phenomena were to be seen only in the bourgeoisie. Furthermore, it was the fault of the Communist Party faction that Reich had gained so much influence. He had done serious work, whereas the faction of Communist physicians had made no efforts in this direction. She stated that substantial changes in practical work were necessary, although Reich's theoretical basis had to be discarded.

Thus it was permissible to steal the people's hearts but perfidious to guarantee their independence from such representatives of dialectical-materialistic theory and revolutionary freedom. A young physician who had been enthusiastic about my work for years stated innocuously that my theory was to be discarded, as the questions had to be asked in a "political" reference. Psychology in Russia, he said, was "materialistic," as opposed to mine.

Following an emphatic remark by the party representative that a schism would develop if the resolution was not accepted unanimously, fifteen votes were cast for the party leadership, seven for me, with three abstentions. This was an enormous victory, since I had no organizational power behind me. [My only weapon was truth about life.]

At the same time, critiques of my youth book began to be received in the organization:

Neue Lehrerzeitung,[11] Berlin, February 1933:

The book, by an author well known through his numerous psychoanalytic and psychopathological works, is written from a special standpoint, compared to other similar works, inasmuch as it views questions of sexuality from the perspective of the class character of prevailing contemporary opinion. Hodann, for example, despite the clear factual explanations in his writings, shows a distinct weakness in regard to demonstrating modes of solving sexual problems. Reich, however, offers a thorough analysis of the social origin of sexual misery and demonstrates the fact that we may hope for sexual emancipation only through a change in the economic and political foundations of society. The book is written in a popular style so that it will function as a guideline, especially for the proletarian youth for whom it was intended. It is also recommended for all teachers and educators desiring an introduction to the sexual question from a Marxist perspective.

The opinion of a female stenotypist:

Absolutely nothing can be said against it. The book is clearly and understandably written. Everyone ought to have a look at it. The format is also excellent.

Die Rote Fahne,[12] Vienna, December 14, 1932:

This book was written in 1931. However, it is still of great current interest because Comrade Reich demonstrates clearly and without reserve the inseparable relationships between sexual distress and the ruling system. But the author also takes pains to give proletarian adolescents as much advice in their sexual misery as is possible within this system. To quote his finest counsel to them, "Fight against this system; then you will also be fighting for your sexual freedom and dignity." For these reasons this informative book must be recommended for

[11] A newspaper for teachers. —*Trans.*
[12] *The Red Banner.* —*Trans.*

Irrationalism in Politics and Society

struggling proletarian youth. [That was embarrassing for the party leadership!]

Critique of a youth in a Charlottenburg plant:

I read the book together with several other fellows. They were enthusiastic and said that something like this had always been lacking until now. The contents are great. You went into everything we had on our minds. We have already become clear on a lot about ourselves just by reading it.

From a youth group leader in Neukölln:

I read your *Sexual Struggle of Youth* with great interest and noticed that it by far surpasses the brochure *Sexual Excitement and Satisfaction* in both content and style. It must be particularly emphasized that almost every chapter is discussed on a Marxist basis [here that means "true" basis] and provides a brilliant field of discussion for proletarian youth organizations, especially since practical examples were selected from KJV and Fichte groups. These examples also reflect the sexual needs of youth in youth organizations.

Although I have no objections in general, I would like, nevertheless, to exercise the right to comment on, or supplement, several questions touched upon in the book. We do hope the book will appear in our youth organizations very shortly. It is the first publication which answers the question "When are adolescents actually mature enough to begin having sexual intercourse?"

The sexual problem is so clearly and understandably solved that it would aid not only proletarian adolescents but many others as well. In my opinion, the final sections seem too much like Communist propaganda. If one were to select a more general approach in these chapters, it would certainly be read by wider circles, as not all youths are Communist. However, I feel that it is most important for the book to reach as many adolescents as possible in order to gain youth for the cause of sexual emancipation.

(signed) Zeltlager

Let us pause for a moment to review the questions raised by such conferences, resolutions, betrayals, etc. They are not localized questions pertaining only to the field of sex-politics. They are the basic questions of all human organizations, and if they remain unanswered there can be no real change but only the illusion of freedom. The infinite difficulties of human life have undermined, until now, every attempt to solve the basic problem of our society, namely the division of its members into classes. The fiasco of the Russian Revolution leaves us in no doubt in this respect. In the conferences and disputes which I have described, one was able to observe the following phenomena:

The people's fear of stepping out of line, of leaving the solid ranks of the masses, regardless of how revolutionary their behavior. This holds true in all circles and realms of life.

The people's pettiness, which stems from a guilty conscience and which is practiced completely unconsciously, as their self-image does not allow them any alternative. The Soviet Russian espionage and sabotage trials which filled the following years were full of these mechanisms and therefore incomprehensible.

The people's attraction to ideas about human freedom, but simultaneous helpless collapse when the first serious difficulties arise. Once again, the contradiction between *yearning for freedom* and the *capability of being free* comes to the fore.

The domination of official political functions by private, highly personal moods and attitudes and hence the utter senselessness of all politics.

The childishness of mass expectations as soon as authoritarian influence is exerted, regardless of the nature of that influence.

The irresponsible willingness of former socialistic organizations to support correct ideas as long as they do not understand them; and their equally prompt readiness to destroy correct ideas once their effect is perceived.

The deep unbridgeable chasm separating the life of the masses from that of their representatives, whom they themselves organized and invested with power.

The forced "bureaucratization" of every mass leader, once he rises above the mass level; the sexual core of every bureaucracy; the irreconcilable contradiction of bureaucracy and natural sexual activity.

The seeming faithlessness of the masses which stems from the insurmountability of real problems; the disdain for the masses on the part of individuals who never took the trouble to trace a social problem to its roots.

Frequently I was on the verge of giving up the entire mass-psychological effort and devoting myself strictly to medical and clinical work. I could have overcome the social guilt feelings, as achievements founded on social conscience are of little permanence. My deep convictions on the correctness of Marxist sociology would also not have restrained me; on the contrary, the unscientific methods of the Marxist party would rather have implemented rapid severance. It was my fervent interest in the peculiar human reactions which bound me. Urgent research depended upon my understanding them, and for this reason I did not resign from any organization or work group with which I had finished, but simply let subsequent events take their necessary course. This provided inestimable insights and I might say strength as well. First, I overcame my personal sensitivity; second, I gathered experience for the future; and finally, I gained mass-psychological insight. *If one wishes to combat the plague one must expose oneself to it.* Beyond all doubt, neurosis and politics did constitute a plague of humanity, but all this appeared as "unproletarian" or "unscientific adventurousness" to established politicians and to my professional colleagues.

There were some precarious situations. In several districts, the Socialist Reichsbannerjugend[13] had united with Communist youth. The parties' leaders were engaged in disgraceful struggles. For example, in December 1932, the Communist Party issued orders for members not to march with the Social Democrats in a large demonstration, but merely to line up along the sidewalk. Against the will of the party, the masses intermingled. People of all classes and professions wanted to fight Fascism. I had put myself and my car at the disposal of an armed formation consisting of the Reichsbanner and Arbeiterwehr. I drew up a leaflet for the combat formations in which I advised separation from the parties and common action against the planned Fascist attack at

[13] National Banner Youth. —*Trans.*

the March elections in Berlin. Several hundred thousand copies were distributed.

The meetings held in Leipzig, Stettin, Dresden, etc., were crowded. On February 24, 1933, I went to Copenhagen, where the Danish student organization had invited me to lecture on the problems of Fascism and race. On the ship, I was interviewed by *Politiken*, the largest Danish government newspaper. I was also to speak at a meeting that *Politiken* wanted to hold. After the first evening with the students there was great enthusiasm, but after the second, when I spoke on Fascism and Germany before a workers' meeting, *Politiken* backed off. It had been too much for the government paper to take. Early on February 28, I returned to Berlin. That evening the Reichstag was set ablaze and the next morning fifteen hundred functionaries and intellectuals were arrested. I escaped arrest only because the Fascists' lists had been drawn up according to the official positions held by those arrested, and I had never held an official position.

The six days following the mass arrests were horrible. The organizations were paralyzed. No one could be found. On March 1, 1933, I accidentally met a Communist Reichstag deputy at a colleague's home. We discussed the question of what to do on March 5, the election day set by Hitler, as Chancellor appointed by Hindenburg. The Communist representative told me that the remaining party leaders had ordered workers' living quarters to be protected and the Fascist columns to be broken up. A worker in the defense formation had informed me that the forty thousand armed workers at our disposal would have been only too glad to intervene if mass demonstrations occurred. But there were no mass demonstrations. The last took place in the middle of February, when one hundred thousand people, in the bitter cold, silently and earnestly marched past the Karl Liebknecht house, where Thälmann and the Central Committee stood in review. The people expected the party to begin the fight. The party knew the masses were passive. Nevertheless it gave orders to the defense formations to break up the Fascist columns. Meanwhile the formations waited for the masses, making intervention dependent upon their actions.

Three good friends of mine, workers who had led defense formations, were among those arrested. Two of them were murdered in the SA barracks on Pape Strasse. Possession of arms and distribution of leaflets (or even aiding in this) were punishable by death. Four days prior to the election I was visited by youths who needed my car to transport arms and leaflets to a Berlin suburb. We agreed that, in case of arrest, the driver would claim the car had been stolen. As they drove off, it suddenly occurred to me that we had not discussed the address from which the car had supposedly been stolen. If they were caught, all would be lost. They were to bring the car to a certain place in the inner city by 1 A.M., at the latest. If they were not there by the appointed time, this would indicate that matters had gone amiss and I was to report my car as stolen. Six hours of dread passed. The individuals who had set out were outstanding men and would have lost their lives had the leaflets been found. I waited at the appointed place. Time passed; it was one o'clock and the car was not in sight. I assumed they had been arrested. What was I to do? I could not report a stolen car because the first questions would surely have concerned where the car had been parked, and that would have exposed the whole plot. There was no escape. I could have fled, but I had neither money nor identification with me. I could not go home, because my apartment was being watched. The SA had already been there. At the time, I was living in various hotels where I registered under a false name. Two days before, my children had been sent to Vienna to their grandparents. My wife was living with friends. On the other hand, not reporting the car as stolen also meant certain catastrophe. I was stricken with fear and soon thereafter overcome by a peculiar icy chill. I decided to wait a bit longer. Another half hour passed and no car. I felt miserable and was about to leave when suddenly I saw the car in the distance. Everything had gone smoothly except that they had had a flat tire on the way back. We went into a bar and had a drink to celebrate. They had also thought of our stupid forgetfulness.

The next day an article on my youth book appeared in the *Völkischer Beobachter*. It was clear that I could not remain in

Berlin any longer. Two friends from the sex-political organization urged me to flee at once. But where was I to go? I had no money. We decided I should first journey south with my wife and cross the border as a tourist in ski clothes. We departed at night. There were several friends on the train but no one greeted anyone else. In a small Bavarian town just before we reached the border, we got out, not knowing whether the border was open or not. We held Austrian passports but no one knew whether lists of people to be arrested had been drawn up. To find this out, we spent two days with an older couple who were enthusiastic about the Nazis. Although Bavaria had not yet been conquered and was still ruled by Held, the SA could be seen everywhere. Newspaper reports indicated that a return to Berlin would be ill-advised. With trepidation we crossed the border. Everything went smoothly with our Austrian passports and we got off the train on the other side. My wife was then to go back to Berlin and let me know whether it was safe for me to return as well. A letter soon arrived telling me not to return under any circumstances. Nevertheless, I crossed the border and went back to Berlin. I had no clothes, underwear, or even the barest essentials for the eventuality of permanent emigration. In Berlin my friends thought I was insane (that was not the first time!). Giving my full name, I registered in a hotel for transients. This seemed the safest thing to do. An Austrian, correctly registered under his full name in a transient hotel, with his passport deposited at the desk, could not be anything but a harmless foreigner who did not know his way around. I sent an innocuous-looking person to my apartment to ascertain whether I could still go there and fetch my clothes. I had heard that the SA had been there again and taken a watch and some books, among them the *Kamasutra* (the manual of Indian love techniques) and one with Japanese woodcuts. This was precisely in line with my diagnosis of the psychic roots of the enthusiasm engendered by National Socialism. The maid had innocently reported the theft to the police and some of the articles were returned. One evening, after dark, I stole into my apartment and packed some clothes. The furniture, library, and car had to remain behind. An invaluable card catalogue and archives with numerous manuscripts had already been taken to safety in various regions of Germany, by friends, prior to my first flight. I was able to have acquaintances send my library to Copenhagen several months later. I stayed on for a few days but could not locate anyone. Nonpolitical acquaintances showed me clearly—although in a friendly manner—that they did not wish any embarrassment. Thus I left for Vienna with only a few marks in my pocket. There I was able to resume my medical practice with no difficulty. Strictly speaking, I was not an "emigrant."

In Vienna the situation was not especially promising. After three years of absence I no longer had contacts and it was necessary to establish myself anew. I lived with friends who were exceptionally helpful but who obviously had no proper perspective on the events in Germany. "Something like that could never happen in Austria." "It would be a shame to leave without a struggle." "In Austria things are making headway." "A revolutionary division of the Schutzbund has just been organized within the Social Democrat Party." "One can learn something from the events in Germany." "The Austrians will defeat Fascism." No one anticipated February 1934, and even less March 1938. Since I did not wish to discourage them, I remained silent, although I did not foresee victory in the near future. The student organization of the Austrian Socialist Party invited me to give a lecture on Fascism. I explained all I knew about it as well as I could, but did not draw any consequences for politics; this could have served no purpose. It was too deep a matter to be understood and mastered practically in a short time, although everyone understood the contradiction within social development. When several friends who were aware of the political consequences asked me to explain them, I declined—not because the police were present, but rather because I refused to rattle off phrases without the prospect of accomplishing anything by doing so. Many illusions about politics, the nature of a party, and the "class struggle" would have to be eliminated before sex-politics and mass psychology could be taken seriously.[14]

[14] 1952: These illusions are still widespread in America.

Early in the summer of 1938, Freud, robbed of his possessions by the SA, had to leave Vienna and flee to London. Most other Viennese psychoanalysts also became homeless emigrants. They had been "apolitical scientists" who did not wish to mix politics and science.

In January 1932, Freud, as editor of the psychoanalytic journal, had attached a prefatory note to my paper on masochism, in which I clinically disproved the death-instinct theory. Thanks to the efforts of German Socialist psychoanalysts, this note was not published. It had read: "Special circumstances constrain the editor, at this point, to remind the reader of otherwise self-evident facts, namely that this journal allows every author who entrusts it with a manuscript for publication the full right of freedom to express his opinions—within the context of psychoanalysis—and does not assume any responsibility for its contents. In the case of Dr. Reich, however, the reader must be informed that said author is a member of the Bolshevist Party. Now, it is known that Bolshevism places restrictions on the freedom of scientific research, similar to those of the Church. Obedience to the party demands that everything be rejected which contradicts the prerequisites of its own doctrine of salvation. It is left to the option of our readers to clear the author of this paper of such suspicions. The editor would have been moved to the same comment had he been presented with a manuscript written by a member of the Society of Jesus."

I knew that Freud's remarks on the Communist Party were correct, but I also knew he was avoiding the same question as the Communists and was, additionally, undertaking nothing against the bureaucratization of the IPV.[15] To take such action one must first have suffered under the bureaucracy one wishes to overcome. I also did not wish to obscure the fact that I had learned much among the Communists, as well as in all other organizations, about evaluating social existence. Hence I refused to rescind my article, or even revise it to avoid embarrassment. Finally it was decided to have Bernfeld write a counter-paper, which was

[15] Internationale Psychoanalytische Vereinigung (International Psychoanalytic Association—IPA). —*Trans.*

published in the journal, together with my article on masochism. Freud's foreword was omitted. Bernfeld did himself great harm with his rejoinder, but my article was universally well received. However, factual ties and organizational ties are two different things. This too is a part of social psychiatry: *An individual's organizational ties are injurious to his factual convictions when the organization begins to contradict the facts.* In my reply to the editors of the journal, I maintained that:

1. My criticism of the death instinct has no relevance to any party and is *clinically* based.

2. I was at complete liberty to give courses on psychoanalytic psychology within the party. In contrast, I had been ordered by the president of the Berlin Psychoanalytic Association to refrain from introducing sociological topics in the professional organization.

3. The direction of my analytic research involved certain social consequences. The death-instinct theory had been formulated to avoid these same consequences. I had already been critical of this theory at a time when I was not yet politically active.

4. Restrictions such as this had never been placed on the philosophically cumbersome articles by the Rev. Pfister or the metaphysician Kolnai. Hence the judgment against my article was biased.

5. My refutation of the death-instinct theory had never been treated factually. The issue was still open.

Eitingon, president of the Association, had already asked me in October 1932 not to admit any candidates to my technical seminar, which was attended by approximately twenty practicing Berlin psychoanalysts. I rejected this unjustified request and he vetoed my election to membership in the Berlin Training Institute. Nevertheless, I gave lectures at the Institute which were very well attended.

In January 1933, I contracted with the Psychoanalytischer Verlag to publish my book *Character Analysis*. When I arrived in Vienna, the director of the house told me that it had been necessary to cancel the contract due to the political situation. Despite my protest, the decision remained unchanged. Since the galley proofs had already been run off, the book could only be "published by the author" and then taken on commission by the IPA publishing house. I had prepaid the printing costs. The action was meant to decrease the influence of my book. They wanted no embarrassment through the use of my name, and this organization of which I was still a member in good standing showed no consideration for my work, my expenditures, or my situation. I could only maintain the principles expressed in my letter of March 17, 1933:

1. The political reaction cloaks psychoanalysis with the term "cultural Bolshevism," and justly so, because the science of analysis endangers the existence of Fascist ideology. The sociological and cultural-political character of psychoanalysis can be neither denied nor concealed. This could only harm scientific work, but could never prevent reactionary political powers from recognizing danger wherever it appears.

2. The cultural-political character of psychoanalysis, in addition to its medical value, has been admitted by every professional organization. Any concealment of this fact is senseless self-sacrifice. A strong group of psychoanalysts exists which is willing to continue the cultural-political struggle. The existence of this group will remain politically embarrassing regardless of whether it is active within or outside of the IPA.

3. In this struggle, psychoanalysis can only side with the worker.[16] It is not the personal existence of analysts which must be secured at all cost, but rather psychoanalysis itself, as a research method. It recognizes but *one* criterion, namely progressive social movement, which, in Germany, is currently paying for its lessons in blood. "The historical process will by no means end with Hitler. If proof of the historical justification of the existence of psychoanalysis and of its sociological function was ever necessary, the current phase of development must furnish it."

I knew that the letter would change nothing, but wished nevertheless to separate myself at all cost from the behavior of

[16] Within the context of work democracy, "worker" means anyone who does *life-important* work, and "Fascist" denotes *any* dictatorial power based on mystical and helpless attitudes in people. It thus includes red Fascism.

Irrationalism in Politics and Society

the profession. No one could know what fate would bring. I harmed myself personally in doing this. My letter could not help but create guilty consciences and thus cause irritation. But this could not be avoided.

The letter did not fail to produce results. Following the lecture which I delivered to Socialist students, I received a letter from the chairman of the Vienna Psychoanalytic Association. Politely but laconically, he demanded that I give no further lectures for Socialist or Communist organizations. This gentleman was a member of the Austrian Social Democratic Party. It always happened that way. For a long while the Social Democrats retarded the progress of decent work, until the advance of Fascism finished off the task. I replied that I was unable to accept this demand unconditionally, but would in any case consult the board of directors. Thereupon I was informed by telephone that my promise to consult with the board was not sufficient and that it was incumbent upon me to agree. In reply to my request for written confirmation, the chairman explained that he had made the request at the suggestion of Freud. I repeated that I could not accept this restriction, whereupon he forbade me to participate in the Association's meetings. He told my wife that if he were in my position he would long since have left the Association. I suggested a consultation with the Vienna executive committee of the IPA, which took place on April 21, 1933. In this meeting I proposed to refrain from all publishing and lecturing activities until the IPA had officially come to a decision as to whether or not my views were compatible with my membership. Until then it had not taken an official stand and worked against me only from behind the scenes. Thus I hoped at least to clarify my position before the profession. This move could not be avoided, and five years later it was shown to have been correct.

For a long time, I had been aware of the fact that my views were my own, although psychoanalysts claimed them as analytic theory while omitting the most significant aspects. This had to be avoided under all circumstances, because the IPA was not willing to bear the consequences. If my opinion was correct that psychoanalysis, by virtue of its very nature, would necessarily be opposed by political reaction, then I had to be allowed complete freedom to express myself. However, if the organization did not wish to identify itself with my viewpoint, then I wanted to bear full responsibility for the issue entirely alone. Anna Freud remarked during the meeting that the tide was against me, but that one could not know whether it would someday turn. For the moment, nothing could be done. The secretariat was to inform me of the organization's position. The information never arrived and the situation remained the same until the termination of my membership. I had not been able to obtain a single official comment. They did not wish to give up, altogether, the possibility of winning laurels as a result of this philosophical conflict, and I was determined not to give them to anyone if the burden of practical responsibility and sacrifice lay on my shoulders.

Embarrassing events accumulated. A young physician from Copenhagen had come to me in Vienna for training. As was the custom, he also visited several prominent colleagues. They advised him not to work with me; I was a Marxist and my pupils would, under certain conditions, not be recognized. Bernfeld, a "Marxist," emphasized this particularly. But the physician came to me in spite of this and is a practicing vegetotherapist today. It was his idea that I come to Copenhagen. He said there were several candidates for analytic training there. This impressed me as being a good solution, so I requested information from Copenhagen on a work permit, and asked Eitingon, the director of the training committee, whether my teaching in Copenhagen would be recognized. His reply was quite contorted and stated that, due to the differences in opinion, my candidates were to be subjected to stricter examination. Leunbach wrote that they were not willing to grant me permission to work because of my lectures. However, I could remain there for six months. Since the agitation about me in Vienna was making the situation distasteful, I decided to go to Copenhagen in any case. Thus it was not the police or a lack of work which caused my emigration from Austria, but my professional colleagues. I knew that Anna Freud, secretary of the IPA, secretly sided with me because she valued my efforts. I wrote her several times but she did not wish to become involved

Irrationalism in Politics and Society

—nor did anyone else in those days. There I stood, without means or a home, and in a highly precarious position professionally. In addition, it had been necessary to borrow money to cover the printing costs of *Character Analysis*. I had almost decided to withhold it, but the publishers convinced me that it absolutely had to appear. For years to come it safeguarded my existence.

I borrowed the money for the journey to Copenhagen and left Vienna on April 30. My papers were in order; there were no difficulties. I traveled via Poland on a freighter. On the first of May I arrived in Copenhagen, where I registered at a hotel. There had already been numerous inquiries and on the following day a number of people requested appointments for treatment. It was not possible to handle this situation at the hotel, and after two days I rented a small apartment and began to work. I particularly wanted to publish *The Mass Psychology of Fascism*. The manuscript needed only to be prepared for the printer, but I was forced to wait until I had earned enough money to finance the printing. Several German emigrants helped me to transfer my Verlag für Sexualpolitik to Copenhagen. Meanwhile, *Character Analysis* was published in Vienna. The book on Fascism appeared in August. Two pupils from Berlin joined me and several others registered in Copenhagen. I was even able to provide for a pupil who later let me down horribly.

I had contacted the Danish Communist Party because emigrants with their wives and children were starving in the streets. I organized contributions from friends, but there were simply too many in need. The Rote Hilfe only supported those who had been recommended by the party in Germany, and gave no help to the others. I began to encounter increasing numbers of desperately shabby individuals. One day, while taking a walk on the Lange Linie, I saw a young man, completely destitute, sitting on a bench, half starved, without money, a place to stay, or hope. He was considering drowning himself. I took him home and supported him for a while. Some time later he wrote a marvelous novel about vagabonds, which I published.

I went to the Danish party and demanded to see the German

representative, but the Danish party official refused to put me in touch with him. I declared that I would not leave the premises under any circumstances until he had accommodated me. He wanted to usher me out, but I protested in such forceful terms that a second party official had to come in and quiet things down. They said I would receive information the next day, which I did.

I met the representative of the German party in the following fashion: In great secrecy they led me into a room. There sat a heavyset man with a stern face who told me to take a seat. He inquired whether I had "party permission" to leave Germany and why I had made such a scene with the Danes. This was a breach of discipline, he said, and merited suspension. He spoke in a strict, overbearing manner. Suddenly I shouted at him to stop being such a bureaucrat and then I would talk with him. I told him to behave decently. Immediately he changed his tone—cowards that bureaucrats are—and became cordial. I did not trust the fellow and later discovered that he was one of the lowest types. They had nothing to say, had driven a party with lofty goals into the ground, and then impertinently claimed to be the future leaders of Germany. The man explained that the information from the Danish party official was correct and that the German party had "offices everywhere to issue party border passes." This was too ridiculous. I declared that it was a lie and that the emigrants had to be cared for *immediately* regardless of whether they were recognized by the party or not. They could not be allowed to starve. I felt it would be time enough later to see what developed. He was not willing to accept this, so I threatened to raise hell if it were not done. He promised to do whatever he could, as scandals had to be avoided at that time.

I knew their mentality. The results of my protest were not particularly profound, but I did hear that more was being done for the refugees. However, my actions gained me the deep hatred of the Danish Communist bureaucrats. [Since then, the red Fascists have slandered my work wherever they could—in Norway, England, the United States, etc.]

I soon experienced the irrationalism of politics. The German "emigrant representative" requested the manuscript of *The Mass*

Psychology of Fascism. The first sentence of the book read: "The German working class has suffered severe defeat." I was called to account for this single, opening sentence. The Comintern resolutions during those months had stated that the German working class had not suffered defeat. The catastrophe in Germany was "merely a transitory defeat in the course of revolutionary progress." An eighteen-year-old mechanic's helper who had just left Germany told me that the Communists still remaining behind had told him that all this was only an interruption, and that the Hitler era would not last six months. Completely convinced, he expected to return in a few weeks.

My expulsion from the Comintern occurred as follows: Prior to my arrival in Copenhagen, the Communist journal of Danish intellectuals, *Plan,* had published my essay "Wohin führt die Nackterziehung?"[17] which had originally appeared in 1927 in the journal *Psychoanalytische Pädagogische Zeitschrift,* and had been translated and published with my permission. The Danish Minister of Justice, Mr. Zahle, was a very ascetic gentleman whose daughters were somewhat less abstemious. For this reason, he vehemently despised everything tinged with the terms "sexual enlightenment," "psychoanalysis," etc. He had had great difficulties with his children, and consequently had the editor of the journal accused of pornography. As usual, the indictment was based on words which were not quite correctly used. In this case it was the word *Wipfi.*[18] The translator had not taken into consideration that, for the layman, sexology is dangerously close to pornography and had translated one or two passages carelessly. In response to an inquiry by *Extrabladet,* I truthfully stated that although the translation did not correspond precisely to my original manuscript, there could be no question of pornography and that the indictment was a serious error. The large magazine *Kulturkampf* published a detailed article by me entitled "Was ist Pornographie?" In a second article I expressly took up the cause of the indicted editor. He was sentenced to serve forty days.

---

[17] "Where Will the Trend toward Nudity in Education Lead?" (Included in *The Sexual Revolution*) —*Trans.*
[18] A German diminutive for penis, used with children. —*Trans.*

Following this, the Danish Communist Party declared that I had betrayed the editor and deserted him. A small Moscow-type trial was set in motion. No one could comment on the issue itself because no one was in the habit of advocating any subject.

On November 21, 1933, the following article was printed by *Arbeiterblad*,[19] with a large spread:

COMMUNIST PARTY
SECRETARIAT OF THE CENTRAL COMMITTEE

Exclusion from the Communist Party of Denmark

In agreement with the Central Committee of the Communist Party of Germany [which had ceased to exist in March], we announce that Dr. Wilhelm Reich has been excluded from the Danish Communist Party [of which I was never a member]. The reasons for this include: His un-Communist and anti-party behavior in a succession of cases; his publication of a counterrevolutionary book; his establishment of a publishing house without party sanction, and additionally, his statement, published by the Danish government press, wherein he renounces his own article published in *Plan*, thus facilitating official and police action against the editor of said *Plan*.

Dr. Reich lives in Denmark and, as the newspapers show, has been granted an immigration visa. [The visa had just been canceled at that time.]

The Party Secretariat

On December 1, 1933, a lengthy review of *The Mass Psychology of Fascism* was published in *Arbeiterblad*. It contained the same statements I had heard in the discussions in Berlin, almost word for word. Among others, the following were added:

> With the cowardice that appears to be the most predominant trait of the author (we recall his behavior in the *Plan* affair), he attempts to obscure the orientation of this book, which in reality constitutes an attack on revolutionary politics. Only a few passages reveal the facts and refer to "the Communist parties" by name—otherwise Reich pre-

[19] *Workers' Newspaper.* —*Trans.*

Irrationalism in Politics and Society 201

fers to aim his blows at a concept he himself has created, namely "vulgar Marxists." . . . Sexuality is the driving force of the human psyche,—in capitalism no normal sexual life exists at all. . . . Reich and his followers will, of course, deny that which is most certain, namely that they are attempting to break down the former basis of Marxist propaganda. However, the book represents, objectively, such serious undermining of the doctrines of Communist propaganda that it must be termed counterrevolutionary. It is twice as dangerous because there is not a trace of proof that Reich's idea would, in reality, reinforce the Communist struggle, even as a supplement. When he cites as proof the interest with which his concepts were greeted by women, children, and the bourgeoisie, it can only be termed naïveté. Every form of discussion and enlightenment pertaining to sex awakens the interest of politically uneducated elements precisely because of capitalistic education!

I did not understand how I could have belonged to this party for so long; but I did understand that the sharp reactionary position toward sexuality it now maintained was prompted by the need for a clear answer demanded by the times, an answer the party was unable to supply. If one reads the above statements carefully, the question arises as to what function this party organization had assumed in the world, since it had completely forgotten to whom it owed its existence.

[SO: The manner in which WR committed grave mistakes in this official break with the red Fascists in 1933 should be carefully observed.
1. He did not say that he had never belonged to the Danish Communist Party and therefore could not be excluded from it. (The German Communist Party had ceased to exist in March 1933.)
2. He did not immediately state publicly that:
    a. the red Fascists had no right whatsoever to control the publishing house of his Institute;
    b. the red Fascists plainly lied when they claimed that he had renounced his article in *Plan;*

c. they lied again when they wrote that he had been given permission to stay in Denmark, thereby insinuating that this was a reward for his betrayal of the editor of *Plan*. His visa had been withdrawn precisely at that time. Here, as he had done before and would do often again, WR manifested one of his most serious weaknesses seen from a militant point of view. He let the plague talk and act without contradicting it, in spite of the existence of clear evidence that the pestilent character was lying, cheating the public, falsifying records, turning upside down and distorting right and left what was actually the truth. He did not deny such public statements simply because he felt himself above such filth. He did not deny them because he was convinced that the truth would sooner or later win out spontaneously, exactly as so many American liberals believe today, thus allowing the politicking scoundrel to go on doing his mischief unopposed. WR also had too much practical work to do, while the political scoundrel did nothing but pestilent politicking. It is this same scoundrel who attacked in Korea, 1950, and then accused the gullible American of being the attacker.]

On April 13, 1935, the following notices were published in the *Reichsgesetzblatt*:[20]

Number 213—April 13, 1935

In accordance with the VO[21] of February 4, 1933, the publications *Was ist Klassenbewusstsein*[22] by Ernst Parell,[23] *Dialektischer Materialismus und Psychoanalyse*,[24] by Wilhelm Reich, Volumes 1 and 2 of the political-psychological series which were published by the Verlag für Sexualpolitik (Copenhagen, Prague, Zurich), as well as all other subsequent publications in this same series, are herewith to be con-

[20] *Official State Information Sheet.* —Trans.
[21] Volksordnung (People's Order). —Trans.
[22] *What Is Class-Consciousness?* —Trans.
[23] A pseudonym for Wilhelm Reich—ed.
[24] *Dialectical Materialism and Psychoanalysis.* —Trans.

Irrationalism in Politics and Society

fiscated by the police and withdrawn from circulation, as the works are liable to endanger public security and order. 41230/35 II 2B 1. Berlin,

April 9, 1935   Gestapo

Number 2146—May 7, 1935

In accordance with the VO of the President of the Republic, of February 28, 1933, the distribution of all foreign publications of the political-psychological series of Sexpol (Verlag für Sexualpolitik, Copenhagen, Denmark; Prague, Czechoslovakia; Zurich, Switzerland) has been prohibited within Germany until further notice. III P 3952/P 53. Berlin, May 6, 1935 RMdj

On January 7, 1934, the following article appeared in the Comintern organ in Prague, *Der Gegenangriff*:

The Results of Association Mongering

. . . In addition to overworked Freudian slogans which are exemplified in National Socialism but could also be equally well applied to all other forms of cultural reaction, we find reiterated confirmation of two facts which are already well known to us: first, that Hitler's transitory success has engulfed numerous members of the petty bourgeoisie, among whom there are also individuals—like Reich—who consider themselves "Communists"; second, that there are certain natural-scientific half-truths which have already been dogmatized within science in the direction of mysticism. When these are applied to social conditions, they assume the sectarian character typical of the propagation of decadent bourgeois phenomena within the workers' movement since the days of the deceased Eugen Dühring. In this they fall into the closest proximity to Fascism. . . .

[According to Reich] the workers' movement sinned by placing the material need of the exploited in the center of its propaganda, while neglecting the "central issue on the cultural front, namely the question of sexuality." But, again according to Reich, one only wins the already leftist industrial proletariat with economic and political solutions. The indifferent masses are to be won over through the demonstration of their sexual need and through the description of a "cultural-bolshevistic" state of unrestricted freedom. We understand very well that bourgeois disintegration is the psychological source of this, but its propagation by Reich, a "Communist," plays perfectly into the hand of Hitler's propaganda. In all earnestness, we are told that Christian workers are best won—as a detailed example illustrates —through proof that their Church is an organization founded for the purpose of blocking their sexuality.

Shortly before this, the journal *Weltbühne* had published a very favorable article on the book. That was embarrassing! This journal, published by intellectuals dependent upon the Comintern, later reversed its position completely. Meanwhile, the first edition of the book was sold out and a second had to be printed. I heard that it was circulating widely in Germany and was highly regarded. I have letters from underground workers in which they expressed complete understanding and appreciation. The book is still being bought today, six years after the catastrophe. But who still reads the Comintern resolutions of that era? Who even read them at the time? This is directed against those individuals who are incapable of looking beyond the present and their immediate environment and who are constantly tied to the apron strings of their organization. Organizations come and go; valid concepts have a development and a future. Today *The Mass Psychology of Fascism* is a recognized book in the struggle against all forms of dictatorship.

Against my better judgment, I myself clung fast to the organization to which I had belonged and for which I had fought. The party became my second home, and it becomes a second home for all who renounce bourgeois security in favor of the struggle for a better future. For many, it becomes the *only* home because they lose sight of the goal beyond. This destroys the organization and transforms it into an apparatus. I clarified these matters for myself in the following way:

I did not doubt for one moment the correctness of the great thoughts and deeds of the founders of the Socialist movement. Every phase of my work, every experience had confirmed their theories. And still the events of almost a decade showed a deep contradiction which I could not resolve, namely the contradiction between the goal and the reality of the movement leading to that goal. Was the goal still valid at all? If so, why was the movement in such contradiction to it? If not, why was it used to justify every action of its representatives? Brandler, the former leader of the German Communist Party, paid me a visit in Copenhagen. We discussed the disaster for hours. Everything he said was correct, in principle; but then why was Hitler the ruler in Germany and not this sympathetically human, intelligent man whose views were so very applicable to the problems of society? Trotsky was also correct, in principle; but why was Stalin in power in the Soviet Union and not he? Was I also to become a furious antagonist of the Communist Party? In principle, I too was correct, and not the inhuman and problematic bureaucrats! Why were they able to lean on powerful organizational support, and not I? *What is the essence of human organization?* Not one had kept its promises to date, neither the great Christian world-community, nor the first or second Socialist International, and now also not the third. All of them had betrayed their objectives and become instruments of suppression. It was obvious that there was no sense in founding a new organization to remove the misery of the old. Trotsky's fourth International seemed to me to have been stillborn and senseless. The nature of organization itself seemed puzzling. Soon I would be able to include the organization of psychoanalysts as well. A number of years had to pass before I felt ready to grasp this enigma.

[1950: Basic Tenets on Red Fascism:

1. Communism in its present form as red Fascism is not a political party like other political parties. It is *organized emotional plague.*

2. This politically organized and militarily armed emotional plague uses conspiracy and spying in all forms in order to destroy human happiness and well-being, just as does every biopath. It is not, as is usually assumed, a political conspiracy to achieve certain rational social ends, as in 1918.

3. If you ask a Liberal or a Socialist or a Republican what his social beliefs are, he will tell you frankly. The red Fascist will not tell you what he is, who he is, what he wants. This proves that hiding is his basic characteristic. Only people who hide by

way of their character structure will operate in and for the Communist Party. It is conspiracy and hiding for its own sake and not a tool to achieve rational ends. To believe otherwise will only lead to disaster.

4. As a special form of the emotional plague, red Fascism uses its basic characterological tool, hiding ("iron curtain"), to exploit the identical pathological attitudes in ordinary people. Thus, the politically organized EP uses the unorganized EP to gratify its morbid needs. Political aims are secondary and are primarily subterfuges for biopathic activities. Proof: The political ends are shifted according to the "political," i.e. emotional plague, need to hide and cause trouble from ambush.

5. The hiding, conspiring, conniving are there *before* any political goals are conceived to veil them.

6. The sole objective of the conspiring is power with no particular social ends. Subjugation of people's lives is not intended, but it is a necessary and automatic result of the lack of rationality in the organization and of the existence of the emotional plague.

7. The organized EP relies upon and uses consistently what is worst in human nature, while it slanders and tries to destroy all that threatens its existence. A fact to the EP is only a matter of convenience; it does not count in itself. Accordingly, there is no respect for facts. Truth is used only to serve a certain line of procedure or to maintain the existence of the emotional filth. It will be discarded as soon as it threatens or even contradicts such ends. This attitude toward fact and truth, history and human welfare, is not specifically a characteristic of red Fascism. It is typical of all politics. Red Fascism differs from other forms of politics in that it eliminates all checks and controls over the abuse of power, thereby enabling the nuisance politician to achieve utmost power. To believe that "peace negotiations" are meant as such is disastrous; they may or they may not be, according to the expediency of the moment. Red Fascism is a power machine using the principle of lie or truth, fact or distortion of fact, honesty or dishonesty, always to the end of conspiracy and abuse.

8. No one can ever hope to excel the pestilent character in

lying and underhanded tactics. Espionage and counterespionage may have their place in present-day social administration. They will never solve the problem of social pathology. Using truth in human affairs will serve to overcome the seemingly unsolvable entanglement created by spying and counterspying. It will also be constructive in establishing a foundation for life-positive human actions.]

Although I had experienced enough of the power of state organizations, in Denmark I saw one of their basic principles clearly for the first time: Representatives of various public interests who are supposedly elected by the common people, enjoy excessive power in their capacity as agents of the state—an illusional but very effective power. The same individuals who elect officials to represent their cause, tacitly invest these officials with power against themselves. In this instance it was demonstrated through a Minister of Justice and two psychiatrists. A Minister of Justice is an individual whom society (and a social-democratically ruled society at that) has invested with the task of safeguarding justice. Psychiatrists are individuals whom society has selected to protect the mental health of the populace. This is the way justice is upheld and health protected:

I had been asked to practice psychoanalysis in Denmark. One of the first persons I saw was a young girl suffering from hysteria. She had already made numerous suicide attempts and now desired treatment from me because no one else had been able to help her. I did not accept her as a patient. However, she visited me again and threatened suicide, so I promised to keep her under observation for four weeks and then to give her my opinion. After the four-week period, in which she progressed well, I discontinued seeing her and advised her to wait until one of my Danish pupils was advanced enough to treat her. She seemed to agree to this. Several days later I heard that she had been placed in a psychiatric ward because of a suicide attempt. She had done this because she *wanted* treatment and was not able to get it. As is customary in such cases, the psychiatrists claimed that this was "the result of treatment" and reported the case to the police, to whom I wrote a detailed letter of explanation. Those very psychiatrists were to decide upon my further activities. The Health Department declared officially that my request for an extension of my residence permit was to be denied. Numerous important personages refused to subscribe to this nonsense, but the Minister of Justice connected the issue with the pornography affair. A meeting of doctors and educators was held and no one wanted me to yield, as they were all interested in my work. However, the bureaucratic machinery won the battle. Since my visa was not extended, I was compelled to leave Denmark. Even the Chief of Police, who was personally deeply interested, declared that nothing could be done. That is apparatus!

I wrote the following letter to the psychiatrists, Clemensen and Schröder:

October 20, 1933

Dr. Wilhelm Reich
Stockholm
Vanadisvägen 42

Professor Schröder and Dr. Clemensen
Copenhagen
Psychiatric Clinic, Commune Hospital

It was your clinic from which a report to the police was made stating that I was supposed to have practiced medicine in Copenhagen. I clarified the case and your misunderstanding of it, as well as your lack of psychoanalytic knowledge, by proving I was unable to cope in any other manner with a hysterical woman who was pressing me. In spite of this, you were able to prevent my stay in Denmark from being extended. In the meantime, you surely will have realized that your actions were contrary to the ethical principles which unite the medical profession throughout the world, and that these actions stemmed from a hatred of psychoanalysis, with which you are completely unacquainted, and from other obvious motives which cannot be mentioned here. You have harmed neither me nor the psychoanalytic movement. You have, however, promoted charlatanism in Denmark and robbed a number of individuals who were seriously interested in and dedicated to science, of the opportunity to acquire knowledge and a scientific technique which could shed a beam of light into the darkness surrounding psychiatry, my professional field. You may pride yourself on having been the first to have undertaken such action against psychoanalysis. The history of science and its struggles will record this as a minute curiosity, and otherwise silently pass it by. It is not worthwhile for us to linger on this subject when even clinical psychiatrists like Bleuler, Pötzl, and Schilder find it difficult to reconcile themselves to your tactics.

Usually, the average conservative psychiatrist is simply a policeman who must guard the mentally ill and also make sure that no reasonable sexological psychiatrist comes too close to them. The actions of these individuals extended far beyond the confines of Denmark, their effect maintained by the law of inertia, as it were. Hence I was provided an example, in my own life, of what occurs when one is caught in the nets of formal bureaucracy.

For the moment, I took leave of my pupils and arranged to continue with them after the New Year (four weeks hence) in Malmö, Sweden, across the sound from Copenhagen. They wanted to hire a boat and allow it to drift into no-man's-land, outside the three-mile limit, in order to continue their studies. And this despite the fact that Freud, in reply to an inquiry, had expressly stated that he had not sent me to Denmark as a teacher, because of my "communistic creed." Thus "logical arguments" accumulated. In Freud's eyes I was a Communist; to the Communists, I was a Freudian. In other words, I was "dangerous." I journeyed to London, not without arousing suspicion at the border (a German!). They were about to make difficulties, but when I explained that I intended to have my car sent after me so that I could tour Europe in the spring, they became friendly. My car was of inestimable value in the future as well.

The analysts who most feared my work lived in London, so it was impossible to settle there. Still, I wished to speak with Jones, the president of the IPA. In Copenhagen—which I had been forced to leave—there remained, as highly respectable representatives of the analytic discipline, the philosopher Neesgard, an outsider and a so-called "wild analyst," and one depth psychologist especially revered among doctors, a gentleman who had spent fourteen days with Groddeck. In London, I met pupils from Berlin and also made my first personal acquaintance with Malinowski. We immediately had a good rapport. He had recommended my book *The Invasion of Compulsory Sex-Morality* in America and thought highly of it, saying that I was the only one whose understanding of his book *The Sexual Life of Savages* had been productive. I felt comfortable among his group of pupils; there was a simple camaraderie. I felt less at home at an ethnologists' meeting where a lecture was given on something concerning the Middle Ages. On this occasion, with no previous warning, Malinowski, after having spoken himself, announced that his friend Reich now had something to say. (We had actually become friends, although I could have clouted him for calling on me unexpectedly.) Since I was trapped, I had no alternative but to speak—and in English at that. I stated what I had just been thinking on the topic at the time and, to my surprise, it went well. I can no longer recall what I said, but Malinowski was satisfied.

The English psychoanalytic group was odd. I attended one meeting, which was conducted with rigid formality. In Jones's home, a meeting with the members of the board of directors was held at which I explained my current views. In *principle,* there was general agreement, especially with the social origin of neurosis, but actually they wanted nothing to do with it. Politics and science, they said, did not belong together. However, despite all my insight, I still did not quite comprehend why research on the social origins of neurosis should be considered "politics." Jones was cordial as usual, but always the gentleman—in other words, no involvement at any cost. Still, he declared that he would vehemently oppose my exclusion from the IPA. I was unaware at the time that my exclusion was already a settled matter, of which Jones must have been cognizant. He also knew of my relationship with Malinowski, who was the first to reject the biological nature of child-parent conflicts and replace it with a sociological interpretation based on his investigation of matriarchal tribes. In opposition to this, Jones had stated years before, in his caustic polemics against Malinowski, that the Oedipus complex had no connection with sociology and was the universal *"fons et origo."* It was also the English group of the IPA which contended that neurotic anxiety in children was biologically based in the weakness of the child's ego as it struggled against the instincts. That was correct thinking for a society which makes children ill and "capable of culture" at the age of six months through strict toilet training.

At this time I was occupied with plans for experimental work. I intended either to confirm or to refute my earlier idea of the electrical nature of the orgasm. In Copenhagen, on the basis of known physiological facts, I had formulated in writing the hypothesis that the orgasm was an electrical discharge. Now I wanted to hear the opinion of a physiologist. I visited Wright, director of an institute at the University of London. When I asked him about the available technical possibilities for conducting electrical charges from the skin and measuring them, he replied, "You are crazy! That's impossible!" He was as unaware as I of the fact that there were stacks of research papers on the Tarchanoff phenomenon in scientific archives. I assumed his experiments pertained only to muscle contractions.

With the exception of Malinowski, everyone I met impressed me as being helpless in the face of events. This atmosphere became universal only after the "Munich Peace" in 1938. People sensed the baseness, the injustice, the political fiasco and human insanity in which they had become ensnared. A paralyzing passivity immobilized even the young Communists who had emigrated to London. All that remained of the grand gesticulations and rhetoric was a lack of comprehension of events.

I went to Paris, where several leading functionaries visited me in my hotel. They were members of the Trotsky party and the SAP (Socialist Party of Germany), which were still associated at that time. All of them had read my *Mass Psychology of Fascism* and were in agreement with my views—theoretically! A few questions sufficed to show me that they were willing to admit the role of irrationalism in politics but refused to formulate the question in practical terms. They agreed that social sexual suppression enslaves and dulls people and thus counteracts rebellion against suppression in general, but the practical answer offered by sex-politics was foreign to them. As human beings they were enthusiastic, but as "politicians" they were completely removed. For the first time I experienced the sharp contradiction between the *human being* and the *functionary* in politicians. It was evident that they wished to enlist me in the party organization, but at the time I was undecided as to the value of a new party connection and a vague feeling restrained me from committing myself.

I attended several meetings of German emigrants. Nothing seemed to have changed. The discussions on the "categories of class-consciousness" and the "role of the avant-garde" continued blithely. I shuddered when I asked myself what kind of psychic structure could experience Hitler in 1933 and not feel that these scholastic discussions were unthinkable. In one of these conversations I interjected an innocuous question: could anyone name five concrete elements of "class consciousness"? One man mentioned "hunger" and that was the extent of the response. After returning to my hotel, I drafted an outline for an article entitled "What Is Class Consciousness?" Two weeks later, in the Tyrol, I finished it, and it was subsequently published under the pseudonym Ernst Parell. It dealt with the structural contradiction within the mass individual, the necessity for mass politics to be oriented toward needs instead of categories, and related experiences from sex-political work in Germany. In this brochure, I assumed a position in favor of the Communist movement, but by then I was already against the Communist apparatus. I felt I belonged to the party, but my position was that of a mistreated and misunderstood member in opposition. The consequences of criticizing the "party" and "politics" in general had not yet been felt. Thus I sought a new social revolutionary organization which was willing to learn productive lessons from the catastrophe. Many of my political-psychological essays of that time were based on this. Further experiences were needed to free me from these illusions completely and to make me realize that the problem of human organization per se was at issue and not merely that of a different organization fashioned after an old pattern. Reactionary developments in the Soviet Union became clearly

Irrationalism in Politics and Society 213

visible only in 1934. Today I know that, in addition to these factual motives, a deep fear of having no organization, i.e. being without a home, restrained me. More than a decade of invested energy and effort in a political organization cannot be relinquished overnight. The Soviet Union still existed as an ideological prop, but this had long since ceased to be a reality. I enjoyed the atmosphere of Paris for a few more days and then left for Basel. Max Hodann had arrived there, having had the good fortune to escape after spending six months in a concentration camp. We made plans for future work, but I noticed that he did not wish to commit himself and was even further removed from awareness of the current catastrophe than I. I told him I intended to publish a journal dealing with political psychology, and organizational collaboration with him seemed possible. But it did not materialize.

In Zurich, I visited Fritz Brupbacher. This sexologist, weathered by experience, never ceased to fascinate me. For decades he had lived through all the joys and sorrows of the workers' movement, and his book *Vierzig Jahre Ketzer*,[25] which was published two years later, is a brilliant account of pettiness in that movement. The conclusion, however, spells resignation; Brupbacher had lost all hope. I countered this by explaining that science had by no means spoken its last word and that, essentially, retrograde development was impossible. Although I did agree with his criticism, the question remained whether or not we would live to see the outcome.

In the Tyrol, I visited my children and former wife after seven months of separation. There were no signs of the miserable events and human reactions which would devastate our lives less than half a year later. In Vienna, six weeks prior to the catastrophe in February, everything was running its usual course. The Communists were preparing the revolution, the Social Democrats were making further concessions in the interests of democracy, and the political reaction made quiet progress while people took no further notice of "historical powers" and the "conflict of productive forces." They were simply depressed and hungry, had

[25] *Forty Years of Heresy.* —Trans.

their family tribulations, and occasionally discussed politics. I wanted to travel to Sweden via Prague, where I hoped to meet friends. I was interested in the reaction of my acquaintances to the events of the times. Nowhere did I find a trace of willingness or determination to understand. There was nothing but illusion about the support to be expected from the Church, the Western powers, the German Army, and, naturally, from the increasing awareness of the factory workers. Belated efforts for a unified front between Communists and Social Democrats occupied current thought. The concept of a Socialist people's front, together with the bourgeoisie, had not yet been born. In conversation, I cautiously attempted to direct attention to irrational mass reactions. *Mass Psychology* had been well received but no hint of understanding could be discovered. *Talk of politics itself seemed to be a part of society's irrationalism.* This question now came to mind for the first time. I was not willing to recognize as valid the comfortable answer that politics was not supposed to interest scientists. Politics was a fact upon which everything depended; but what was it, really? How did it function? Thus I sought the rational core of leftist politics, using as a criterion the understanding of the adverse mass reaction in Germany. There *was* no understanding, and what is more, the question was successfully rejected.

I was very much surprised that a previously enthusiastic adherent of my work in Germany, who had even been an opponent of party leadership, had completely swung about. Later I understood that following one problem continuously becomes a severe mental strain and that a flight home to the party momentarily relieves that strain.

To spare myself the long detour across Poland, I wanted to travel through Germany. People said this was madness, but I felt that if no lists were kept at the borders, I might risk it. Actually, this was not justified because the possibility of being arrested existed everywhere. Nevertheless, when I was informed that no lists were being kept, I decided to try it. I was a bit uneasy at the border but nothing happened. In Berlin, I had a three-hour stopover. The scene on the streets was distressing. There were soldiers everywhere; people looked depressed; their movements were lethargic; there was nervous loitering. A female acquaintance had been notified of my arrival and we spent some time sitting in the first-class restaurant at the station. As I was boarding the train for Denmark, a man passed by who looked at me as if he were startled. I thought I recognized the face but could not place it and did not know whether I should greet him. Many Communists had turned Fascist. Entire Arbeiterwehr squads had enlisted in the SA. No comrades were left. What was conviction worth? *How was it possible to risk one's life for one idea for years and then, suddenly, risk it just as enthusiastically for another?* Allusions to corruption, lack of conviction, etc., were meaningless. Was not the nature of the parties in general a systematization of various contradictory sentiments? Was it not merely a case of world-views at war with each other, apparently in the interest of material things? But tens of thousands had changed from championing one view to advocating its opposite. Everything was in a state of flux, nothing seemed constant, and, meanwhile, old friends and acquaintances innocently continued to cling to organizations amidst the chaos. How to explain all this? Impossible! Perhaps I was only imagining it. The existence of classes, and class struggle, was beyond all doubt! But the individuals whose well-being was involved drifted from one side to the other, without direction, as though unconscious. I knew that on both sides of the German border there were workers in various fields who maintained illegal ties to party groups and risked their lives in doing so. However, when I read their reports in official publications, I was convinced that this was not reality but fantasy, or overvaluation of reality by individuals starved for social liberty. There is a deep schism between these individuals and the great masses; the two are unrelated. On the one side, there is death-defying loyalty and enthusiasm and, on the other, apathy and the capability of being influenced by the comfortable concepts of medieval ideology. How is this gap to be closed—and when? Is it solely dependent upon the self-sacrificing political activity of a group of revolutionary enthusiasts? Are the doubts of self-satisfied intellectuals in regard to this nerve-racking struggle justified? Certainly not! They have nothing with which to replace it. Where does the answer lie? Only the course of events itself will show—and only those who are free of illusion will be able to perceive it. For those who doubt because of fear, it will remain a mystery. The train passed through the familiar German countryside. Externally, nothing appeared to have changed, and yet, a continent was quaking.

In Trälleborg, I reached Swedish soil accompanied by Elsa Lindenberg, who had joined me in Berlin. I planned to settle at first in Malmö and then decide where to go. Malmö was not especially enticing. I could have stayed in London, but my German pupil Dr. Käthe Misch had told me that Jones usurped the work of all well-known colleagues. Furthermore, London was puritanical and I was living with my companion without benefit of a marriage license. Neither of us had the desire to marry. We were very happy together without a marriage certificate because we knew that it was more than a formality; it conferred the right to exploit and subjugate another human being. We did not want this. In addition, there were Danish pupils waiting for me, among whom I had a feeling of well-being. They had gradually begun to comprehend my work and were extremely loyal. Letters arrived from colleagues and former pupils in Berlin saying that Malmö, which was closer, was better than far-off London. In short, I preferred a state of dull asylum to a new career in a cosmopolitan city. Nor was I to regret my decision, although once again it seemed to the conventional mind a "mad" reaction.

A pupil from Copenhagen awaited me in Malmö. He had reserved two separate rooms for Elsa Lindenberg and me in a small hotel on the market square. As I entered the town I became afraid. It was common, everyday, ungrounded fear. Malmö is one of those little towns in which boredom breeds Fascism. I was to stay there for six months; at least it was better than a concentration camp. The hotel was horrible: stiff, cold, and full of older, unattached women who observed us with prying eyes. Several elderly, well-dressed gentlemen, some equipped with monocles and walking sticks, made civilized conversation with the ladies who were knitting. We ate supper quickly, each of us concealing our fear of the town and the hotel. It was exactly the opposite of the atmosphere in which we had previously been alone and able to breathe freely.

We clung to the letters we received and to our connections with people all over the globe. In October 1933 (two months earlier) the editor of *Weltbühne* had written a letter full of unshakable confidence and without the slightest insight into the future. Two years later he was mentally and politically destroyed. Several doctors in Copenhagen were interested in my work, but the neurological association canceled an invitation for me to give a lecture when it became known that the Minister of Justice was personally opposed to me. The *Zeitschrift für Sozialforschung*[26] in Frankfurt had been forced to take refuge in Paris and I reestablished contact with it there. The director of the University Institute for Psychology in Norway wrote me a letter referring a female pupil for treatment. My book *Character Analysis* was beginning to exert some influence. Four years later, when character analysis had developed into vegetotherapy, this same director became an enemy. A female analyst in Oslo had recommended a very well-known man to me for study and was to visit me shortly in Malmö with him. I received a letter of recognition from Friedrich Kraus, a famous internist in Berlin.

There was much to be done. I arranged my room as an office, and since my library was in Copenhagen, my friends agreed to bring me whatever I needed. My companion, to whom I was very grateful for the attitude she displayed during these times, was afraid she might be unable to continue the work she had begun in Copenhagen. Then it occurred to a friend of mine that my pupils could take her across the border as a Dane. This arrangement worked successfully during the six-month period when she was not permitted legally on Danish soil. I was always alone four days a week and had ample free time for scientific work. My pupils had arranged to visit me every other day for one and a half hours. The journey across the sound and back took about three hours. The ship's crew, the police on both sides,

[26] *Journal of Social Research.* —Trans.

professors, and hygienists knew exactly what was going on. News of our activity had spread rapidly. People were amazed but did not understand.

Leunbach had brought my car over from Copenhagen. On our free days we made long excursions into the countryside of southern Sweden. Late one Sunday night, we saw two girls walking down the road exhausted. I stopped the car and offered them a lift. Soon a conversation developed on the value of marriage. They were unmarried but hoped to have a home of their own soon. Living with their parents was difficult because there was so little they were allowed to do. On the other hand, it was pleasant to have their mothers take care of the entire household. I asked whether we could meet again and they replied that it would be a pleasure. Since I was always alone, my companion-wife suggested that I phone them. Perhaps this would help me overcome my loneliness. One day I did call, and although one of them was busy the other said she would be glad to meet me at the station. We met and wandered together through the streets, conversing in English. Suddenly she grew uneasy. "Someone is following us," she said. I turned around to look. She was right; a tall distinguished gentleman with a walking stick and derby was following us at a distance of approximately ten paces. She recognized him as her uncle. After a short while, I stopped and asked her to introduce me. Our conversation ended then, but the uncle was of greater interest to me. When he caught up with us this gentleman was quite embarrassed. We invited him to join us. After about ten minutes of conventional pleasantries, he excused himself and left. Then she began to complain: it was always that way; she could not even take a walk alone; no doubt her mother had asked him to protect her; he had been present when I had called; but she was no longer a child, she was twenty-three years old and attending the university. She began to cry and asked me to excuse her. I tried to find out whether there would be unpleasantness at home. She would be able to bear it, she said, although the situation was really no longer tolerable. (This was not a bolshevist, but an apolitical woman!) She would have liked to talk with me at greater length because she never met people other than those she already knew to the point of boredom. She asked to be remembered to my wife and said she would perhaps call me sometime. Every small town is like Malmö, and from that time on I abandoned all attempts to make friends. It was more dangerous than criminal activity.

My publications were known in the small university town of Lund. The student organization Clarté had even translated some of them. Discussion groups on my work were held regularly. When the wife of a history professor heard that I was living in Malmö in exile, she invited me to visit them at home. I soon established a good rapport with her husband; university professors are quite amiable people in their homes. They had an eighteen-year-old daughter, full of modern ideas, but the mother watched her closely and the ideas were soon stifled. They had read *The Invasion of Compulsory Sex-Morality, Character Analysis*, etc., and were extremely interested. We made several excursions into the country and then I suddenly thought I noticed the first indications of a problem in our relationship. So I allowed the relationship to cool, professing that I was inundated with work. I did not always act with such foresight.

The police could not bear the situation. Those two foreigners who had been living in a hotel for six weeks were unmarried—and yet "married." Every day visitors came by ferry from Denmark. Now, in Malmö the police had little to do. It was a calm, undemanding town, lacking even prostitution; a town in which civilization could doze in "peace and quiet." There was no crime. At ten o'clock in the evening the youth walked the streets separated into groups of the same sex and merely giggled at each other, feeling bold in a bashful way. Men in their twenties stood on the corners and made remarks about the girls. Thus the police had nothing to do and it had to attract attention that two German-speaking people had been living in a hotel for weeks, that they received regular visitors, that they possessed valid passports but were living in Malmö nevertheless, that they gave no one any trouble and were properly registered with the police. This was too conspicuous; the couple had to be put under surveillance. Therefore a detective was hired to observe them from behind the curtains in an office on the opposite side of the street, which did not go unnoticed by me. Then an undercover man—easily recognizable as such—was posted in front of the entrance of the hotel. I walked past him every day and looked him innocently in the eye. He acted as if he did not know who he was and what he was doing there; he even acted as if he had not noticed that I knew what he was doing. This attracted even more attention and suspicion. This German quietly walks past our detective and acts as if nothing had happened. They would take more severe measures. They began to intercept my pupils at the door, take them to the Chief of Police, and ask them what they were doing. ("Democracy"!) What was this German doing in Malmö living "up there with a lady" out of wedlock, and the visitors lying on the sofa? Psychoanalytic training? What strange thing is that? Another one of those bolshevist affairs! My pupils quietly answered their questions. Finally they called me in also and asked the same questions. I could only react by posing the question "What am I accused of?" "Nothing!" "Then, why the questioning?" Embarrassment! Yes, why were they questioning me, actually? Further questions. My reply: "'I would like to state, expressly, my willingness to provide any information you may want. But first I must know what your accusations or suspicions are!" "Who is being questioned here, you or me?" the uniform replied. "So you *are* asking questions! What am I accused of?" Great embarrassment! Then they became friendlier. "Well, it's nothing serious," or something similar. I told them, "Do what you like. You may see my papers whenever you wish," and left. That aroused even more suspicion; peculiar fellow, that German. Once when I was taking a walk along the harbor I was stopped. "Your passport, please!"

In May, my time had expired; I could no longer remain in Sweden without special permission. I requested an extension. A request for permission to return four weeks prior to the end of the six-month period of mandatory absence had already been submitted to the Danish Minister of Justice and had been denied without any explanation. Meanwhile, neither the police nor the psychiatrists had been idle. I could not understand what I was accused of according to their laws. In April, the police in Malmö attempted to search my quarters. It happened in this way: My colleague Philipson was with me for an analytic session. Suddenly, there was a brisk knock at the door. "Police, open up." Two typical detectives quickly entered the room. "We have to search this room! And who is this man?" I controlled my rage at this manifestation of anonymous power and invited the gentlemen to inspect my desk. The manuscript of *Über den Urgegensatz des vegetativen Lebens*[27] was in the typewriter. They lurched for it with an incredibly naïve gesture of curiosity, read a few lines, looked disappointed, and were about to search further. At this, I stood in their way and demanded a search warrant. Since they had none, they were embarrassed and disappeared mumbling something which was supposed to be an apology. The next day I heard that Philipson's apartment had also been searched at the same time, naturally to no avail. Our "criminal activities" were simply a type with which they were not yet familiar. The Danish and Swedish police had coordinated their actions. And all this effort simply because they did not understand the meaning of the term "psychoanalysis."

My request for an extension of my visa was denied by the police. This was unpleasant even if not dangerous. It is difficult to interrupt analytic work without complications. I protested at the Ministry for Immigration, but no one actually knew why I had not received an extension. Bureaucratic decisions are governed by their own laws. Once an office has made a decision, the course which the matter then takes is no longer related to the issue involved, but is handled according to article, paragraph, and alphabetical file. It now became necessary to mobilize a different set of formalities to counteract this. The Chief of Police summoned Elsa Lindenberg and me to appear. A great ceremony was enacted. The all-powerful one sat upon a podium not unlike a judge's bench, obviously self-conscious but striking a Napo-

[27] *On the Basic Antithesis of Vegetative Life.* —Trans.

leonic pose. To his right and left there were stenographers and two officers as witnesses. We had to stand in certain places. He then read the interdiction: I was to leave Sweden by May 24. I said nothing and we left.

Our friend Sigurd Hoel, who was in Malmö, immediately contacted a lawyer, but as the lawyer himself was more afraid of the police and the law than a criminal, we dismissed him. Hoel then immediately sent telegrams to Ström, a Swedish parliamentary delegate, as well as to Freud and Malinowski and our friends in Oslo. Two well-known journalists from Copenhagen came to Malmö and visited the Chief of Police together with Hoel. Did he not know, they asked, that he had a future Nobel prizewinner on his hands? The official was deeply alarmed and was duped by the ploy—as I believed it to be—although my friends were actually convinced that I was a potential Nobel prizewinner. He said in a calming manner that I should put in another request and that it would certainly be granted. Meanwhile, there had been a flurry of telegrams to and from Ström. The matter had reached the Minister of Justice and he wished to be kept informed. In the case of extradition, I was to appeal to his ministry. I did not understand why he did not simply give orders to extend my visa, but those are state secrets and incomprehensible to common mortals. Ström informed Hoel by letter that the denial of my request was traceable to "information" supplied by a "personal enemy" of mine. Affairs of state! Later I was told that the psychiatrists in Copenhagen had contacted the Swedish Ministry of Health. Thus an anti-sexual complex can influence the functioning of government.

Malinowski wrote a cordial letter. Freud, however, wrote only, "I am unable to voice support of your protest in the matter of Dr. Wilhelm Reich." The whole affair was ridiculous. It made me appear dangerous, which I was not. It destroyed the façade of highly respected institutions and was disgusting. To save face, the Chief of Police "granted" further residence until an official decision had been reached on the appeal which I was now to submit to the Minister of Immigration. I declined. Without further negotiations, I remained undisturbed in the hotel until I had settled my affairs. Hoel and I had arranged for me to journey illegally to Copenhagen during the summer vacation and from there to a house in the country. On June 4, 1934, I drove to Helsingör, where I was not known. It was a Sunday, my car had Danish license plates, and a Dane and a Norwegian were in the car with me. We started a loud involved conversation in Danish. Everything went smoothly and we had a good laugh on the other side of the border. In Sletten, I lived under the pseudonym Peter Stein. All the official police officers were aware of this but they seemed secretly to be wishing me luck. I was expecting a visit from my children, whom I had not seen in many months.

Wilhelm Reich in Sweden, 1934

Psychoanalytic Opposition Congress, Easter 1934. At left, Elsa Lindenberg; third from left, Reich; second from right, Otto Fenichel

Reich in the laboratory with Roger Du Teil, Oslo

8

The Psychoanalytic Congress in Lucerne, August 1934

[SO: There are few things more tragic than man's failure due to ignorance to act rationally when the correct answer is right around the corner and the ignorance is caused by fear of seeing truth in time.

At the Lucerne Congress of the psychoanalysts the development of the conflicts within the International Psychoanalytic Association reached its climax in the elimination of WR from the organization for depth psychology, in the circumstances under which it was accomplished, and in the fact that *with WR the libido theory of Sigmund Freud (SF) became homeless.*

We follow WR with amazement on his tortured path in 1934. He does not seem to know what is hitting him, why, or how. He is gullible and trusting like a child, to a degree incredible in a man who is already a famous psychiatrist. He refuses to quit SF's organization. He wants them to throw him out. At the time, this appears stupid, self-damaging, and unintelligible. Things are not usually done that way. To get rid of somebody you do not like, you must convince him that he'd better resign "of his own free will," that he take a "sick leave," that he declare his loyalty and let everything run its course peacefully without unnecessary upheaval. WR somehow senses that the scandal should be associated with the psychoanalytic movement for all time. He knows that he is the sole representative of natural-scientific psychoanalytic theory. He does not yet know that it will lead him to the discovery of the life energy. He also cannot possibly know that as a consequence of this struggle the situation in psychiatry sixteen years later in the United States will reflect his position: The death-instinct theory, which was established as an evasion of the grave social consequences of psychoanalysis and completely subscribed to in 1934, is dead as a doornail in 1950, except for a few powerless adherents.

The "Marxist opposition" is gone, forgotten. All its surviving participants are silent. Otto Fenichel, who led it in a political rather than a factual, scientific manner, abandoned WR's troubled ship in 1934. But the social consequences of the psychoanalytic libido theory of 1920 are alive and factually rooted in American society in the practical handling of the genitality of children in their first puberty.

WR's book on character analysis, which the IPA refused to publish out of fear of the Nazis and because of Paul Federn's continuous machinations from 1924 through 1934, has become the most important textbook on psychoanalytic medical technique, acknowledged all over the world as a "classic." Every psychiatrist is eager to assure everybody that he is "practicing character analysis." However, the psychiatric world is still afraid to mention the words "orgasm" and "Wilhelm Reich."

WR's orgonomy flourishes in the United States. The discovery of the life energy, accomplished through the consistent pursuit of SF's much disliked libido theory, is on the verge of full public recognition. It has saved many lives and will save countless more.

WR's book *The Mass Psychology of Fascism*, which was not allowed to be displayed at Lucerne in 1934 and was condemned as "counterrevolutionary" by the red Fascists in Moscow, 1933, has appeared in three editions and sold many thousands of copies in Europe and the United States. It was mentioned in 1949 by the New York newspaper *PM* as the book most frequently requested in the New York Public Library. It has made a significant contribution toward establishing the use of psychology in sociology. This was inconceivable in 1927 when, following those crucial talks with Freud, WR started on his journey through the realm of sociology.

Character Analysis and *The Mass Psychology of Fascism*, both firmly based on SF's libido theory, have gone a long way in precluding victories of the ascetic and monastic trends of the Catholic Church and red Fascism in the United States. Churches of many denominations were induced to go with the times and to acknowledge the existence of the genital function in childhood. Puberty is still in bad straits, handled by ignorant policemen and heredity-oriented, anti-life court psychiatrists, à la Scharffenberg in Norway. But the doors are wide open for future educators and physicians to secure happiness in love for the unborn generations, WR's "children of the future."

And last but not least, SF's truly natural-scientific thinking in psychiatry, represented by his adherence to the concept of a "psychic energy," has become a lasting acquisition of the science of man. The recording of sexual currents on the oscillograph by WR furnished proof of the bioelectric nature of human emotions. (Later studies, which included the use of the GM counter, established that this energy was not electromagnetic but a new form of physical energy.)

These are great strides in the struggle toward clarity about and protection of human life. Compared with them, the events at Lucerne, dramatic and tragic as they were at the time, appear in a rather peculiar light.

There was general surprise over WR's exclusion. Anna Freud called it a "great injustice." Federn and Jones had finally triumphed after many years of mole-like digging. They would never have succeeded under normal conditions. SF had been misled into a major blunder, running contrary to his insights and hopes in the 1920's. As the truly great scientific pioneer he was, SF had early sensed the developments which WR was to make a reality after 1934: the secure rooting of depth psychology in natural science.]

In order to make comprehensible my exclusion from the IPA, I must first return to my efforts in Malmö. Three significant lines emerged in the development of my work: the founding of the journal *Zeitschrift für Politische Psychologie und Sexualökonomie*,[1] preliminaries to my conflict with the IPA, of which I was still a member, and finally, the first concrete beginnings of sex-economic biophysiology.

The situation was no longer tolerable without a periodical to disseminate my views. Numerous papers were waiting to be published and the problems of political psychology were pressing for discussion. I knew that no journal would publish articles by me; moreover, I wanted to be independent. A publishing house for sex-economy was therefore established in Copenhagen. It was directed by a German immigrant, a teacher who had collaborated with me in Berlin and had lost his job in 1933.

At that time there still existed a group of "dialectical-materialistic psychoanalysts." In Berlin, I had left the psychoanalyst Otto Fenichel the responsibility for uniting this group. I myself had introduced him to Marxist sociology and he seemed ready to take over the task. In 1933 he had moved to Oslo. I proposed a meeting with the Scandinavian psychoanalysts for Easter 1934. The proposal was accepted and Schjelderup, himself a psychoanalyst, and director of the University Institute for Psychology in Oslo, arranged for the meeting to convene in rooms at the university. Our friend Dr. Edith Jacobson, a diligent participant in the movement, came from Berlin. (Her later misfortune in having to spend two years in a German prison lies heavily on my conscience.) She was a woman of exceptional intelligence and deep humanity. Organizational strife in the following years was unable to alter our good relationship. [SO 1951: Unfortunately, she later succumbed to the malignant practices of a few psychoanalysts from the Viennese circle who continued, with a zest worthy of a better cause, to slander WR's good name.] She came to Malmö and we journeyed together to the meeting in Oslo, a two-and-a-half-day drive through the Nordic countryside. All of us were full of questions and concern because we knew that psychoanalysis, as a movement, was not withstanding the test of time. We also felt particularly responsible for its fate,

[1] *Journal for Political Psychology and Sex-Economy.* —*Trans.*

since we had formed the radical scientific wing—if indeed that is the proper expression—as opposed to the ethical philosophers and aesthetes in the Berlin Association. Our group was closely knit through friendship and a common cause. We realized that psychoanalysis was a science and not a *Weltanschauung*—and to this we held firmly. It was, however, opposed as a *Weltanschauung*, particularly by the National Socialists, because it could have powerful sociological consequences. The fact that it did not have them was due to the inhibition exerted by the theory of the death instinct, which appeared to be the ideal way of evading social issues. In addition, it desolated clinical work, thus driving the best young analysts into my camp. I had proven the non-existence of the death instinct, but it had not yet been replaced by a better theory.

Anyone who enters a completely equipped scientific workshop and effortlessly harvests its fruit can rarely understand what the loyalty of the opposition implies. This opposition acted in the firm conviction that it was not advocating a new direction of clear insight but, on the contrary, an adherence to the strict natural-scientific path. We all believed the cause could still be saved within the international association. Diligent, valid, clinical work was to prove its superiority; the rest, we felt, would fall into place. But we had calculated without taking into account the political developments of the times. The events to come confirmed our basic tenet, namely that science is never entirely objective and certainly never independent of political currents. Nevertheless, we had illusions, and we still had no experience in the role of "organization." The comedy played by the Malmö police chief was to repeat itself, although no one would have dared to predict the events of August 1934. Today, I realize we were all stricken with the disease which I call "feeling of belonging"—in that no one really wanted to leave the organization. To try to pursue an oppositional cause without risking this means being a Social Democrat, i.e., acting "as if." All I had previously felt about the role of so-called tactics, and later experienced personally, I owe to Fenichel's "leadership" of the psychoanalytic

The Psychoanalytic Congress in Lucerne, August 1934

opposition. But I am unable to spare myself the accusation of having been stupid and uncritically trusting.

During that time I was dominated by a serious characterological weakness. I assumed it to be self-evident that all those who joined the movement would exhibit the personal independence and willingness to run risks which I had developed through numerous painful experiences. My profession and nature had equipped me to sense harmful attitudes in an associate long before they became obvious even to the individual himself. I reacted to this in two ways: If I felt personally close to the individual involved, I told myself that what I perceived was untrue, i.e. I repressed the knowledge. However, either the course of events would regularly confirm my feelings, or I would be unable to ward them off and would sever the relationship in the correct conviction that the individual was "a traitor to the cause." My only mistake was in believing that the co-worker was already betraying the cause at the time and in not waiting until his change of heart revealed itself clearly to everyone. Thus I frequently broke off a relationship at a time when no one understood the reason for my action. In the case of Otto Fenichel, I had a vague inkling at the beginning of our political-psychological work that he was characterologically and structurally unable to cope with a cause which demanded forthrightness, a willingness to take risks, and exceptional freedom from personal and organizational commitments. These are generally valid issues and they rule the developmental course of all organizations. An organization is formed around a cause in order to secure for it protection, the opportunity for propagation, and, furthermore, a home. Simultaneously, however, this creates a contradiction. A new cause is vital and continues to develop as long as it remains independent. This includes independence from the personal involvements of its advocates. If it has a great number of advocates, the interference of personal inhibitions is increased and this, in turn, inhibits the free course of development. It begins at first with retardation, progresses to gentle exclusion of radical, raging elements, and finally ends in a reversal of its direction and an adaptation to the very issues against which it was originally created. If organizing occurs too late, valuable co-workers are lost whose only fault lies in being unable to work without dependence upon a home, and in being incapable of standing alone. If organization occurs too soon, retardation and reversal also begin too early, i.e. before the cause has had ample time to pass through the pioneer phase. In the opposition, all forces which are critical of established order must first consolidate their theories into new productive concepts before an innovation is ready to risk trial as a replacement of the old. In this, the old is first negated where it is false. Simultaneously, however, an honest opposition will know exactly what it wishes to (or feels constrained to) appropriate from the old and will be willing to develop this further. There are no values which can be considered unequivocally right or unequivocally wrong; time changes much regarding "right" and "wrong." "Right" today can become "wrong" tomorrow and vice versa. On the other hand, a new concept cannot, in its function as critic, answer all questions immediately, because of the difficulty of the questions confronting it. It should not even attempt to answer all questions, as this would paralyze it from the start. Thus, for example, it is impossible for a person who wishes to defeat Fascism to have at his fingertips all the positive measures with which Fascism is to be replaced. The main issue is that criticism must correspond to the facts and that the positive constructs may not be utopias. But criticism must not only correspond to real processes in the world; it must not lie only in forward development. An opposition movement of a group within a stagnating or obsolete organization must do more; it must seek, find, and know exactly which other forces in the world are striving independently for the same goals. Only then is there hope of securing unification of the group movement within the social process. At this stage, the most important objective is to elaborate one's standpoint as opposed to that of the stagnant organization. Since all innovation is not merely negation of the old but also continuation of the old in certain areas, common ground must always be given proper consideration. Anyone who opposes a cause and claims that he only

The Psychoanalytic Congress in Lucerne, August 1934   231

wishes to advocate common ground in a more efficient manner, however, is a fool, because he cannot advocate it better than the previous organization did. If he sees nothing but common ground within the movement which he criticizes, he would do better to remain silent, because it is stronger than he. The art lies in formulating and advocating the opposition in a manner that will secure the sympathy of the best forces in the organization. This cannot be replaced by tactics, but is founded on absolute honesty and consistency despite the threat of temporary failure. In other words, one must have the strength to stand alone, never forgetting that members of obsolete organizations live in severe conflict. They love the organization to which they belong and identify with it; the organization, in turn, offers them protection and security. They themselves are more or less oppositional with varying degrees of clarity. Thus they automatically sympathize with an individual who knows their organization and who points out where it is ineffective and how issues could be handled better. If this individual shows any weakness, oppositional games are played but no serious movement is created which transcends the organization. The members of an organization have sympathy, whether secret or overt, only with an opposition leader who indicates that he is also ready for absolute enmity. For example, numerous prominent members of the Social Democratic Party sympathized with the Communists as long as the Communists could be taken as serious opposition. One of the strong points of the Fascist movement was the fact that it had no such difficulties to overcome with an opposition, because it did not advocate progress but rather, the comfort of regression. It raised no new problems but merely revived age-old modes of life. All that was new in Fascism was the revolutionary form it gave to old issues. Through this, it enjoyed all the advantages— at first!

In the case of psychoanalysis, the situation was particularly complex. Fenichel did not comprehend that it was not a matter of a few friends who created an opposition movement together, and that the objective was not to show consideration for individuals but to clearly establish some decisive principles. Thus he led the opposition in a manner in which no one, if possible, was even to know of its existence. The group was to remain "secret," and its members were to call themselves "Marxist analysts." The name, however, was not important. Of importance were the issues, the critical judgments, and the development of insight. I must give a somewhat more detailed description of situations which are today unimportant in themselves but which are typical and could be repeated at any time within our movement. In addition, they are historically significant for the evaluation of individuals who once played a role or who could again become active in the future. These descriptions will also be useful in preventing similar processes from recurring.

To make my exclusion from the international organization of psychoanalysts comprehensible, I must set forth my scientific position in 1934. Until now, it may have appeared that political conflicts were the essential factors. Nowhere had a factual exposition of the opposition to my work been presented. The beginnings of my theory of political psychology were scattered, intermingled with other people's views, and still lacked important foundations which were only elaborated during the following years. The period between 1930, the year of my first conflict with Freud, and 1934, the year of the Congress at Lucerne, had effected great changes. I no longer felt committed to the organization and had been forced into solitude. Being alone is beneficial for the maturation of serious thoughts which one does not seek but which, rather, force themselves upon one. The dissolution of ties to the illusional home offered by a professional organization necessitates seeking new paths, not only in one's material existence but in one's spiritual existence as well. The description of some sex-economic problems which fascinated me at the time should illustrate the reason why, in 1934, I lost literally all of my friends in professional circles. It should demonstrate the fact that it was not a lack of affability, but inner coercion, motivated both by clarity and by vagueness, in my attitudes toward the work. The following five years justified me completely.

My social work in Germany had shown me that sex-politics based on clear scientific knowledge, and presented simply, constitute a sharp weapon against Fascist irrationalism. Fascist mass-psychological practices employ unconscious instinctual forces, especially sexual longing. I knew the mass-psychological technique of providing the means of giving this yearning *real*, instead of mystical, expression. The mechanisms which Fascism used as a devilish means of enslaving people were the same which drove people to my meetings. What Fascism diverted into mystical negation of life I directed toward the goal of happiness in life, with sexual happiness at its core.

It is harmful in working with the masses to complicate problems and to overemphasize the difficulties involved in their solution. This paralyzes the mass individual, who has already become fainthearted in the face of social power. However, behind the scenes in social work, every difficulty must be grasped, formulated, and solved according to the existent body of knowledge. Marxism, which was economics and not sexology or psychology, could neither grasp the problem nor solve it. Psychoanalysis provided all the means to comprehend unconscious mental activity. But first of all, it had bogged down in false theories; second, it had rejected organizational social work; and third, it did not understand economic problems. Thus, to maintain the long-established classification of psychology within sociology and to free depth psychology from incorrect concepts in order to employ it more effectively became the objective. The group of so-called Marxist psychoanalysts lived under the illusion that psychoanalysis and Marxism, psychology and sociology, were to be united. I was not completely without fault in this. I had described these relationships previously in various papers but had not put the matter into any organizational framework. The Marxist psychoanalysts lived and worked in the organizational worlds of both psychoanalysis and the Marxist workers' movement. There was no organization for my work. Hence the attitude of Marxist analysts necessarily remained a mechanistic, eclectic synthesis of Freud and Marx. I had already freed myself from this, but to execute the matter correctly would have meant losing many very valuable co-workers who were not prepared to support the beginning of a third movement. On the contrary, my work during those years bore the mark of the difficulties created by the organizational commitments of my collaborators. The term "Sexpol" had been introduced long before and signified the "organization of sex-politics," although it had no presidents and secretaries. I could have suggested such offices, but a vague feeling restrained me from making commitments. The structure of the old organizations seemed impractical for my work and to devise a different organizational form seemed impossible and fruitless. It would not have been consistent with the issues, for Sexpol required something entirely new, although I did not know what. The problem remains unsolved today. However, applying the concept of self-government in forming an organization was rewarding and the overall consideration of the problem led to formulations about the human organizational problem per se which I shall later describe.

I felt that the current forms of organization, as well as the reactions of people within them, were irrational and therefore that sex-economy, which was someday to become an important instrument in the struggle against irrationalism, must not be allowed to suffocate before birth. All organizations have goals, but our goals lay in the work itself. Deriving social consequences from scientific insight was our first goal; the second was advocacy of those consequences; third, and most important, was establishing science and scientific insight as the only valid principle in guiding society. Neither the Marxist organization nor the psychoanalytic was a suitable framework, as both rejected my sex-economic theories. Neither wished to be associated with my goals. They did agree, theoretically, that "politics should be scientific" but not that sex-economic insight bore consequences. For this reason, the tone of all objections to me implied that I drew political, i.e. social, consequences from my science. My exclusion from both groups was based on this. In simple terms, they rejected a sex-economic ordering of infantile and adolescent life,[2] and thus upheld everything that had its source in the disorder of this life—among other things, Fascism. Sanction of my work and objectives would have implied, for Marxism, the inclusion of the psychology of the unconscious and sexology, and consequently a refashioning of Marxist philosophy in accordance with conditions in the twentieth, rather than the nineteenth, century. Acceptance of my work by psychoanalysis would have implied the following: compatibility of social outlook and science, renunciation of the doctrine of the biological nature of perversions and child-parent conflicts, acceptance of a plan for an economic system in which corresponding cultural policies could develop, i.e. work democracy, renunciation of the death-instinct theory and its replacement by my theory of the *social origins of anxiety and suffering*. Furthermore, acceptance of my clinically founded orgasm theory would have required a radical transformation of psychoanalytic technique into character analysis, and later into vegetotherapy. This would have led inevitably to research in biophysiology. The analysts were not prepared for this. In short, sex-economy had become a new discipline and had purged itself of theories which, when traced to their origins, were no longer in accord with it. The specific innovations of sex-economy germinated during the period of the Lucerne Congress. I shall mention only the essentials: The orgasm formula, which could also be considered the life formula itself; the bioelectric (later orgonotic) nature of sexuality and anxiety; the comprehension of organic diseases such as rheumatism ("muscular armoring") and cancer. At the time I had as yet no knowledge of the bions. It is understandable that my inner urge for intellectual independence was strong. My friends and co-workers basically understood nothing of the developments in my research. Whatever they did know and affirm, they uncritically

---

[2] 1952: The tragic rationale in this rejection was dealt with in *The Murder of Christ*, to some extent at least. The oranur experiment revealed the core of the trouble to be human bioenergetic structure which fears and resists expansion.

categorized as either Marxist or psychoanalytic. They did not consider—nor did they wish to consider—that these organizations no longer cared about my work, and actually opposed it. By allying my work with these organizations, they appeared to be attempting to create the alibi that they intended only "improvement," certainly not rebellion. The course of events, however, followed the laws of all development. The new, germinating from the old, first opposes the old with hostility. Following the resolution of the conflict, the new then becomes independent and begins to determine its own direction. If it is wise and prudent, it retains vital elements of the old. If it feels insecure, it denies its origins and intellectual homeland. I attempted to resolve this problem correctly in my paper "Überblick über das Forschungsgebiet der Sexualökonomie."[3]

This was my inner position. Outwardly, I still clung to the organizations through numerous friends, and was dependent upon them. The complete separation of sex-economic theory did not occur until four years later, following the monstrous campaign by its adversaries in Oslo.

I would like to relate another part of the history of the opposition movement within the IPA. Although, in itself, of interest only to historiographers of psychoanalysis, it assumes a basic significance for us because it contains the universal characteristics seen in all opposition movements. We must expect that someday, when the pioneer phase of sex-economy and political psychology has passed, an opposition and factions will arise. It is useful to provide them with an understanding of their actions beforehand and to demonstrate their well-intended desires and practical weaknesses. If this opposition is objectively correct, then it should gain an easier victory than we did. If, on the other hand, its advocates and factual issues are weak and incapable of extending the lines of strict scientific research better than we, then it deserves to fail. In this case somewhat less harm will have been done. We shall attempt to illustrate this in the picture presented by the opposition psychoanalysts between 1932 and 1934

[3] "Synopsis of the Sex-economic Field of Research."—*Trans.*

and in the consequences which might have resulted had they been successful.

The basic problem of every serious opposition movement is to maintain a balance between practice and principle. The former is determined by the multitude of daily events and human commitments, and the latter by the natural course of development of the cause. Frequently they contradict one another. As the founder of the opposition, I was unable to solve this conflict. In the end I sided with the principles of the cause itself. The opposition analysts stagnated in practical and personal matters. Later they were replaced by other scientific workers. The situation produced great excitement, literally tears, and often it was painful.

Let us return to the Oslo convention at Eastertime 1934. Only two reports were given, one by Fenichel and the other by me. Fenichel spoke first and limited himself to criticizing scientific as well as organizational conditions in the IPA. Later he compiled them in one of the circular letters which he sent, as the leader of the opposition, to its members. I have culled several typical examples from that letter. In doing so, I am breaching a confidence because Fenichel wished that his oppositional work become known to no one through the letters except to the addressees. They were to be burned after reading. I once asked him, "Do you really think you can keep the existence of our faction a secret?" His reply to this (in the circular letter of April 1934) was:

"I feel it is impossible to keep our mutual correspondence and exchange of opinions a secret, but it is—and must be—possible to keep secret the identity of the participants and the views expressed as well as the mode of exchanging opinions, which is unconventional in bourgeois science."

This implied illegality of the Communist type. However, we were not politicians struggling with the police, but scientific workers advocating definite views which I always felt were well known. No member of the IPA was unaware of my views. Naïvely, I believed Fenichel had meant to keep the promises he made when he assumed leadership. He had not only declared his solidarity with my views but had written positive criticisms of my papers in the journal. There was no opposition platform in the IPA other than mine. Could he have been interested only in the "leadership of the opposition" and not in my views? Slowly this thought took hold until finally I could not shake myself free from it. Fenichel was attempting, with the help of my colleagues' sympathy for my clinical and sociological research with which they identified, which showed them the future . . . with that help he wanted to . . . what? . . . To be the "leader of the opposition"? . . . Nonsense! Opposition without a factual stand is suicide! But it did exist, and not only in the psychoanalytic movement. Suddenly, I discovered that most opposition movements within parties and societies are not founded on facts. They have no contribution to make and have nothing better with which to replace the objects of their criticism. They simply want to be the "leaders," regardless of ways and means. What structure was capable of that kind of mischief? I was soon to find out.

Fenichel's criticism of psychoanalysis in 1934 was correct. I had made the same points repeatedly between 1924 and 1934, namely that social conditions were reflected in the conflicts of psychoanalysis. An insecure existence and fear of the dangers produced by the revolutionary consequences of the theory rekindle old resistance in analysts which makes them forget their analytic knowledge. Göring, leader of the German psychotherapists, expected his members "to have read Adolf Hitler's basic work, *Mein Kampf*, in all scientific earnestness." Künkel (individual psychologist, characterologist), Schultz-Hencke (psychoanalyst, ethical philosopher), and Weizsäcker were made members of the German professional organization and all Jewish analysts were removed from leading positions. During one meeting, a German psychoanalyst had proposed that all Jewish members hand in their resignations. Schultz-Hencke had become national commissar. (He had always been a firm advocate of "value-ethics"!) Böhm, a German analyst, went to England to see Jones, the president of the IPA, and explained that only through very adept maneuvering, had he succeeded in preventing the destruction of the entire organization and the detention of analysts in concentration camps. According to Fenichel, Böhm would have been especially proud to become the "leader" of German psychoanalysis. Among other remarks, he had stated that psychoanalysis "serves the purpose of educating the heroic individual." Under such circumstances, the emigrant members of the German Association were in favor of its dissolution. Most resigned, and National Socialism undertook to look after the further development of psychoanalysis.

What follows is a description of a scientific organization which had once been a center of the search for truth and had remained apolitical: In Austria, which was not yet fascistic, some writings by the Fascist Weizsäcker were given preference, by the Jewish editors of the journal, over papers stemming from the radical group. In 1938 many of these editors were constrained to flee, but there was no Weizsäcker to save them although they had, in a highly academic manner, considered it correct to "build bridges to previous opponents." According to Fenichel's report, Weizsäcker had stated in a hundred-page paper that an Oedipus complex does exist but he had also emphasized that there was more in this world than just natural science. Natural science, he said, should practice modesty because not everything under the sun is accessible through natural-scientific methods. We might add, for example, National Socialist mysticism. Fenichel wanted to criticize Federn severely for recommending that children take a deep breath to avoid erections. His critique was not allowed to be published. The editors of *Imago* had rejected Roheim's report on my ethnological research because it was laced with personal disparagements. However, the great events in the world determined that the report would be subsequently published nevertheless. It contained the famous sentence in which he stated that it was not true (as I had said) that private enterprise created neurosis; on the contrary, he said, neurosis created capitalism. Papers by members of the opposition were not accepted.

May these examples suffice, chosen from many. They were taken from circulating letters and are evidence of so-called analytic gossip. We waited for the forthcoming congress to hear proposals for concrete measures. Members of the opposition were critical of Fenichel because he was emphasizing personal issues and neglecting the factual. There was not a word about my constructive criticism of psychoanalysis, about the orgasm theory, the ethnological criticism, the discovery of the social origin of neurosis, or the mass psychology of Fascism. He even wrote, "Nothing new in the field of sexology has been published since Freud." At that, I suddenly understood: Fenichel was determined to usurp my claims but to suffocate my theory through silence [a program he later carried out extensively in America]. I therefore defined clearly before my colleagues the omissions of which Fenichel had been guilty, and presented a synopsis of my constructive criticism: above all, prophylaxis of the neurosis, not therapy of the neurosis; the dynamics of neurosis require an energy viewpoint, i.e. the orgasm theory; the standard technique is inadequate because it does not consider sexual stasis; etc.

In the discussion period Fenichel was greatly embarrassed and apologized, saying he had "forgotten" to mention the orgasm theory. From that point on I became aware of a process which had previously escaped me. I later detected this same process in many individuals, i.e. revolutionizing, due to unsatisfied ambitions and a lack of originality, which easily lures people into joining an opposition. Envy tempts them to usurp others' ideas and cowardice inveigles them into making more promises than they can keep. The unavoidable consequence is betrayal: unconscious betrayal, obscured by tactical theories designed to cover the personal motives.

Sensing trouble, I wrote a letter to the group, which Fenichel published in the newsletter. In it, I stated that the struggle between scientific and mystical factions in psychoanalysis was an old issue which had begun in 1925 when the theory of the orgasm was formulated. I felt that the conflict would develop into a crisis at the forthcoming congress due to the pressure of political events. The language of objective science usually prevents philosophical conflicts from being discussed openly in scientific circles. A great deal of experience is needed to distinguish between scientific differences stemming from a lack of factual knowledge and those based on philosophical views. Within a scientific organization, a struggle cannot be carried on with the usual political weapons. Proving that one faction was "reactionary-Hitlerian" or the other "revolutionary-Marxist" was not important; it was important to prove that scientific knowledge was being inhibited by unconscious adherence to a philosophical position. Again, it was not the philosophy but the attitude toward finding the truth that was significant here. Only at this point is there a parting of the ways toward the "right" or "left." In this context it would be unimportant whether or not the French group mistreated the emigrants, but extremely important that their incorrect assertions had been preferred for publication over correct ones. One had to be forthright. My own critical standpoint had been clinically and theoretically firm since 1924. All other members of the opposition should assume a stable factual position as well. It was impossible to be "oppositional" without knowing what one was opposing or simply to oppose purely formal organizational incidents. (It was not until four years later that I was able to formulate this clearly: Sentiment and organization are not important, but only advocacy of the cause.)

Furthermore, I stated, Fenichel's actions were disquieting. He always attempted to keep Freud personally out of the conflict. It was self-evident that we did not honor and defend Freud less because he had of late been advocating unacceptable views. All the scientific errors of Roheim, Laforgue, etc., were traceable to Freud. If his work was to be rescued for posterity, then honesty toward Freud himself was indispensable. Only when it had been proven how and where Freud the scientist and Freud the conservative philosopher contradicted each other could one's claims bear fruit. My personal experiences with Freud had convinced me that he would also prefer this attitude.

I also mentioned that I bore full responsibility for the entire conflict. The differences had already been clear even when it was still generally believed that the situation was under control and that my "aggression" alone was to blame. It was my duty to protect my work under all circumstances. Numerous elements of the orgasm theory had been accepted without comprehension in order to destroy it. The work had developed into sex-economy and political psychology, which did indeed contain the best scientific features and traditions of psychoanalysis but had outgrown them.

Thus my path was laid out. Since very few opposition analysts shared my scientific standpoint, my position, should a conflict arise at the Congress, would differ somewhat from that of the others. My suggestion for behavior when we convened was: no petty organizational-political criticism; advocacy of the strictest demands of research together with factual, impersonal, but uncompromising criticism of opponents; organizational unification of all opposition analysts, forming a tightly knit organization within the IPA. Additional requirements for practicing analysts were: an orderly sex-economy (because of the catastrophic influence of sexually unhealthy analysts); training in the correct application of psychoanalysis in sociology and vice versa; extensive sexological training (which very few analysts had). Priests, and those physicians and educators with reactionary sexual attitudes, were not to be allowed to practice psychoanalysis, because this would be inconsistent with the work.

After a lengthy discussion there was agreement on all the essential points I had made. (Circulating letter of April 1934, p. 6.) Let us now examine the events of the Congress. Unnoticed by all, the leader of the opposition had made a prediction in a single statement. "In regard to Reich's letter, an agreement will also be reached that it is absolutely necessary to draft a platform from which we can pursue our goals. We (i.e. Otto Fenichel[4]) feel, however, that this may be postponed in order not to *burden, at this time* (tactician!), *the necessarily broad discussion of practical questions* (?). Such a platform ought *not* to contain theories, e.g. Reich's position on the death instinct and anxiety, which one would feel compelled to believe dogmatically (!!), but rather . . . our opinions on the historical-scientific significance of psychoanalysis, its research methods and natural-scientific tenets." (!!) But he did not mention *which* tenets he was referring to;

[4] This and subsequent parenthetical comments in this paragraph are Wilhelm Reich's. —Ed.

The Psychoanalytic Congress in Lucerne, August 1934   243

only "opinions on the historical-scientific significance . . . research methods . . . natural-scientific tenets."

Empty phrases! Words instead of scientific convictions! High-flown rhetoric instead of a simple statement of position! Fenichel lacked factual conviction and thus involved several very intelligent and decent opposition analysts in a situation which made no sense to them. When I read the lines quoted above, I knew what lay ahead. After that, nothing the opposition did at the Congress surprised me. Although the opposition had sprung up around my scientific research, I was the only one to advocate it at the Congress. The defection occurred with the most ingenuous sentiments.

It had been decided to register as many speeches by the opposition as possible in order to emphasize clearly "our views" and their deviation from established theory. In the event of a sabotage of my lecture, the entire group was to protest. In the business meeting a resolution was to be placed before the board of directors expressing the opposition's apprehensiveness in regard to the future of psychoanalysis. In addition, an explanation of the IPA's behavior during the Copenhagen pornography affair was to be requested.

In June, Fenichel gave a lecture before our Copenhagen group which revealed to everyone his complete lack of understanding of the orgasm problem. He was sharply corrected; later he gained support in Prague, where no one could contradict him. At the end of June, I wrote one more letter of warning to the group but did not mail it. It was useless. I knew that all hoped for the best but that they were not really willing to do anything about it. I was still unsuspecting.

On August 1, shortly before the Congress, I received a letter from Müller-Braunschweig, the secretary of the German Association. The publishing house wished to print a roster for the Congress and I was not to be surprised if I did not find my name on the list of German members. "It would please me if you would show understanding for the situation by waiving any possible personal sensitivity in the interest of the psychoanalytic cause in

Germany, and consent to this measure. Your renown as a capable scientist and author is so great in the world of international psychoanalytic academia that this procedure could not harm you in the slightest way." In addition to this, he continued, the recognition of the Scandinavian group at the Congress and the future appearance of my name on their membership lists would make the issue entirely meaningless. All this impressed me as an emergency measure which was understandable. Membership in Scandinavia seemed certain. Later, I marveled at my own naïveté and inexperience in political psychology which did not allow me to interpret the maneuver correctly.

When I arrived in Lucerne on August 25 and attended the reception on August 26, the situation appeared to be in perfect order. Greetings of colleagues from near and far were cordial, as always. No one sensed any differences of opinion. On the evening before the Congress, the German secretary took me aside and informed me, in an embarrassed manner, that the German executive committee had resolved to exclude me from the society. This automatically canceled my membership in the international organization and meant that I could no longer participate in the business meeting. I asked why I had not been informed and the reasons for my exclusion. The secretary merely shrugged his shoulders in embarrassment. I immediately knew what was going on. That evening at dinner I told several colleagues. They could not believe it. It had to be a mistake. And, anyway, any other group would naturally accept me as a member. The directorate of the international organization would certainly not condone it. But it did! More and more colleagues heard about the situation. Müller-Braunschweig was overrun with questions as I sent those who would not believe it to him, one after the other.

The "opposition" held a consultation. What was to be done in this new situation?

Without doubt, the most fertile and practical mode of action would be to advocate the cause in the lectures. One female colleague spoke on the "biological foundations of Freud's anxiety theory." She had already contacted me in 1931 in Berlin and felt, at the time, that my understanding of stasis anxiety was the correct extension of the Freudian anxiety theory into the biological realm. She was interested in physiological experimentation and already had some results. These confirmed completely my view that anxiety corresponds to a state of excitation in the vegetative system and is the direct antithesis of sexuality. We recall that Freud had rejected this theory. At the Congress, the same colleague who had related this problem to my research, gave a clear, accurate description of it, but mentioned neither my name nor the titles of my works. After the lecture she came to me in embarrassment and apologized, saying she had planned to mention me but it had "slipped her mind." I quieted her with a few noncommittal phrases.

Another female analyst from the opposition, who was a good friend of mine, spoke on "the problem of therapy in child analysis." Since children lack the social means to gratify their instincts, they are unable to attain the goal of adult treatment, namely, readiness and capacity to experience genital pleasure. Quite correct! But this theory was the very core of the differences between the IPA and me, and neither my name nor my work was mentioned. When I inquired why she had not mentioned my name, she asked me in astonishment where she could have done so. I said no more. The cause had, after all, been successfully advocated. But this comfort was self-deception.

Fenichel spoke on the problems of anxiety. We know how pivotal a role the question of neurotic anxiety played in the thinking of opposition members. Fenichel made no reference to my theories.

A certain analyst, Gerö, who had followed me when I emigrated in order to study character analysis and test it on himself, spoke on "the theory and technique of character analysis." The following excerpt from his published thesis contains the only place where my priority in the entire issue was mentioned: "These formal elements have been stressed by Ferenczi, Fenichel, and Reich." Later, he became an enemy. When my paper on the orgasm reflex appeared, in which the content of his thesis (originally borrowed from me) was thoroughly elaborated, he stated that I had gone off "on a tangent."

It may seem petty to mention these incidents. In this context they are only intended as examples of the peculiarity of human structure, *which takes wherever it can and gives only when it must*. This is an unconscious process, and if fair dealing is mentioned it is taken as an insult. Above all, human structure refuses to bear the responsibility for what it has been given.

Meanwhile, I discovered that I had been excluded *a year before* in a secret meeting of the German executive committee. The directorate of the international organization, headed by Jones, enthusiastically seized the opportunity to follow suit.

I feel constrained to go into these details, as the individuals responsible later attempted to place the guilt upon my shoulders. They spread the rumor that I myself had requested exclusion. May this illuminate the backstage activity in a "democratic-parliamentary" organization! Dictators simply exclude or shoot people, but democratic dictators murder on the sly with less courage and willingness to assume responsibility. Let us recall that Jones had told me expressly, in London, that he would oppose my exclusion under all circumstances.

I had someone ask Jones whether I could still give my lecture and participate in the business meeting. He replied that I could give the lecture as a *guest* but could not participate in the business meeting. Jones himself seemed quite concerned. I was told he had apprehensively sought advice about what to do if I were to come anyway and throw out the president. They actually thought I was capable of that. I must confess that I later regretted not having done so. I spoke to Bibring, Hartmann, and Kris about it. What would happen if I really did it? I asked, not mentioning a word about Jones's remark. They were startled and patiently persuaded me to maintain my dignity. In this way I realized the purpose of precepts such as dignity, modesty, and politeness, namely to better camouflage the impertinence of cultivated people. Finally I quieted them by saying it was not worth the effort.

The situation in the executive committee was in disarray. Everyone had a guilty conscience, but Federn felt guiltiest. He,

Jones, and Eitingon[5] spoke caustically and disparagingly about me, saying that I seduced all my female patients, that I was a psychopath, etc., etc. The Norwegians were furious. My only question was: Why then had these men allowed me to live and work for twelve years as a prominent member of the IPA? It was ugly and despicable.

Only the Norwegian analysts, Raknes, Nic Hoel, and Schjelderup behaved decently. They said I could become a member of the Norwegian Association whenever I wished. I warned them that they had no firsthand knowledge of the significance of the issue and its explosive qualities. What they were currently exposed to comprised only a fraction of the whole. Nevertheless, they did not retreat. Schjelderup had studied character-analytic technique with me the summer before the Congress and wanted me to continue my work in Norway. At that time, I had already made plans to conduct my bioelectric experiments and said that if he could offer me the possibility of carrying them out in his institute, I would come. Still, I warned him once again. None of us could have imagined that three years later a vicious campaign would erupt in Norway because of these experiments and that Schjelderup would emerge as an antagonist. The reader will ask whether I was not at fault, since so many prominent individuals joined me, only to leave me later on. May the facts speak for themselves. They reveal the real problem of social psychiatry.

When my exclusion was no longer doubted, a deep gulf, filled with a peculiar respect and skittishness, formed around my person. It was almost physically perceptible. Everyone else was standing on the other side. My friends shed tears, but soon took comfort. Only a few found their way back to me, for example Ellen Siersted, an untiring and forthright individual. Dr. Nic Hoel also visited me in my room and brought flowers. I was very grateful to her.

The formal course of my exclusion ran as follows: To prevent my attending the business meeting, the executive committee

[5] 1952: Eitingon, later, in a letter (December 29, 1935) denied that he had participated in the procedures against me.

decided to appoint an international commission to meet with me privately. This took place on the day before the actual business meeting. As had been the case earlier in Vienna, the objective of the committee was to persuade me to renounce my membership voluntarily; this would have made it more convenient for them. I explained my position: From the standpoint of the death-instinct theorists, I fully understood my exclusion from the IPA, which was already in effect. My views differed so significantly from those of psychoanalysis in 1934 that communication was hardly possible any longer. However, I simultaneously emphasized that *I viewed myself as the legitimate representative of natural-scientific psychoanalytic thought and from that standpoint did not accept my exclusion.* Since strictly formal, official steps could no longer be taken, I demanded that the reasons for my exclusion be printed in the journal. (The chairman of the committee promised to do this but the promise was never kept.) My orgasm theory and the views deriving from it did not contradict clinical psychoanalysis in any way (today I realize that they *did* contradict it on essential issues), but they were incompatible with the death-instinct theory. Compulsory repression of sexuality could only originate either in a biological instinct or in social processes. It was inconceivable for both to be responsible simultaneously unless one assumed a highly improbable hereditary transmission of very early social influences.

Since the directorate of the IPA did not wish to support my views and had, on the contrary, already secretly excluded me, I stated that I preferred to carry on alone and call my theory *sex-economy.*

Hushed excitement pervaded the meeting. Afterward, Anna Freud is reported to have said, "A great injustice has been done here." But, as the secretary of the IPA, she did nothing in accord with this statement.

In the business meeting the next day, nothing happened. My situation was not mentioned. Fenichel's feeble resolution came to naught. The only conflict was between Nic Hoel and Jones.

From then on, I resolved to maintain the following position:

1. Always to emphasize the historical and factual elements common to psychoanalysis and sex-economy.
2. To strictly accentuate the existing differences in sexual theory and the concept of anxiety.
3. To claim what may evolve in the future as my own with the same fidelity with which I acknowledge what we share in common.

On the fourth day of the Congress, I gave my lecture, which was later published by Sexpol Verlag under the title "Psychischer Kontakt und vegetative Strömung."[6] I began with the words: "After fourteen years of membership, I shall now address the Congress as a guest speaker for the first time . . ." I was given more attention than ever before. The atmosphere that pervaded the auditorium was the same as in the committee session. One participant remarked that this Congress had stood "under my star." He was correct. An organization burdened with problems, having set out to influence the future, does not condone a farce such as my exclusion without severe consequences. They emerged one by one. I had the feeling that the IPA had excluded the sexual theory, the vital nerve of psychoanalysis. And now the strict natural-scientific sexual theory was being presented in a guest lecture in its own homeland to an uncomprehending audience. My lecture dealt with the problems which had arisen in my medical practice during the transition from research on character in neurosis to the basic somatic mechanism of psychic illness. The topic of the lecture became the point of departure for establishing the bioelectric nature of sexuality experimentally. At this Congress, and in this very speech, the initial steps were taken toward the fulfillment of Freud's hopes that analytic psychology would someday be placed on an organic foundation. I must add that it was the first time a large scientific audience had heard reflections and facts which later combined psychic and somatic functions into a natural-scientific unity. I was not completely aware of this myself at the time, nor did I realize that the

[6] "Psychic Contact and Vegetative Current." This paper is included in the 3rd, enlarged edition of *Character Analysis*. —*Trans*.

problems of contactlessness, as well as those of vegetative current, also touched upon the core of schizophrenia and cancer in a new [bioenergetic] way.

At the end of the allotted speaking time, I was not quite finished and requested permission to continue. The response was enthusiastic applause. There was no negative criticism during my lecture. Afterward, I was informed that at least half of the audience had not understood me in the least, but that the other half had realized which path I was following.

One of my former Viennese students, Dr. Bergler, spoke on "Thanatos" in dreams. After the lecture, I posed the question whether he had ever seen evidence of the death instinct. "No, certainly not!" he replied. "It is only a theory." "Well then, why are you talking about it?" I queried.

The organization had not based my exclusion on either my scientific views or my political sympathies. There were many in the IPA with diverse scientific views, and many Communists as well. The incompatibility with IPA membership lay in my *having derived social consequences from scientific findings,* i.e. the development of sex-politics from scientific sex-economy. [Twelve years later, my socio-sexual theories were generally recognized and partially applied in America.] I did not understand why my sex-political views were more dangerous or harmful than Communism or false scientific theory. I *really* could not grasp it. I had never indulged in political activities in the common sense of the word; I had only done social-hygiene work as a physician and was far from demanding political leadership or attempting to gain power. Respect for politics was still deeply embedded within me. My organism had not yet comprehended that science is more decisive than politics, that it is science, not politics, which poses the real threat to the misery at hand, that science even threatens politics, that these respectable "apolitical scientists" had executed radical political-tactical maneuvers by excluding a serious, forthright quest for truth, that they were actually supporting the spiritual depravity which had recently begun to undermine Europe. Nor did I realize that they constituted a part of the great politically active and yet so unconscious masses which, while drowning in an ocean of meaningless phraseology, formed the broad shoulders upon which politics and diplomacy were riding the world to ruin. Only during the following years was I capable of frankly professing the revolutionary character of science and only very gradually did I begin to grasp the significance of the connection between the vegetative sensations of human beings, their lack of contact and yearning for a rescuer, and the political impact of slogans such as "the surge of pure Aryan blood" or "the call of homeland and native soil." And this, despite the fact that I had written a three-hundred-page book on the mass psychology of Fascism. Slowly, however, filled with my experience of the insane events at the Lucerne Congress, I comprehended it. Fear of bearing the responsibility for so great an insight had prevented my assuming the burden immediately.

I took leave of my children and journeyed with my companion to Denmark via France. She had suffered greatly under the situation and had supported me in a simple human manner without much comment, for which I was very grateful.

We arrived in Copenhagen late at night. It was raining and we had no place of our own. For several days we stayed with friends to whom we related the events. But gradually we sensed that they were beginning to grow cool. Coincidence and not factual necessity had driven them to me and would also drive them away again. Later, this actually happened. We packed clothing and books and left for Norway. I was detained at the Swedish border. Allegedly I had been extradited from Sweden and was not permitted to journey through it. I telegraphed Oslo and Stockholm immediately. The border guard was taken aback because I had named a university professor and a parliamentary representative. What is an exiled machinist, one employee among millions in a German factory, to do under such circumstances? Finally a crossing was permitted with no further complications. In Oslo we lodged in another of those horrible small hotels which seem especially equipped to crush even the strongest spirit. It was the end of October 1934.

The Norwegian Psychoanalytic Society invited me to their meetings, but I attended only infrequently, as I was fully occupied preparing for the biophysical experiments. After approximately two months, Schjelderup invited me to lecture to the faculty of the Psychology Department. Following several lectures, an unbelievably base, harassing article was published in the Norwegian Fascist newspaper *ABC*. (They even printed a purported picture of me, actually the face of an idiot.) Although it was only a small local newspaper, the article reappeared four years later in the file which the police had gathered to use against me. However, the Norwegian analysts were loyal. During this time a conversation with Schjelderup raised the question of whether I should apply for membership. The Norwegians were willing, he said, although they had encountered great difficulties at the Congress and had been told that they would be recognized as members of the international organization only on condition that they pledged not to accept me. The Norwegians had rejected this out of hand and replied that they would accept no provisos. Either they would be accepted unconditionally or they would refuse. Here, for the first time, I became acquainted with the general Norwegian mentality, although during recent years it had begun to make concessions to European Fascism. I drafted a formal letter to the Norwegian group with the suggestion that they first discuss the question of my membership with me in order to ensure complete awareness of all possible consequences. I was in the best position to provide the necessary information. There was one man, however, who circulated from member to member and agitated against my acceptance. To one of the members he said I had only come to Norway to steal all his patients; to another he said I had gone mad. This rumor was started by none other than the "leader of Marxist psychoanalysts," Otto Fenichel himself. His behavior cost him dearly and aroused loathing wherever he went. Finally, in the summer of 1935 he was forced to leave Oslo because he could no longer earn a living there. I must emphasize that I took no steps to counteract his behavior.

When I noticed that the members of the Norwegian Psychoanalytic Society were becoming hesitant, I suggested that they drop the issue of my admission. I could exist without it and

The Psychoanalytic Congress in Lucerne, August 1934   253

perhaps it was better not to provoke any conflicts. I never regretted this decision. They attended the evening classes I held on clinical work and we remained good friends. Almost all of them were studying the well-advanced technique of character analysis and were at the time grappling with the problem of mastering physical rigidities. The experimental biophysiological research, so highly significant for the development of social psychiatry, began at this time. I dissolved all my ties to psychoanalysis while simultaneously providing a solid foundation for its correct clinical insights.

My naïveté about people, however, was not yet at an end. It contributed to the disturbing and hazardous events which began in the Oslo Psychiatric Society in the autumn of 1937 and kept the Norwegian public in a state of suspense for almost a year. As a result, it became difficult for me to appear at meetings of the society or even in public, but almost overnight my work was advanced a decade. To ensure a thorough evaluation of the political-psychological mechanisms of the Oslo campaign against my research, it will be necessary first to render a description of my biological work.

9

Toward Biogenesis

THE NORWEGIAN PRESS CAMPAIGN

After moving from Malmö, Sweden, to Oslo, Norway, in the late autumn of 1934, my research was suspended between heaven and hell, figuratively speaking. On the one side, friends and admirers of my work advocated at least two Nobel Prizes, while on the other, my enemies were advocating with equal intensity the necessity for extradition, police investigation, and surveillance. And there were enemies everywhere: neurologists who hated sex, court psychiatrists who believed in the hereditary nature of "criminal intercourse in puberty," Fascist police officials who hated "foreigners," etc. Viewed from the present, irrationalism in social life during the twentieth century of "culture and civilization" assumed gigantic dimensions in the struggle of armored life against the discovery of biological energy (and therewith biogenesis). Friends and remote observers lauded the discovery of the bions as the greatest scientific achievement in centuries. The Norwegian Chief of Police, Konstad [a Fascist who later faced execution for collaboration with the Nazis], considered me a most dangerous enemy of law and order. The discovery of the bions and of the cancer process occurred "on the run," so to speak, in the short intervals between emigrations. My own life impulses must have developed enormous powers to enable me to survive the period between 1934 and 1944. For several reasons it is imperative to describe this period.

Toward Biogenesis

The struggle over the issue of biogenesis exposes the riddle of why science had been unsuccessful until that time in discovering the life process itself. It also demonstrates the horrible effect of the emotional plague on human existence and it will serve the purpose of inactivating numerous false rumors about me which circulated during this period and were actively spread and utilized by the enemies of unarmored life. Finally, it illustrates the position of unarmored life in our social order.

I have procrastinated for years in compiling the details of and describing the infamous "Norwegian press campaign" against my research. Whenever I was working with a bion preparation, observing orgone energy, discovering, pondering, and systematizing the interrelationship of life functions, or the place of living matter in non-living nature, the clamorous "campaign" seemed utterly ludicrous. It had been answered unequivocally in the events that followed, e.g., the discovery of the secret of the cancer cell (1938–39), the discovery of the atmospheric orgone, the temperature difference in the orgone accumulator (1940), the healing effects of the orgone accumulator on blood and tissue, etc. The individuals who irrationally opposed my research in that campaign can no longer be viewed in a heroic light. To have entered into a debate with them in 1937 would have meant trying to shoot sparrows with a cannon. I was also not particularly interested in burdening the history of science with the names of insignificant persons. The furious struggle against me was very painful indeed. All manner of insult, suspicion, and calumny was employed, but it was futile to parry invective with invective. Although in 1937 I could not have anticipated the momentous events to occur in my future research, I was already aware of an enormous responsibility. I am not one of those individuals who hypocritically profess the virtues of clemency and submission. I can use invective as well as anyone else and must admit that I often felt a desire to castigate some of the advocates of pseudoscience when they carried matters too far. I am by no means a mild-mannered saint, but an inexplicable feeling restrained me from intervening in this type of "scientific debate," a feeling I recognized in amazement, only many years later, as the basic attitude of unarmored life—after hundreds of observations and experiments had confirmed my first vague notions.

The attitude of unarmored life toward life's aberrations, toward the malicious actions of armored human animals, is one of indifference or incomprehension, alienation, and occasionally pity. I have observed this basic attitude in small healthy children in the face of life's distortions and monstrosities, e.g., a young boy of four was happily playing on the street when several aggressive, obstreperous children approached him and demanded that he bring them a glass of water. He did it willingly, but when he handed them the water they shouted and threw it into his face, without any provocation. Some of the children laughed maliciously; others stood by embarrassed, saying nothing. No one, neither a child nor one of the many adults who witnessed the incident, interfered. The little boy stood still at first and then walked away, tears in his eyes, uncomprehending. On another day I saw the same child being pestered for no reason by an obviously nervous and sadistic boy. But this time he turned on his tormentor, threw him to the ground, gave him a thorough trouncing, and then walked off quietly. [Kindly life had finally abandoned its misplaced tolerance and goodwill; *it had begun to fight.* One day, sooner or later, all the kind and good-natured boys everywhere will start beating the hell out of the malicious, cowardly "big boys" and make them run screaming.]

During the campaign, I was a guest in a foreign country. True, I had been invited to teach at a university there, but the false sympathy, mingled with envy and fear of competition, always lurked behind the word "refugee"—the stigma of every alien. The campaign aggravated this painful situation. I had indeed fled from the German Fascists to Scandinavia, but I tried to bother my host country as little as possible. During my five-year stay in Norway, I lectured to university students on only two occasions. I did not write for newspapers, although I was requested to do so. I did not found a Norwegian-language journal but voluntarily limited myself to a German publication which was hardly read in Scandinavia because most people could not

Toward Biogenesis

read German. I worked quietly in my laboratory but would not allow myself to be denied the right to invite students to seminars and small lectures held privately. After all, I was living in a democratic country ruled by a Socialist Labor Party government. At the time of the press campaign, I discussed my withdrawal with friends. One of them, the poet Arnulf Överland, remarked, "I have never heard such clamorous silence." This comment struck the heart of the matter. If I had simply mingled in public, pursuing the innocent tasks of daily life, nothing would have happened. It was my very quietness which provoked my opponents to make as much noise as possible.

Wherever armored life presides over the scene of social intercourse, all activity is essentially traceable to:

1. A surfeit of words and concepts which serve only to distract from the simple basic principles of life.

2. Tense enthusiasm wherever armored beings encounter the uncomplicated laws of unarmored life.

3. Complete inability of armored individuals to utilize these simple laws in a practical manner, resulting in disappointment and hateful persecution of everything even vaguely reminiscent of unarmored living.

These three typical modes of behavior exemplify all the symptoms of the emotional plague. It will be demonstrated that the natural, truly uncomplicated laws of existence lack social recognition and protection, that truth may be purloined by every type of biopathic ideology, and that twentieth-century legislation has neither an interest in nor an understanding of unarmored functioning. I did not devise these pathological mechanisms of human life, but first experienced them as one of their many astonished victims. It was the responsibility for my great discovery which forced me to find the winding, secret paths along which the biopathic human animal stalks, attempting to destroy his own existence and well-being by slandering the giver of life.

I have already described the effect of the struggle against my work on the life process in Germany, Denmark, and Sweden. Among the opponents of unarmored life, the struggle was always waged under the cloak of political slogans because, unfortunately, my work occurred during an epoch in which the "political fugitive" was spotlighted by every police force in the world. It was asking too much to expect a government official to keep the question of the political fugitive separate from the question of biogenesis, when even a professor of cancer pathology was unable to make this distinction.

Between autumn 1934 and the beginning of 1937, for approximately three years, my research had the necessary peace in which to develop. The great campaign against the bion theory commenced in May 1937. It was preceded by generally insignificant skirmishes from which I could have deduced the impending danger had I not been overly naïve in adhering to my faith in the objectivity of scientific circles. I was theoretically aware of the fact that mechanistic science is itself an offspring of mechanistic civilization in regard to its methodology, but I was still unacquainted with its practices.

Healthy children, in whom life functions freely, discover and utilize the living process as if it were a game. By playfully setting his or her speech organs in motion, the child learns to form words—words which at first have no meaning, wrong words, not words in the sense of strict academic linguistics, but nevertheless sounds from which "correct" words proceed under environmental influence. Until the age of three, children are the greatest scientific discoverers. Their only tool is a lively bioenergy. Handling a spoon or a chair, opening and closing doors, selecting food, stroking, cuddling, and playing are not due to heredity. The same children, raised in a different cultural milieu, would derive other meaning from their activities. Children are the greatest natural researchers, and the greatest natural researchers are, first of all, children playfully conquering new fields of knowledge like infants mastering their new surroundings. Consider Leeuwenhoek, Faraday, Edison, among others.

The bionous nature of all matter that is allowed to swell was also discovered playfully. Anyone watching me on the lonely evenings when I "discovered" the bions would simply have shaken his head. No "serious scientist" would have paid me the slightest attention. The practical effects of cosmic orgone energy

Toward Biogenesis

on tissues, on growth in plants and animals, on biopathic decay in cancer, etc., are the result of that biological "playfulness" in 1935. I played in this way:

Over the course of the year 1935, I confirmed, by means of an oscillograph, the hypothesis which I had formulated on the basis of my sex-economic research, namely that the life process is determined by a four-beat rhythm, in the sequence: mechanical tension—charge—discharge—mechanical relaxation. This system of mechanical and bioenergetic functions did not exist in the non-living realm. The approach to the problem of biogenesis was to be sought in connection with this life formula—assuming the formula to be correct. Finding such an approach to biogenesis would, in turn, naturally confirm the validity of my formula for sexuality and the life process. In the case that no such approach could be found, the formula could still be correct, but it would remain sterile, for a time at least.

In 1935 I owned only one oscillograph, which I placed in the center of my small, fifteen-foot-square study amid a pile of books and manuscripts. I am not mentioning these details for the sake of sensationalism, but rather to contrast sharply the beginnings of such great scientific developments with the glory of official palaces and the monuments of politicians. I was not the first discoverer forced to work under such conditions while the drones of social life had millions at their disposal. I am dedicated to the living process and to honest work, but after thirty years of hard, dangerous research on the human organism, I do not feel obliged to bow before social absurdities.

During the winter of 1934–35 I had spent almost three thousand Norwegian kroner of my earnings as a teacher of biopsychiatry for the construction of the oscillograph. This, however, was not disturbing, because I loved my work and required little in my personal life. In my prominent position I earned enough to support my children and myself and, in addition, to afford the luxury of an oscillograph. But now I needed a microscope. A pupil, Dr. Lotte Liebeck, who had come to Oslo to study with me and had participated as a subject in the bioelectric experiments, was intensely interested in the work and offered to give me a microscope. Thus, at the end of 1935, I obtained a magnificent binocular Leitz research microscope with basic equipment for microphotography. Before using it, I first had to refresh the knowledge of microscopy I had acquired sixteen years before as a medical student in Vienna and had long since forgotten. The instrument met the usual requirements of magnification to 1500×. The day it arrived I began to check my hypothesis. I can still recall the evening I sat alone in my apartment brooding deeply over how to arrange the experiment. While I was playing with the microscope, with no idea of what to do, and placing everything within reach under the objective lens, it suddenly struck me that living organisms subsist on organic substances, i.e. substances which were once alive themselves. If living organisms continue to draw life energy from nourishment which had been living matter itself, then, I felt with increasing certainty, there had to be a connection. Food contains "chemical substances" which the organism assimilates and incorporates into its body fluids. This is a material, chemical process which has already been thoroughly investigated by science. I knew that the chemistry of foodstuffs could not be observed through a microscope, but I asked myself how it was possible for foodstuffs to pass through the walls of the intestines into the fluids circulating in a living organism. How does this occur? I had not yet considered the riddle of the osmosis of the contents of the intestines through the intestine wall,[1] which physiology had not yet solved. If the human intellect could always be aware of all the problems of natural science during its playful experimentation, a good many questions would be more easily answered.

The simplest procedure, I thought, would be to observe various foodstuffs under the microscope. Fortunately I did not possess any biochemical equipment that would enable me to study foodstuffs neatly broken down into fats, carbohydrates, and proteins. I say "fortunately" because if I had proceeded in a "strictly scientific" manner instead of naïvely and playfully, I would never have discovered the bionous nature of all matter that has been

[1] Cf. *The Cancer Biopathy* (Farrar, Straus & Giroux, 1973), pp. 361–64.

allowed to swell. Fats would have revealed nothing because they are composed exclusively of fat globules; sugar would have dissolved into molecules, and neither muscle tissue nor egg white would have revealed bions. My actions were not particularly well considered, but I was tormented by the basic question of the relationship between foodstuffs and the organism. It was "crazy"! I threw meat, potatoes, all kinds of vegetables, milk, and eggs into a pot, filled it with water, boiled it for half an hour, took a sample, and rushed it to the microscope. What I saw seemed as insane as the entire venture. I had expected to be able to differentiate clearly between the various substances. But pure chance —usually called fate—enabled my endeavor to take a giant step forward. *The sample contained nothing but vesicles.* All were of the same type although different in size. There were also large bubbles and shapes which I recognized as starch. The mixture I had brewed was thus an essentially homogeneous mass. The individual vesicles shone in a blue to blue-green hue. At first I discarded this with the "explanation" that it was due to a refraction of light, exactly the way strict natural scientists still "explain away" the blue or blue-green glimmer of biological colloids. My first orgone-physical conclusion was correct, namely that organic substances, when boiled, disintegrate, i.e. swell, into vesicles. I was on the track of the "bions."

I adjusted the microscope to a magnification of 1500×. Motion within the contents of the vesicles was now clearly visible, but not clear enough to allow me to draw conclusions. I inquired of the Leitz company as to the magnification of their strongest objective and was informed that it was 150×, whereupon I immediately ordered it. Together with a 16×, or perhaps a 25× ocular, I could achieve a magnification in the vicinity of 5000×. Although I was aware that no structures are clearly resolvable over a magnification of 2000×, it was not seeing the finer structures themselves which interested me but *seeing the motion within the bions.* Although I have often emphasized this differentiation between structure and movement in the evaluation of microscopic objects, the objection can still be heard that I did not know how to use a microscope because I was unaware that there is a limit to microscopic observation using light. Prejudices are as deeply embedded as lice in an animal's fur, and the greater the ignorance, the greater the arrogance. Since mechanistic researchers focus totally and exclusively on the dead structures of stained tissues, they do not understand that there is also movement and that the fine motion in a particle which is not yet noticeable at a magnification of 2000× is, however, visible at a magnification of 3000×.

I owe the discovery of biological energy and with it of cosmic orgone energy to this *differentiation between structure and movement,* a differentiation which appears foreign and "unscientific" to mechanistic thinkers. The *inner* motion which I discovered in my bions also solved the question of "Brownian movement." In the nineteenth century Brown observed that very small India-ink particles move from place to place. He was entirely correct in viewing this motion as an indication of life forces. Soon, however, mechanistic physicists seized the issue, destroyed Brown's very fertile theory, and transformed its living quality into dead mechanics. They argued that the movement of the tiny particles is caused by "bombardment of the molecules in the liquid." Thus a momentous discovery was stifled for decades; their delicate calculations of the distances traveled by the Brownian particles could not change this. Only in the 1940's did I realize that the destructive mechanisms of armored life had participated in the physicists' procedures and that their attitude was due to the general evasion of everything that merely reminds one of orgone energy.

In my bions it was not the external but rather the internal motion which was significant. The "bombardment of molecules" would not suffice to explain internal motility such as vibration, expansion, contraction, convulsion, etc. Just as preoccupation with matter had limited the mechanist to microscopic observations below 1500×, the mechanistic bombardment theory also barricaded access to the origins of the inner motility of swollen matter and therewith access to bioenergy.

In another work I have described in great detail the development of protozoa from bions and that of bions from matter and

Toward Biogenesis 263

mass-free orgone energy, and hence may limit myself to a brief summary at this point. It was logical that I continue to add more, and very diverse, substances to my mixture and then cook them. Finally there was nothing but blue, glimmering, internally agitated vesicles. Next I began to swell various substances in water slowly, at room temperature. The appearance of bions now occurred much more slowly, over the course of days or weeks, depending on the hardness of the substance. However, disintegration into bions always occurred, regardless of the material I subjected to swelling. Gradually it became evident that *the internal motility was to be attributed to an energy freed from formed matter during heating or swelling.* For this reason I also termed the bions "energy vesicles." [The term "orgone" did not yet exist.] *The internal motility was an effect of work, and work is inconceivable without energy.* I intentionally avoided determining what type of energy I had encountered. There was ample time for that. Meticulous observation alone could produce further clarification.

The swelling of moss and blades of grass revealed the development of protozoa from bions, i.e. natural organization in biogenesis. My observations and microphotography left no doubt as to this; but to be absolutely certain, I requested amoeba cultures from the Botanical Institute in Oslo. An assistant there was very friendly and said that the simplest method of obtaining amoebae was to make grass infusions. I then asked him, momentarily completely naïve and unaware—that is, without ulterior motive— how the protozoa came into the infusion. "From the air, of course," he replied in astonishment. "And how do they get into the air?" I asked. "We don't know" was the answer. He did not tell me that as yet no one had succeeded in cultivating protozoa from air. Therefore I was confronted with the task of preparing numerous air-contamination cultures to convince myself that there were no protozoal germs in the air.

[During the following years I tried hundreds of times to obtain protozoa from the air, with no success. This fact burdens the "air infection" theorists with the task of proving their contention that protozoa develop from "air germs."

Today, before any student of orgone biophysics and biogenesis is admitted to advanced biogenetic work at the Orgone Institute, he must attempt to prove that protozoa, cancer cells, plasmatic flakes, bions, T-bacilli, "cysts," etc., can be obtained through "air infection." Only when he is convinced by ample air-culture experiments that there is no such thing as protozoa in the air will he be able to resist the many influences exerted upon him by his social environment, relinquish his anxieties about "impurities," and study nature as it functions. Only then will he be able to judge intelligently where air infection is actually valid. In such cases, he will adhere to strict sterilization. But he will no longer misinterpret every microscopic observation which clearly demonstrates biogenesis as "only air infection." The extent and intricacy of the evasions made possible by neglecting to prove to oneself the possibilities of actual air infection are unbelievable. This evasiveness must be completely removed, in student and professor of biology alike, if one intends to get through the mire of "air infection" beliefs.

The problem is more complicated in the case of rot bacteria (fusiformis, subtilis, etc.). It is possible to obtain such bacteria from the air. However, it is not easy to do so. And even if it is accomplished the next logical question is *"How do bacteria get into the air?"* This inescapable question provokes an irrational response instead of a factual answer. No one has even tried to answer it. Orgonomy offers the following explanation: The dust "particles" in the air arise from all kinds of decayed organic matter. We obtain rot bacteria from the air through hydration and decay of the dust bions just as we do in any decaying bion preparation.

The air-germ theorist simply refuses to consider this argument and sometimes resorts instead to slander. However, from now on this question will trouble every serious biologist. It can no longer be circumvented.

All this has nothing whatsoever to do with "spontaneous generation." Nor has the theory that life originates from non-living nature ever been disproved. Neither Pasteur nor anyone

Toward Biogenesis

else has claimed this. What Pasteur did in his quarrel with Bastian was to behave like a man who maintains that a certain alive, mobile horse is not alive, contrary to all appearances. When the owner of the horse insists that it is alive, the man takes an ax, bashes in the horse's head, and then triumphantly says: "Now it is obvious to anyone that the horse is dead." This story is analogous to the function of sterilizing living matter in biogenetic research. Fortunately, orgonomic biology has broken the spell. Bions arise from completely sterilized material through swelling, as in Experiment XX after freezing of the yellow bion water. It may take months or years before protozoa appear in sterile preparations, but they are there. The spontaneous decay of living tissue into bions and then into rot bacteria can be observed microscopically and reproduced experimentally. This process goes on constantly in all nature, and in many diseases. The helplessness of erroneous bacteriological theory in the face of such diseases as cancer will sooner or later bring about the defeat of the adherents of the air-infection theory. Unseen air germs cannot possibly prevail against clearly visible bionous processes. One wonders how many human lives will be lost before an end is put to this incredible mismanagement of scientific matters.]

At the time I respected mechanistic natural science and its representatives. They were forthright, diligent men and women who carried on their experimental work with care. Only in the following years did I free myself from a dangerous error to which I had clung, not entirely without irrational reasons. I knew I had encountered the problem of biogenesis and that this problem was the central issue not only of all biological sciences but of natural science itself. It was obvious that I was not sufficiently equipped for *this* problem despite more than one and a half decades of natural-scientific and philosophic training. It was too much, far too much for one person, even considering my capacity for work and my experience. I was as yet unaware that I was afraid of the problem. I felt I had to gain the cooperation of established scientific institutions if I were to succeed. Phenomena which I could not comprehend were appearing with increasing frequency, but I did not know that mechanistic researchers also have no explanations for these phenomena nor do they even realize they exist. I was still to be made aware of this in a dangerous way.

From the multitude of these momentous new facts I shall select only one to orient the reader. The phenomenon I have chosen led later to the discovery of the origin of cancer. As students of orgone biophysics know, cancer tumors are traceable to the general cancerous shrinking biopathy, which in turn is traceable to a tendency toward decay in blood and tissues. Painstaking clinical examination indicated that this tendency toward decay was itself rooted in a sharp decline of the pulsatory function and with it the energy metabolism of the organism. *Thus the key to the problem of cancer was the problem of decay* or, expressed more "scientifically," the nature of bodily degeneration and putrefaction of living tissue. When I encountered my bions I had no idea that decay is too "commonplace" and "unscientific" to be investigated by medicine, bacteriology, biology, and biophysics.

Decay is a universal, natural process. All living substance ascends to a greater or lesser height and then gradually declines, leading finally to death and tissue disintegration through decay. There is no sterilization in nature and no "air infection." But mechanistic biologists and bacteriologists do not consider themselves scientists until they have carefully sterilized everything. Because of the fact that these natural scientists neatly, properly, and meticulously exclude all possibility of decay or "air infection" from their preparations with the strictest precision of the mechanistic age, the greatest discovery in biology slipped through their fingers, namely the simple explanation that the cancer process is rooted in the premature decay of blood and tissues; that, in other words, the cancerous organism suffers a "living death." It was the "air germ" theory, rigidly and mechanically applied, and the theorem *"omnis cellula ex cellula"* which caused cancer research, and all other biogenetic research, to become sterile in the strictest sense of the word. We shall soon see the enormous role played by the "banal rot bacteria" not only in cancer research but also in the campaign of armored life against unarmored life processes, of mechanistic science against orgonomic functionalism.

At first I worked under completely non-sterile conditions. I observed tissues in their natural state, cooked and uncooked, using no sterilization. Today I realize I would never have been confronted with the cancer problem had I adhered exclusively to the observation of sterile preparations as the law of strict biology requires. I watched rot bacteria appear in my preparations. Under high magnification one could distinctly follow the disintegration of tissue into vesicles and then directly into long rod-like shapes. [This process has been filmed. If only my opponents would care to look into the microscope they could see the formation of rot bacteria clearly and unequivocally.] The observation left no room for doubt. With one blow it overthrew a mountain of false, mechanistic, biological concepts. To convince myself experimentally that I was correct, I sterilized an egg-white preparation, kept it sterile, and discovered that even the strictest precautionary measures could not prevent auto-disintegration of the protein under certain internal conditions and the appearance of rot bacteria. I painted fresh eggs with lacquer and tar, but sooner or later they decomposed. All the substances I sterilized degenerated sooner or later for internal, not external reasons. I prepared a sterile mixture of substances which has since become the famous preparation 6c.[2] The rot bacteria appeared within a few minutes. I heated coal to incandescence and added it to the swelling solution. Five minutes later I was able to observe and Gram-stain short mobile organisms which were later called T-bacilli. Thus *there was no doubt as to the internal origin of the decay,* although it was still entirely unclear to which energy forces it was to be attributed.

I now made my first "tactical" error by yielding to Dr. Odd Havrevold's urgent suggestion that I ask the Oslo Bacteriological Institute to identify the micro-organisms. I must beg the reader's understanding as to why I regard this as a serious mistake. De-

[2] Communicated to the French Academy of Science, 1937.

spite a basic knowledge of bacteriology, I was not a specialist. The appearance of biologically stainable micro-organisms shortly after a bion preparation had been made, naturally excluded the possibility of so-called air infection because the latter would require at least twenty-four hours for bacteria to appear. I was aware of this fact but could not make the decision alone as to whether the micro-organisms resulting from my experimentation were identical with known forms or represented essentially new ones. Had a well-equipped laboratory and, above all, sufficient funds been at my disposal, I would have employed a bacteriologist to conduct the necessary tests. However, I did not have the money and had preferred to wait and to avoid contact with "official" science because of several unfortunate experiences, which I would like to describe briefly.

When I succeeded in producing bions from preparation 6c in the last months of 1936, I asked friends in Copenhagen to request the Biological Institute, headed by Dr. Albert Fischer, to allow me the use of its microphotographic equipment in order to study on rapid-motion film the development of bions from matter which had been allowed to swell. Fischer's response was friendly and I went to Copenhagen to demonstrate experiment 6c. Shortly before I began, Fischer asked a cynical question about what sort of a paste I was planning to brew. This was typical of the basic attitude of classical biology. I was tempted to walk out but then accepted his pacifying apology and continued. The substances were mixed and the preparation cooked. Then difficulties arose because Fischer's microscope magnified only to 1500× and thus revealed the shapes themselves but not their internal motility. This required magnification of at least 2000×. Fischer grew nervous and raised the issue of the limits of useful magnification. I replied that my objective was to observe motility and not to identify structure. [This lack of distinction between the functional (movement) and the mechanical-static (structure) lingered on for years in all discussions of high-power microscopy.] One of Fischer's assistants suggested a Giemsa stain, which was immediately made, revealing forms that reacted positively. This demonstration clearly made a deep impression, but subsequent events demonstrated that prejudice in favor of the "air germ" theory was overpowering.

I returned to Oslo and asked Dr. Leunbach [a Danish physician and early friend of orgonomy] to keep open the channels to Fischer. Soon a letter arrived from Leunbach informing me that Fischer's reaction had been very peculiar. He had accused me of "lacking critical judgment" and of "fantasizing," claiming that I had requested ridiculously high magnification. Supposedly, I had described observations of spindle formations and cell divisions. All motility, he said, was the movement of the liquid, and my contentions were the "old fairy tales" from the era prior to Pasteur—untenable mixtures of psychology and biology.

To prevent false rumors, I refuted all Fischer's claims in a letter to Leunbach on January 9, 1937, although I continued to believe (inexcusably) in the objectivity of natural scientists. It would have been better to react defensively and curtly. Fischer had simply attempted to explain away obvious facts. He denied the Giemsa stain, paid no attention to the appearance of rods and cocci a few minutes after the preparation had been made, and resorted to portraying the entire experiment in a ridiculous light. Unfortunately, I did not dream of how new, how revolutionary and comprehensive my experiment was.

I also encountered the mechanistic natural scientists' fear of moving life during an experiment with coal bions, in the presence of the Norwegian cancer pathologist Leif Kreyberg. This demonstration was the direct cause of his reversal from cooperation to hate-filled animosity. He had brought me a cancer preparation (as he had often done before) and I asked him whether he wanted to view the cancer cells under high magnification, which had not been available to him previously. I had focused on a spindle formation moving across the field slowly and jerkily. He looked through the microscope at 4000× and did not recognize the forms as cancer cells.

He asked to see my coal bions. I heated a fresh coal-dust preparation to incandescence and added it to the swelling solution. Several minutes later I took a small sample and adjusted the microscope to 3000×. The bions were extremely motile, contractile, and manifested a blue glimmer. [These characteristics are familiar today to those who have observed coal bions.] Kreyberg looked through the microscope and was taken aback. "I would like to see your 'broth,' " he said, implying that he believed it to be a contaminated solution. This astonished me because he had seen the clear solution himself. Furthermore, it is impossible to confuse a coal bion with any known particulate matter obtained from the air. Still, I yielded to his demands and put a drop of the solution under the microscope at the same magnification. Naturally there was nothing to be seen. Kreyberg walked away obviously shaken. Previously he had asked me for a coal-bion culture to examine at home. I hesitated slightly, knowing he would have no idea of what to do with it. I did, however, give him a sample of the culture grown on agar. His evaluation of this pure culture clearly demonstrated the verbal idiom of bacteriology. In his later campaign against me, he claimed the bion culture had contained "only staphylococci." Only staphylococci! In this way Kreyberg rejected the novelty of motile cancer cells at $4000\times$, as well as the incident with the coal bions. He made absolutely no mention of them—an outrageous crime for an individual who called himself "objective" and "scientific." He further omitted reporting that the "staphylococci" represented a "pure culture," whereas air infection usually produces mixed cultures. Nor was he aware that during the process of killing, drying, and staining bions all differences disappear, leaving behind only round, blue forms, which are indeed similar to staphylococci. Kreyberg demonstrated his ignorance—which in a typical way he attributed to me—by believing he had understood a phenomenon when he had only known its name. [He did not understand that the word "staphylococci" says nothing about the origin of the form.] He shared this basic mistake with all mechanistic researchers. He withheld from the public the fact that it is possible to observe vesicles forming from matter under a microscope, although I had published these findings. In short, this man revealed himself as an insolent neurotic who concealed his own ignorance and his inclination for intrigue by accusing me of charlatanism. He was desperately afraid that I was actually correct. [Later, in his efforts to discredit me, he even resorted to gross lies.] What puzzles me is not his behavior but that of the public, including several of my close friends, who invested this man with authority simply because he was an official in a public cancer hospital. [In such hands rests the fate of thousands suffering from cancer.]

Despite these two experiences at the end of 1936, I agreed to Havrevold's suggestion to send the bacteriologist Thjötta bion preparations for identification of the forms.[3] I sent him an uncooked bion preparation 6a, in which rods had appeared a few minutes after the mixture had been made. His oral report to Havrevold stated that it contained simple rods, i.e. subtilis and proteus as found in decaying matter. At the time, as mentioned above, I had not the slightest idea of the enormous significance of these "simple rods" for the entire cancer problem. I simply followed the development of phenomena and sought the aid of specialists in an unpardonably innocent fashion. As yet, nothing was known of orgone energy and therefore I was also unaware of armored life's deathly fear of the orgone, the life energy itself.

The so-called air infection of the unsterile bion preparation 6 proved to be the key to the cancer problem. Let us therefore summarize briefly the arguments which render my opponents' theoretical position invalid; they were elaborated in the second volume of *The Discovery of the Orgone: The Cancer Biopathy*.

1. The cancer process is a long-drawn-out process of decay within the organism due to bioenergetic shrinking of the life system. In the course of this degeneration and decomposition of living protein, rot bacteria develop which slowly degenerate further into T-bacilli, which can be observed in and cultivated from the tissues, including the blood, of every cancer patient. The cancer cell itself is a protozoon formed in animal tissues just as protozoa are organized from decaying plant tissue.

2. No cancer cells or protozoa of any kind can or will ever be

[3] Instead of restricting himself to a simple identification of the organisms in the preparation, he misused this opportunity in the interest of the air-germ theory. Unasked and unauthorized, he issued a public statement to the effect that he "had controlled Reich's experiments" and found "nothing but simple bacilli." His statements had nothing whatsoever to do with our request to identify the organisms.

found "in the air." Every effort to obtain protozoa from the air has failed in my laboratory, and there is no proof in the literature of classical biology that protozoa were actually found in the air. This claim is pure invention on the part of prejudiced scientists. It serves to maintain a defunct view of life which sharply distinguishes the organic from the inorganic, in origin as well as function. Orgonomy has proved by microscopic observation and sterile experiments that primordial life develops through many phases from bions, i.e. energy vesicles. No proof to the contrary has even been adduced. No airborne protozoa or cancer cells have ever been demonstrated. The burden of counter-proof now rests squarely on the shoulders of the air-germ theorists. If they wish to maintain their position, they must prove that cancer cells and protozoa exist in the air. If they cannot prove this, it is logical to assume that cancer cells arise somehow within the organism. It is exactly at this point that malignant irrationalism enters the scene in debates about orgonomic observations. As long as opponents of orgonomy refuse to look into microscopes, however, their objections cannot be taken seriously.

These opponents should be reminded that we are no longer living in the beginning of the age of bacteriology; we are living in its decline. The theory of infection from the air has exhausted its usefulness. It has become a barrier which obstructs the understanding and healing of diseases such as cancer, high blood pressure, rheumatic fever, etc. We are now facing an entirely new set of problems grouped around the natural function of endogenous infection and decay. These afflictions are no longer parasitic in origin; they are bioenergetic and emotional, i.e. functional. Thus, we are entering a new age in medicine and biology. The guiding line of these new developments will, of necessity, be the functions (still to be elaborated) of the concrete, measurable, manageable, visible life energy, orgone energy.

The discovery in 1940 of an energy in the atmosphere with the specific qualities of life (pulsation, orgonomic potential, constant higher heat potential, etc.) not only confirmed the microscopic phenomena in bions, but put an end to all narrow-minded, shortsighted prattle about unseen and unproven "air germs" as

Toward Biogenesis

the source of primordial life, such as amoebae, trichomonads, colpidiae, etc. It eliminated an empty slogan which had obfuscated clear-cut facts for decades and blocked any advance toward an understanding of biogenesis. In 1945 when Experiment XX revealed the formation of plasmatic matter from sterile, autoclaved, and frozen bion water, it became clear that all organic life emerges from orgone energy which has absorbed water, concentrated into bions, and continues to pulsate within flexible membranes. Life *does* come "from the air and from the soil," not as unseen air germs, but as cosmic life energy.

I do not know what I may appear to the world; but to myself I seem to have been only like a boy playing on the seashore, and diverting myself in now and then finding a smoother pebble or a prettier shell than ordinary whilst the great ocean of truth lay all undiscovered before me.

—Isaac Newton

Index

ABC, 252
abortion, 109–11, 151
adolescents, 73, 111–15, 122–3, 153–54, 164, 174–9, 184–5, 226, 235
Aigner, 44
air infection, 263–6, 268–73
Analysis of the Christ Dogma, 136
Arbeiterblad, 200
Arbeiterhilfe, 30
Arbeiterwehr, 81–7, 115, 148, 187, 215
Association for Birth Control, 150
Association of Socialist Physicians, 138
Austria, 11, 22–9, 32–4, 38–47, 120, 239; *see also* names of places in and under Social Democrats

Bachofen, Johann Jakob, 72, 121
Barash, 123
Bastian, 265
Bauer, Otto, 31, 35, 39–40, 43–4, 78, 95
Bergler, Edmund, 250
Berlin, 118, 152, 158, 180, 188; Reich and, 135–57, 189–91, 214–15; marches and demonstrations in, 141, 143–4, 147–8, 162
Berlin Training Institute, 193
Bernfeld, Siegfried, 137, 192–3, 196
Bibring, Edward, 246
biogenesis, 254–5, 258–9, 263–6, 273
biological energy, discovery of, 262

bions, 254–73, 172n; movement and structure in, 261, 268–70; and Brownian Movement, 262; protozoa from, 262–73
biopathy, cancer, 12, 266, 271
birth control, 108, 111–12, 151, 168
Bischoff, 154
Bleuler, Eugen, 209
Bloch, 17
Böhm, 238–9
Brandler, 205
Braun, Otto, 159
Brupbacher, Fritz, 213

cancer, 235, 250, 254–5, 258–9, 265–67, 269–72
Capital, 48, 53, 183
Chalk Triangle, The, 156, 175
Chamberlain, Neville, 75–6, 171
Character Analysis, 193–4, 197, 217, 219, 225–6
character analysis, 73, 217, 225, 235, 245, 247, 253
Charlottenburg, 154, 156, 175
children, rearing of, 7, 12, 58, 100, 107, 154; and neuroses, 211; healthy, 256, 258; *see also under* sexuality
Christian Center Party, 153, 178–9, 181
Christian Democrats, 169, 177, 181
Christian Party, 150, 156–7
Christian Socialists, 34–5, 37–40, 43–4, 46, 78–81, 116

INDEX

Clemensen, Dr., 208
Communists (ism), 4, 10, 11, 29–30, 33, 36n, 37–8, 43–6, 79, 81–4, 86, 88, 91, 96–7, 101, 106, 111, 116–17, 119, 137–9, 141–55, 158–9, 162, 165, 168–70, 172, 175–7, 180, 182–3, 185, 187–8, 192–5, 201, 205–6, 211–15, 231, 250; *see also under* Reich "Contributions to the Understanding of . . . ," 18
Copenhagen, Reich and, 188, 191, 196, 205, 207–8, 251
Copernicus, 64
Coué, Émile, 36, 46
Crime and Custom in Savage Society, 121
cultural Bolshevism, 194
Cunow, 22

Daladier, Édouard, 171
death-instinct theory, 28, 73, 91, 192–3, 225, 228, 235, 242, 248, 250
decay, and cancer, 266–7
dialectical materialism, 136–7, 146, 183, 227
Dialectical Materialism and Psychoanalysis, 73, 202
Discovery of the Orgone, The, 271
Dollfuss, Engelbert, 79, 116, 159
Domes, 78
Dresden, resolution and letters from, 176–9
Dühring, Eugen, 203
Duncker, Franz, 11, 147
Dusseldorf, conference in, 152

economics, 15–17, 31, 46, 50–68, 70, 72, 82, 88–9, 91, 100–1, 106, 120, 123, 125, 128–9, 131, 133, 139–42, 162–5, 171–2, 180, 184, 203, 233, 235
Edison, Thomas, 258
Eitingon, Max, 193, 196, 247
Ellis, Havelock, 17
emotional plague, 3, 4, 12, 14, 49–50, 60, 69, 89, 99, 108, 167, 205–6, 255, 257

energy vesicles, and blue-green color, 161, *see also* bions
Engels, Friedrich, epigraph, 11, 13, 22, 72, 121, 128–9, 131, 137n
eugenics, 17, 109, 151
Experiment XX, 265, 273

family, 16–17, 28, 72, 74, 100–1, 104–6, 129, 133, 149, 165, 167–71
Faraday, Michael, 258
Fascism (ists), 11, 17, 18, 29–30, 32, 35, 42–3, 46, 48–9, 61n, 64, 77, 94–5, 119–20, 137–9, 149, 159, 161–2, 167–70, 172–4, 187–8, 191, 194–5, 194n, 201, 203, 205–6, 215, 225–6, 230–1, 233, 235, 240, 251–52, 256; *see also* red Fascism
Federn, Paul, 20, 74, 225–6, 239, 246–7
Fenichel, Otto, 136–7, 225, 227–9, 231–2, 237–43, 245, 248, 252
films, 64–5, 147
Fischer, Albert, 268–9
Forel, Auguste, 17
"free-will" theory,.68–9
Freud, Anna, 196, 226, 248
Freud, Sigmund, 6, 13, 18–20, 27–28, 43, 46, 53, 67–8, 70, 72–4, 103–5, 128, 163, 192, 222, 225–26, 234, 240–1, 244–5, 249; and Reich, 46, 72–5, 192–3, 195, 209, 222, 224, 226, 232
Freudians, 15, 19, 63, 70–2, 203
Friedjung, Karl, 20
Friedländer, Dr., 180
Fromm, Erich, 136
Funktion des Orgasmus, Die, 18, 18n

Galileo, 64
Gegenangriff, Der, 203
genitality, 19–20
German National Association, minutes of conference of, 180–3
Germany, 11, 29, 42, 97–9, 120, 133–64, 167, 171, 188, 191, 194, 205; *see also* Berlin, Fascism, *and* Hitler

Gerö, 245
Göring, Hermann, 238
Grailer, 44
Groddeck, Georg, 210
Group Psychology and Ego Analysis, 27
Grube, 176
Gürtler, 43–4

Hartleb, 43
Hartmann, Heinz, 246
Havrevold, Odd, 267, 271
Heimwehr, 79–81
Hirschfeld, Magnus, 17, 151
Hitler, Adolf, 13, 17, 38, 42–3, 46, 69, 75, 87, 116, 133–4, 147, 158–63, 165–6, 168, 170–1, 180, 188–9, 194, 199, 203–5, 212, 238
Hodann, Max, 184, 213
Hoel, Nic, 247–8
Hoel, Sigurd, 222–3
Horthy, Miklós, 159

IFA, 152, 154
illusion, 69–70, 76, 163
Imago, 73, 239
International Psychoanalytic Association, 135, 192, 209, 211, 224–5, 228, 236–9, 242–3, 249–50; Reich and, 194–6, 210, 227, 232, 238, 241, 245–8; Reich's expulsion from,, 244–50
"Introduction of Soviet Democracy," 48
Invasion of Compulsory Sex-Morality, The, 15, 60n, 73, 127, 156, 175, 183, 210, 217
Iroquois, 121, 127–8
irrationalism, 6–9, 18, 64, 67, 69–70, 82, 88–91, 96, 98–9, 147, 163, 167, 171, 214, 233–4, 254, 272; *see also under* politics

Jacobson, Edith, 227
Jews, 160, 165–8, 238
Jones, Ernest, 74, 209–10, 216, 226, 238, 246–8

Journal of the Academy of Sciences, 73

Kautsky, Karl Johann, 11, 22
Kolnai, 193
Konstad, 254
Krafft-Ebing, Richard von, 17
Kraus, Friedrich, 217
Kreyberg, Leif, 269–70
Kris, Ernst, 246
Künkel, 238
Kunschak, 43

Laforgue, René, 241
Lantos, Barbara, 136
Lebensraum, 17
Le Bon, 27
Lenin, Nikolai, 13, 17, 46, 138
Leeuwenhoek, Anton van, 258
Leunbach, J. H., 150, 196, 218, 269
Liebeck, Lotte, 259–60
life, armored and unarmored, 254–7, 262, 267, 271
Lindenberg, Elsa, 216–19, 221, 251
London, Reich to, 209–11
Lucerne, Congress in, 224, 226, 232, 235, 239–40, 242–51
Ludwig, Feuerbach, epigraph,

Malinowski, Bronislaw, 11, 74, 119–22, 210–11, 222
Malmö, Reich in, 209, 216–22, 226–27
Malthus, Thomas, 111
Man, Hendrik de, 16
marriage, 106, 121, 123–9, 149, 151, 154, 218
Marx, Karl, 10, 15, 16, 34, 48–72, 111, 183, 234
Marxist psychoanalysts, 233
Marxist Workers' University, 139
Marxists (ism), 16, 17, 19, 24, 31, 45, 48–72, 89, 94, 100–1, 119, 131, 136, 140, 147, 163–5, 167, 182, 184–5, 187, 196, 201, 225, 227, 232–6
masochism, Freud's reaction to Reich's paper on, 192

280 INDEX

Mass Psychology of Fascism, The, 9, 17, 73, 146, 165, 197–9, 204, 211, 214, 225–6; reviews of, 200–1, 203–4
matriarchy, 121, 127–9
matter, swelling of, 261–3
"meat grinder," the, 7
Mehring, Franz, 22
Mein Kampf, 147, 159–60, 163, 166, 238
Meng, 20
microscope, experiments with, 259–63, 267–9
Misch, Käthe, 216
Morgan, Lewis, 72, 121, 127
Müller-Braunschweig, Carl, 243–4
Murder of Christ, The, 235n
Mutterrecht, Das, 72
mysticism, 69–70, 72, 76, 203, 239

National Socialists (ism), 75, 97, 143, 147, 153–4, 157–9, 163, 165–69, 171–2, 174, 178, 181, 190, 203, 225, 228, 239
natural science, 5–9, 13, 15–16, 50, 59, 67–8, 70, 76, 89–90, 203, 224, 226, 228, 239, 242–3, 248–9, 261, 265–6, 269
Nazi, *see* National Socialist
Neesgard, 209
Neue Generation, 151
Neugebauer, 147
neuroses, 6, 19, 58, 102, 104–5, 108, 112, 114, 129, 138, 187, 210–11, 239–40, 249
Nietzsche, Friedrich, 7
Norway, press campaign in, 255–8; Reich in, *see* Oslo
Norwegian Psychoanalytic Society, 247, 251–3

Oedipus complex, 74, 100–1, 104, 111, 114, 211, 239
On the Basic Antithesis of Vegetative Life, 221
One World, 91n
oranur experiment, 3, 235n

orgasm, electrical nature of, 211; formula, 235
orgasm theory, Fenichel and the, 240–5
orgastic potency, 17
orgone accumulator, 255; temperature difference in the, 255
orgone energy, *see* orgonomy
orgonomy, 3–6, 9, 10, 12, 51, 62, 71–72, 136, 172n, 211, 225, 235, 240–41, 243, 245, 248, 255, 258–9, 262–7, 269, 271–3
Origin of the Family, The, 72
Oslo, Reich in, 251, 254–7; meeting at, 227–8, 237
Oslo Bacteriological Institute, 267
Oslo Psychiatric Society, 252
Överland, Arnulf, 257

Parell, Ernst, 202, 212
Paris, Reich to, 211–13
Pasteur, Louis, 264–5, 269
Pestalozzi, Johann, 7
Pfister, Rev., 193
Philipson, Tage, 221
Pitzl, 78
Plan, 199–202
PM, 225
politics (ians) 4, 49–50, 58–62, 75–76, 82, 88–9, 115, 117, 131, 172, 184, 187, 192–5, 202–3, 205–6, 210, 213–14, 228, 234, 251; Reich and, 5, 8–14, 31, 37, 44, 75, 89–92, 101–3, 106–7, 111, 115–17, 134–5, 141–9, 174, 187, 191, 212, 214, 232, 250; irrationalism of, 8, 9, 14, 24, 33, 34, 75, 89, 101–2, 198–9; work vs., 8–9, 13, 82; catastrophe of, 8, 22–9, 32–4, 38–47; population, 17, 111, 151, 154; *see also names of parties*
Politken, 188
Polyclinic, 74, 100, 104, 111
pornography, 199, 208, 243
Pötzl, Otto, 209
psychiatry, social, 11–12, 172–224; *see also* psychoanalysis and psychology

Index

psychic energy, concept of and Freud, 226
"Psychischer Kontakt und vegetative Strömung," 249
psychoanalysis, 4, 100–4, 107, 111, 114, 119, 135–6, 138, 192–5, 220–21, 225–8, 231–3, 235–6, 238–41, 244, 249
Psychoanalytischer Verlag, 193–4
psychology, 15–20, 43, 53, 63, 66–8, 71–5, 88–9, 128, 145, 153, 172, 183, 269; political, 9, 13, 82, 120, 163; mass, 10, 59, 82, 90, 92, 120, 136, 145, 149, 163, 174, 187, 191, 233, 240, 251
puberty, 226
Putsch, 137

race, theory of, 17, 160, 165–7, 170, 188
Raknes, Ola, 247
red Fascism (ists), 11; basic tenets on, 205–7
"Red Wedding," 95, 144
Reich, Wilhelm, as silent observer, 3–4; explanation by, for present book, 5–14; and Communism, 10–11, 19, 29–32, 91–2, 101, 110, 117, 119, 135, 145–6, 148–50, 152–5, 177, 197–205, 209; and psychoanalysts (is), 19, 74–5, 119, 135–8, 192–6, 205, 207–11, 224–8, 232, 235–7, 240–53; and workers' strikes, 23–9, 31–3, 81–7; and seminar, 74–5, 193; and Nazi ideology, 173–5; prohibition on publications of, 175–6, 182, 202–3; comments on theory of, 180–3; critiques of books of, 184–5, 189, 200–1, 203–4; danger to, in Berlin, 189–91; paper of, on masochism, 192–3; pseudonyms of, 202, 212, 223; travels of, 213–16, 223, 251, see also under place names; visits of, with family, 213, 223, 251; see also under items throughout
Reichsbannerjugend, 187

Reichsgesetzblatt, 202
Reichstag, fire at, 188
Renner, Karl, 77–8
Ricardo, David, 60
Roheim, Geza, 74, 122, 127, 239, 241
Rot Sport, 175
Rote Fahne, 91, 184
Rote Hilfe, 30, 197
Rotfrontkämpferbund, 138, 143, 158
Rousseau, Jean-Jacques, 7
Ruben-Wolff, Marta, 183
Russia, 13, 36, 38, 41, 46, 50, 61–2, 69–70, 89, 111, 120, 123, 131, 133, 137–8, 142–3, 155, 158, 165, 170, 172, 183, 186, 205, 212–13
Russian Revolution, 7, 17, 30, 35–6, 74, 131, 186

SA, 147–8, 158–9, 189–90, 192, 215
Sauerland, Kurt, 146
Schattendorf, 22–3
Schilder, Paul, 209
schizophrenia, 7, 250
Schjelderup, Harald, 227, 247, 252
Schmitz, Dr., 78
Schneider, 154
Schober, Johann, 115
Schröder, Professor, 208
Schultz-Hencke, 238
Schutzbund, 22–4, 26, 32, 39, 78–80, 82–4, 87, 115–17, 191
Seipel, Ignaz, 33, 38
Seitz, Karl, 26, 33, 77–8, 95
sex-counseling centers, 73–4, 97–9, 107–8, 112, 115
sexual currents, recording of, 226
sex-economy, 6, 7, 9, 12–14, 17, 51, 59, 71–4, 91, 104, 108, 119–20, 122, 130–2, 135, 167–9, 227, 232–36, 241–2, 248–50, 259; and political concepts, 9
sex-morality, 122, 125, 130, 132
sex-politics, 119–20, 130, 133–4, 142, 149–57, 170, 175, 177–9, 181–3, 185, 191, 212, 234, 250; see also Sexpol
Sex and Repression, 121

INDEX

Sexpol 30, 101–2, 119, 149–50, 234, 249
sexual energy, concept of, 136
Sexual Life of Savages, 121, 210
Sexual Revolution, The, 17, 20, 21n, 60n, 73, 109, 167
Sexual Struggle of Youth, The, 147n, 156–7, 175, 177n, 181; critique of, 184–5
sexuality, 16–21, 71–2, 102–4, 106–8, 120–33, 151, 168–9, 172–4, 176, 178–81, 184–6, 199, 201, 203–4, 235, 240, 245, 259; suppression of, 20–1, 73, 100, 105, 121–3, 125, 130–3, 211–12, 248; children and adolescents and, 20, 103–4, 108, 111–15, 122–3, 125, 129, 156, 225–6, 239, 245
Siersted, Ellen, 247
Smith, Adam, 60
Social Democrats, 20, 37–8, 44, 46, 95, 142–3, 150, 153, 157–8, 169, 172, 175, 177–8, 187, 191, 213–14, 228, 231; in Austria, 22–9, 32–5, 38–47, 75–87, 115–17, 195
Socialism, 37, 42, 45, 50, 61, 69, 86, 88, 95, 101, 109, 120, 140, 153, 160, 162–3, 170; and Freud, 19–20
Socialist Society for Sex-Counseling and Sex-Research, 73, 107
Socialists, 10, 11, 35, 36n, 37–8, 41, 43, 60–1, 78–80, 97, 100, 117, 134–5, 137, 139, 144, 157, 159, 161, 164, 175, 187, 191, 195, 204–5, 211
sociology, 5, 15–18, 21, 31, 59–64, 67–8, 71–2, 74, 82, 92, 102, 113, 128, 136, 187, 211, 226–8, 233, 242
Soviet Union, *see* Russia
Stalin, Joseph, 120, 138, 146, 205
Steidle, 80–1
Stein, Peter, 223
Stöcker, Helene, 151
Streicher, Julius, 166
Ström, 222
syphilis, 166

Tarchanoff phenomenon, 211
T-bacilli, 264
Thälmann, Ernst, 81, 141, 188
Thjötta, 271
Trobriand Islanders, 11, 119, 122–7, 129
Trotsky, Leon, 205, 211

"Überblick über das Forschungsgebiet der Sexualökonomie," 236
unemployed, 92–6, 98–9, 105, 162, 181
United States, emotional plague and police in, 99; students from, to Vienna, 102–3; and Fascism, 137; and Reich theory, 225–6, 250
Unter dem Banner des Marxismus, 73
Untermensch, 161, 166
Urgesellschaft, 72
Ursprung der Familie, Der, 121

value, surplus, use, and exchange, 49–51, 53–63, 70
Varga, 106
vegetative energy, 172, 172n
vegetotherapy, 7, 217, 235
Verlag für Sexualpolitik, 156, 197, 202
vesicles, 261, 263, 267, 270, 272
Vienna, 20, 23–9, 31–3, 102–3, 107–8, 191–2, 213
Vienna Psychoanalytic Association, letter to Reich from, 195
Vierzig Jahre Ketzer, 213
Völkischer Beobachter, 189
Voltaire, 7
Vougoin, 80

Wallisch, 79
Weber, Max, 15
Weinert, Erich, 144
Weizsäcker, 238–9
Weltbühne, 204, 217
What Is Class-Consciousness?, 202, 212

Index 283

"When Your Child Asks Questions," 156, 175
Wiener-Neustadt, demonstrations in, 80–7
Willkie, Wendell, 91n
Wittfogel, Karl August, 145, 147
work democracy, 9–12, 24, 51n, 57–59, 75; 82, 98, 194n, 235
work-power, 49–51, 53–9, 61–3, 66–67, 70, 183
Workers' Cultural Congress, 155
Workers' Cultural Press, 155–6

World League for Sexual Reform, 150
Wright, Almroth E., 211

youth, see adolescents
Youth Publishers, 155

Zadniker, 103–7
Zahle, Carl Theodor, 199
Zeitschrift für Politische Psychologie und Sexualökonomie, 227
Zeitschrift für Sozialforschung, 217